# Best Human Resource Management Practices in Latin America

Latin America today presents a dynamic, challenging business landscape. Although foreign investment in the region has risen, Asia's increasing role in the global economy is a challenge to Latin America's competitiveness. At the same time, *translatina* firms – Latin American transnational companies – continue to grow in capital and influence.

In this context, the role of human resource management strategies used in the region demands further study. This original research collection explores the tensions between the strategic HRM policies demanded by global competition and local approaches rooted in Latin American cultural values. The book uses a selection of real-life case studies, plus quantitative data, to understand the unique challenges of human resource management in Latin America, exploring:

- The relationship between political, economic, and social forces, and HR practices
- Lessons from successful HRM practices in the region
- The role of HRM practices for business strategy in Latin America
- National development and HRM practices
- Diverse, specific social and cultural contexts

Written by regionally-based academics with intimate knowledge of the cultural and business landscapes, this is an excellent overview of current HRM practices in a changing region, and will be important reading for students of human resource management, and business and management.

**Anabella Davila** is Professor of Organizational Theory and Business History at the Graduate School of Business Administration and Leadership at Tecnologico de Monterrey, Mexico. She co-edited *Managing Human Resources in Latin America* (Routledge, 2005) with Marta M. Elvira and has been a member of the Mexican National Researchers System since 1999.

**Marta M. Elvira** is Academic Dean at Lexington College in Chicago. She serves on the editorial boards of the *Journal of Management Research* and the *Business Journal of Hispanic Research*. Her articles have appeared in journals such as *Academy of Management Journal, Industrial Relations, Work and Occupations* and *Organization Science*.

# Best Human Resource Management Practices in Latin America

Edited by Anabella Davila and
Marta M. Elvira

Routledge
Taylor & Francis Group

LONDON AND NEW YORK

First published 2009 by Routledge
2 Park Square, Milton Park, Abingdon, Oxon, OX14 4RN

Simultaneously published in the USA and Canada
by Routledge
270 Madison Avenue, New York, NY 10016

*Routledge is an imprint of the Taylor & Francis Group,
an informa business*

© 2009 Anabella Davila and Marta M. Elvira

Typeset in Times New Roman by Keyword Group Ltd
Printed and bound in Great Britain by TJ International Ltd,
Padstow, Cornwall

*British Library Cataloguing in Publication Data*
A catalogue record for this book is available from the British Library

*Library of Congress Cataloging in Publication Data*
Best human resource management practices in Latin America / edited by
Anabella Davila and Marta M. Elvira.
p. cm.
Includes bibliographical references.
ISBN 978-0-415-40060-2 (hardback) — ISBN 978-0-415-40062-6 (pbk.)
1. Personnel management—Latin America—Case studies. I. Dávila,
Anabella. II. Elvira, Marta M., 1965-
HF5549.2.L29B47 2008
658.30098—dc 22
2008002204

ISBN 10: 0-415-40062-7 (pbk)
ISBN 10: 0-415-40060-0 (hbk)
ISBN 13: 978-0-415-40062-6 (pbk)
ISBN 13: 978-0-415-40060-2 (hbk)

To Richard Alexander, Miriam Alejandra, Julia Rosario,
Marina Catherine, Sara Mae, and Ana Karina,
my lovely nephew and nieces.

To Chemi and Maria Paz, and their children Sergio
and Miguel – my beloved nephews.

# Contents

# Illustrations

## Figures

## Tables

# Contributors

**Veneta Andonova** is a Professor at Universidad de los Andes, Bogota, Colombia.

**Luis Felipe Avella** is a Researcher at Universidad de los Andes, Bogota, Colombia.

**Lourdes Casanova** is a Lecturer at INSEAD, France.

**Anabella Davila** is a Professor at Tecnologico de Monterrey, Campus Monterrey, and Campus Ciudad de Mexico, Mexico.

**Jose Camilo Davila** is an Assistant Professor at Universidad de los Andes, Bogota, Colombia.

**Marta M. Elvira** is the Academic Dean at Lexington College, Chicago, USA.

**Carolyn Erdener** is an Assistant Professor at Middle East Technical University, Northern Cyprus Campus, USA.

**Rodolf Gabrish** is an Assistant Professor at Fundação Dom Cabral, Minas, Brazil.

**Henry Gomez-Samper** is a Professor Emeritus at Institute for Advanced Studies in Administration (IESA), in Caracas, Venezuela.

**Jorge A. Gonzalez** is an Assistant Professor at University of San Francisco, USA.

**Roberto Gonzalez-Duarte** is a Professor of International Management at the Pontifical Catholic University, Minas Gerais, Brazil.

**Roberto Gutierrez** is a Professor at Universidad de los Andes, Bogota, Colombia.

**Jorge M. Herrera** is an Assistant Professor at Embry-Riddle Aeronautical University, USA.

**John C. Ickis** is a Professor at INCAE Business School, Costa Rica.

**Amparo Jiménez** is an Associate Professor at University of Quebec at Montreal, Montreal, Canada.

**Francisco A. Leguizamon** is a Professor at INCAE Business School, Costa Rica.

**Enrique Ogliastri** is a Professor at INCAE Business School, Costa Rica, and Instituto de Empresa Business School, Spain.

**Asbjørn Osland** is a Professor at San Jose State University, USA.

**Joyce S. Osland** is the Lucas Endowed Professor of Global Leadership at San Jose State University, USA.

**Lorena R. Perez-Floriano** is a Visiting Scholar, University of California, Irvine, USA.

**Jacobo Ramirez** is a Professor at Tecnologico de Monterrey, Campus Monterrey, Mexico, and Copenhagen Business School, Denmark.

**Pramila Rao** is an Assistant Professor at Marymount University, Arlington, Virginia, USA.

**Betania Tanure** is a Professor at Fundação Dom Cabral and PUC, Minas, Brazil.

**Laura Zapata-Cantú** is an Assistant Professor at Tecnologico de Monterrey, Campus Monterrey, Mexico.

# Foreword

Latin America's economy surprises us always. Today the region seems engaged in a unique development process. Democracy, open economies, and higher education are growing, if perhaps in different ways from what is typically expected. Because political, economic, and social elements in Latin America are tightly interwoven, understanding its development requires more than a single perspective. We, therefore, need groundbreaking theoretical frameworks for explaining Latin American business environments.

*Best Human Resource Management Practices in Latin America* portrays the development of a management model in Latin America focusing on human resource management practices. Davila and Elvira coordinate a team of scholars presenting original work that aims to understand how firms struggle and succeed when managing human resources in this challenging environment. Through exemplary case research and quantitative studies, chapter authors identify what works best for firms operating in a number of Latin American countries. Each chapter deepens our understanding of different human resource practices and the approaches developed by successful firms. Best human resource management practices in Latin America are found in outstanding firms. Notable are the cases that deal with Latin America's evolving best practices, such as recently arrived multinationals using local management talent, successful middle-sized indigenous firms in non-traditional industries, and profitable firms that overcome conflict-ridden social environments.

International human resource management as a discipline advances and enriches our learning by examining the international arena for new knowledge, particularly in emerging economies where it adds value to what we know about domestic human resource management. This book is a solid anchor to further the discipline in Latin America, a region relatively overlooked by international scholars and researchers. Besides innovative, cross-disciplinary approaches to managing human resources, this book also provides an understanding of Latin America's business context and the intricacies involved in successfully managing firms in the region. *Best Human Resource Management Practices in Latin America* will be a must-read for scholars and practitioners engaged in managing human resources in Latin America.

Mary Ann Von Glinow
Knight Ridder Eminent Scholar Chair in International Management and
Director, Center for International Business Education and Research
Florida International University
2008

# 1 Best HRM practices in Latin America

## An introduction

*Anabella Davila and Marta M. Elvira*

Latin American economies play a strategic role for foreign investors in the global context. Many multinational corporations (MNCs) currently operate in the region, attracted by its geographic position as well as by economic and political changes. Nonetheless, Asia's increasing role in the global economy has undermined Latin America's competitiveness, mainly in low-cost manufacturing industries. Latin American countries, in turn, have responded to this threat by turning foreign direct investment (FDI) into value-added industries and developing business infrastructure. Today, Latin America presents a different business landscape eager to be redefined – both globally and locally.

As happens in other business areas, the field of human resources management (HRM) and, specifically, international HRM (IHRM) is evolving, partly due to increasing levels of business globalization and internationalization. HRM is paramount to the future success of business organizations in Latin America. Scholars consistently stress that effective personal and social relationships are key to successful HRM processes in this economically expanding region. However, tensions between the strategic approach demanded by *global* competition and *local* approaches to HRM, rooted in Latin American cultural values, have received little research attention. Data are needed in order to understand which HRM practices work best in Latin America. Our purpose in this book is to present and discuss the best HRM practices used both by MNCs in the region and by outstanding regional firms via original, in-depth case study research. We also aim to highlight the theoretical implications for IHRM that emerge from these case studies.

## Latin America's economic environment

In 2006 the Economic Commission for Latin America and the Caribbean (CEPAL in Spanish) reported that the region continued the upward trend of attracting foreign direct investment (FDI). FDI reached $72,440 million, and increased 1.5 percent relative to 2005. However, the region's portion of global FDI volume decreased by 8 percent (FDI in the rest of the world is estimated to have increased by 34 percent).

This fall in FDI share could be attributed to a diminished interest of foreign MNCs or to the region's inability to compete efficiently for foreign investment.

The 2006 CEPAL report also shows that although MNCs have high participation in the largest Latin American companies, their sales are decreasing. MNCs are withdrawing or reducing operations in important industrial sectors such as telecommunications (e.g. France Telecom, Verizon, BellSouth, AT&T, TIM), electric power (e.g. EDF, PPL), water (e.g. Suez), retail (e.g. Royal, Ahold, Sonae), banking (e.g. Bank of America), and natural resources (e.g. Royal Dutch Shell, ENI, Total). Foreign firms worry about conflicts arising from new natural resource exploitation requirements, which limit foreign investors' control, and about the weakness of international arbitration procedures to mediate disagreements between foreign investors and local governments (CEPAL, 2007).

This economic environment affects Latin American business strategy in several ways. For example, foreign MNCs might no longer benefit from developing strategic alliances with local firms, a generally recommended mode of entry into a new country; similarly, the region's attractors would have to be focused exclusively on low value-added activities of a global supply chain. Competitiveness in attracting international investment can no longer rely on passive public policies, such as natural resources advantages, or horizontal economic incentives, such as economic opening, liberalization, deregulation, or privatization stimulus (CEPAL, 2007). There is an urgent need to activate basic public policies, led by local governments yet inclusive of other intermediate bodies, to help develop firm competencies and attract high-quality international investment. CEPAL's proposal is to have local authorities determine how to approach MNCs to encourage investment in the region.

The 2006 CEPAL report ends with a positive look at the future based on a discernible trend in Latin America toward recovering its economic stability in terms of FDI and the noticeable increment of FDI by Latin American MNCs. It appears that regional companies are internationalizing faster than was the case in the past: The so-called *translatinas* are the main source of this type of FDI. These two trends demonstrate that the region is adapting to globalization through active participation in the process. We surmise that one way of moving forward is increasing human capital development in the region. This proposal has important implications for developing managerial competencies and HRM systems within firms.

In this book, we aim to understand how competitive Latin American firms that operate within this economically challenging environment develop effective HRM strategies, that is, strategies that focus on developing competitive advantages through people (Pfeffer, 1994).

## Outstanding Latin American corporations

Translatina firms – Latin American trans-national firms – are showing international competency not only across the region but also in developed markets such as the US, Europe, and China. For example, Cemex (Mexico) acquired the Australian Rinker Group, becoming the top concrete producer in the world and the second in terms of sales. Interbrew (Belgium) merged with Ambev (Brazil) to create InBev, becoming the number one beer producer in the world. Companhia Vale do Rio Doce (CVRD) (Brazil), a world leader in iron ore and pellet production and commercialization that also owns the largest nickel reserves on the planet, acquired Canada's INCO and Australia's AMCI Holdings PTY. Alfa (Mexico) made important acquisitions in 2007 through its auto parts division in the US, the Czech Republic, Poland, and China. TELMEX (Mexico) has invested significantly in Argentina, Brazil, Colombia, Chile, and Peru to develop telecommunications across Latin America. Tenaris (Argentina), a steel and pipe tubing manufacturer, acquired Maverick Tube Corp. in the US. Concha & Toro (Chile) has been the leading wine brand imported in the USA for three consecutive years. Grupo Kola Real (Peru) operates in Mexico, Ecuador, Venezuela, Costa Rica, Panama, and Nicaragua. Big Cola, the main soft-drink product of this company, competes with 45 percent lower prices than its main US competitors. PDVSA (Venezuela), the state-owned oil company, is investing in oil refineries in Argentina, Belize, Brazil, and Uruguay, while constructing a gas pipeline in Colombia. Thus, although foreign MNCs appear less interested in Latin America, local private and state-owned companies are becoming prominent in terms of FDI.

Some of these Latin American multinationals are listed in the *Forbes 2000* list of 'The World's Leading Companies', including firms from Brazil (22), Chile (6), Colombia (2), Mexico (17), Panama (2) and Venezuela (2). Moreover, 3 Brazilian and 4 Mexican companies are listed in the *Global Performers List*. These corporations have developed key HR practices that leverage their international expansion. These firms have also achieved successful operations through what we call a *hybrid* management model, that is, a model that combines modern human resource practices responsive to global competition and traditional Latin American practices derived from cultural work values.

## Foreign MNCs in Latin America

According to CEPAL, multinational corporations account for approximately 50 percent of registered sales and 40 percent of exports. Different sectors account for the level of industrial competitiveness to attract FDI. Natural resources investments in oil and gas are concentrated in Venezuela, Trinidad, and Tobago, Argentina and the Andean countries, whereas investments in minerals are concentrated in Chile, Argentina, and Peru. Investment in goods and services involve the region's largest markets, such as Brazil and Mexico. These products include automobiles, processed food, beverages and chemical products, and also financial, telecommunications, retail, electricity and gas distribution services. Manufacturing third-tier suppliers are mostly located in Mexico and the Caribbean.

Interestingly, in 2007 the Great Place to Work Institute reports that MNCs occupied 19 out of the 25 top places in Latin America. The report contains important implications for HRM in the region. On the one hand, there seems to be a great potential for worldwide operations management by local talent. On the other hand, MNCs appear to understand how social capital generates a competitive advantage not only for recruiting and retaining employees, but also for generating organizational commitment and a harmonious work climate. Thus, there is a need for research into HRM practices within MNCs as well as into successful Latin American firms' organizational contexts.

## HR institutional development as a managerial discipline

The practice of HR in Latin America has strong institutional endorsement. Professional associations exist for promoting HR advancement, such as the Mexican Association of Human Resources Management (www.amedirh.com.mx). In addition, the discipline is well established academically. Major institutions of higher education offer academic programs at the undergraduate and graduate levels in the HRM area with a focus on IRHM. Finally, government agencies in each country oversee and promote appropriate HRM practices (e.g. mandatory labor training programs).

However, little research has focused on the development of the discipline itself. Latin American HR practices developed along with the region's industrialization. In some countries, this process began when foreign investment arrived; in other countries, it began with the indigenous economic transition from agriculture to manufacturing. In both cases, HR practices have been widely influenced by dominant global theories or foreign multinationals' imported practices. Thus, not surprisingly, implementing such HR practices in their original design has often failed (Elvira and Davila, 2005). With the challenges discussed above and the need for international competitiveness, we are set to analyze, explain, and further the implementation of knowledge about current best practices as a necessary step in expanding HRM research in Latin America.

## Outstanding firms and their HR practices

This book presents research on HR practices used by top-performing corporations in Latin America. The main research design in all chapter contributions is the case study approach. Contributing researchers either chose a specific HR practice for in-depth analysis or the overall HR system in its organizational and social context. In his seminal work, Yin suggests a case study approach for research aiming to understand complex social phenomena: "case study allows an investigation to retain the holistic and meaningful characteristics of real-life events" (1994: 3). This inquiry method is generally used when the boundaries between a phenomenon and its context are not clearly evident, and when multiple sources of evidence are used (Yin, 1994). The case study approach is also critical for developing novel theory deriving "from juxtaposition of contradictory or paradoxical evidence" (Eisenhardt, 1989: 546). Eisenhardt similarly recommends the case study research approach for theory building when "little is known about a phenomenon, current perspectives seem inadequate because they have little empirical substantiation, or they conflict with each other or common sense" (1989: 548).

Therefore, we contribute to HRM theoretical development through the case study research strategy to understand the complexity in which HR practices are managed in Latin America. Based on the work of expert scholars in the HR subjects and countries that we invited to participate, this book progresses along the following theoretical and empirical HRM issues: the relationship between environmental – political, economic, and social – forces and HR practices (Chapters 2, 3, and 4); the lessons from successful firm HR practices in Latin America (Chapter 5); the role of HR practices for business strategy in Latin America's corporations (Chapters 6, 8, and 9); the relationship between HR practices and countries' development (Chapter 7); and some HR practices emerging from factors unique to the Latin American business and social context (Chapters 10, 11, 12, 13, and 14).

## Summary of the book and contributions

*Best Human Resource Management Practices in Latin America* is organized in fourteen chapters according to various research themes. First, we present work focusing on novel HRM strategies for managing environmental constraints affecting companies in Latin America. Then we present studies describing MNCs' experience managing HR successfully in the region. Next, we introduce two case studies showing integrative approaches to HRM systems. The remaining chapters focus on in-depth understanding of specific HRM practices using qualitative and quantitative methods. Before concluding, we highlight a singular chapter portraying the career of business professors in Latin America. This invited chapter aims to explain business schools in the region, their interests and concerns toward research, and the contextual factors that affect scholarly careers, which in turn provide the background for understanding the incipient stage of HRM research.

In Chapter 2, A. Osland, J. S. Osland, Tanure, and Gabrish describe a land dispute involving multiple stakeholders and a Norwegian firm operating in Brazil, Aracruz Celulose, S.A. Stakeholder management theory is the framework for this case analysis, in which unclear property rights constitute an externality thwarting value optimization. The authors speak of "situational stakeholder management" to describe this demand for greater management attention in highly complex settings. They discuss the role of the HR executive in this context and the implications for HRM practice and research.

In Chapter 3, Andonova, Gutierrez, and Avella study three Colombian companies that have managed their employment relationships in an innovative manner, to attain competitive advantage and simultaneously contribute to a more peaceful business environment. They illustrate their arguments with the experience of Hacienda Gavilanes, Indupalma and Hocol. The authors discuss how "corporate social responsibility" imposes new demands on HR departments in Latin America, which are often accountable for managing stakeholders' demands. The role of HR departments is crucial when national and local institutions fail to enforce basic property rights, and to provide protection and security. In such circumstances, employment conflicts tend to escalate into wider social, political, and economic clashes. Therefore, attending to employment relationships becomes much more important than has traditionally been recognized in HRM research.

In Chapter 4, Jiménez and Davila study Cerro Matoso, S.A., a Colombian company in the natural resource exploitation sector that successfully uses strategic human resources management (SHRM) practices to deal with an unstable and turbulent socio-political environment. Stakeholder management theory again becomes relevant. Three empirical elements are set out that justify the relevance of stakeholder management in reconciling economic and social imperatives: (1) acceptance of the inherent contradictions between social responsibility and economic imperatives in defining an HRM strategy; (2) implementation of management systems that foster the integration of SHRM, organizational culture, and institutional context; and (3) participation of senior management in the process of defining progressive SHRM practices (e.g. skill management in the context of change, employment security, workplace health and safety, and democracy in the workplace).

In Chapter 5, Casanova examines in detail Telefónica's historical development in Latin America and identifies key aspects of its HRM practices that have contributed to its success. In particular, the author examines executive staffing practices. The company's HR policies and practices have played a key role in its ability to dominate the region's telecommunications sector through several major economic crises and in the face of pressure from powerful American competitors. Among other experiences, the case offers important lessons for managing international expatriates in Latin America.

In Chapter 6, Tanure and Gonzalez-Duarte offer a detailed description of why and how HRM may take on a strategic role within merger and acquisition (M&A) processes. The success of these deals depends to a large extent on the successful management of people-related issues. To become effectively a strategic partner in M&As, HRM should participate in the negotiation, not merely the integration, phase. In addition, HRM needs to formulate people-management policies that are consistent with the determining reason for the acquisition and the consequent integration strategy adopted. To illustrate these arguments, the authors study ABN AMRO's acquisition of two banks – a Brazilian bank and a subsidiary of an Italian bank in Brazil.

In Chapter 7, Leguizamon, Ickis, and Ogliastri overview HR practices through Grupo San Nicolás's history. In this case study authors examine the company's HR practices, their interplay with the environment, and the results achieved, as recounted by company executives, middle managers, line workers, and outside observers. They conclude that four factors account for this Central American business group's high performance. First, HR practices such as training and development appear to have increased employee productivity. Second, San Nicolás's management has been careful to adapt new practices to company culture and to the volatile social, political, and economic environment of El Salvador. Third, there is an understanding of the interrelated nature of HR practices adopted: these practices are not isolated but form a coherent whole that leverages performance. Fourth, the mutual reinforcement of these practices, sustained by a set of shared values and guiding principles, has served as an inspiration for the organization.

In Chapter 8, Ramirez and Zapata-Cantú present an exploratory case study of the configuration of high-performance HR practices in Novo Nordisk Mexico, a Danish pharmaceutical firm. The firm has established in Mexico its "Novo Nordisk Way of Management" (NNWoM), which is rooted in Danish culture. Mexican and Danish economic developments, social factors, and organizational culture differ markedly, however. In Mexico, Novo Nordisk faces barriers that could slow its ability to implement a high-performance HR system. However, Novo Nordisk Mexico has been ranked as one of the best places to work in Mexico according to Great Place to Work Institute México (2007). This case study examines how Novo Nordisk Mexico implements its HR system. It introduces the firm's main values (openness and participation), which create a strong corporate culture in support of the HRM system and practices. The effects of contextual factors on HRM operations are also examined.

In Chapter 9, Davila and Elvira draw on an empirical study of performance-management (PM) systems in CompuSoluciones, a medium-size Mexican IT consulting firm also chosen by the Great Place to Work Institute of Mexico as an outstanding company in 2007. A key theme emerging in the study is that combining different PM practices is necessary to align individual and organizational performance. CompuSoluciones PM strategies do so, shedding light on the fundamental research question of how to appraise knowledge workers and the output they produce.

In Chapter 10, Gonzalez and Perez-Floriano describe the experience of TransInc Corporation (real name omitted) in South America, focusing on factors that exemplify the development of safety systems in Argentina and Brazil. The authors argue that "best" HRM practices in this industry are synonymous with "safest" practices. The development, implementation, or transformation of safety systems must emphasize the development of trust. This trust can only flourish through the acknowledgment of local culture and the cultivation of personal relationships among employees, a personal (albeit hierarchical) relationship between management and employees, and by allowing such relationships to generate interpersonal trust and strong personal relations.

In Chapter 11, Rao examines staffing practices used to fill the CEO, vice president, and all director positions below the vice presidential level (or equivalent) in US-Mexican joint ventures located in Mexico. The study, based on a survey of HR directors, reveals that current executive staffing practices are influenced both by national culture and staffing practices from other multinationals.

In Chapter 12, Herrera and Erdener discuss how the conflicting ethical beliefs that organizations face operating internationally require greater knowledge and respect for ethical systems across the world. The authors explore these issues within the context of HRM in Latin America. They review relevant literature and then present preliminary results of a new study designed to contribute to the development of best ethical practices in HRM in Latin America, including data on how business ethics is currently taught and practiced.

In Chapter 13, Gomez-Samper, IESA's (Venezuela) emeritus professor, honors us with his thoughtful consideration of external and internal challenges currently facing leading Latin American business schools and professors' careers within the same. The author offers an expert personal view of the region's business schools relative to the demands of international accreditation agencies; academic market, resources for research and curricula development; and social and political factors influencing business environment and, by extension, business schools. Based on IESA's own environment, Gomez-Samper articulates how Latin America's political turns impact business programs and the progress of scholarship.

In Chapter 14, we conclude with an analysis of overarching themes for HRM theory development in Latin America. HRM practices naturally differ among case studies of different organizations and thus challenge knowledge convergence. Several contextual elements bring into question the use of a singular theoretical view for HRM theory. To understand management in Latin America, theory needs to encompass a unique context characterized by economic and political instability, the role of the enterprise as a social institution, and the value of the individual within the society. Our concluding chapter's tone is optimistic and pragmatic, building on a "new humanism" approach and Santiso's (2006) description of Latin America's "political economy of the possible": Latin American organizations are open to new ideas and systems, willing to experiment in the search for what works and keeping an attitude of hope.

As co-editors, we think that the most effective use of this book is in academic courses and training programs. For example, undergraduate and graduate courses on international HRM would find useful theoretical and empirical frameworks in each chapter. Executive training programs for expatriates or managers can examine the need to approach Latin American HRM with a contextual view of the region. Additionally, the book is a good source of new company data guided by a grounded theory approach and international understanding. The research network represented by the book contributors has continued to grow since we started working on our prior book *Managing Human Resources in Latin America* (Elvira and Davila, 2005). We are grateful to all the new network members researching HRM in Latin America. Their commitment, responsiveness, and professionalism inspired us during this writing process. Because of this collective work, we are able to offer what we think is the most comprehensive view of HRM in companies in Latin America.

Our gratitude extends to all the individuals, organizations, and institutions that allowed us to approach them as researchers: Their generous sharing of time and resources for these chapters, as well as their encouragement and support during the preparation of this manuscript, is genuinely appreciated. Special thanks to Francesca Heslop, the managing editor from Routledge who gave us her trust and encouragement in the early stages of this project; to Emma Joyce for her guidance; to Simon Alexander and Russell A. George for adopting us during the last stages of the project and for their kind guidance. Many thanks also to Josephine Kujawa, librarian at Lexington College, whose professional and friendly support helped progress greatly. Finally, our gratefulness to our own institutions, Tecnologico de Monterrey, Campus Monterrey, Mexico, and Lexington College, Chicago.

# References

CEPAL (2007) *La Inversión Extranjera en America Latina y el Caribe 2006* [Foreign investment in Latin America and the Caribbean], Unidad de Inversiones y Estrategias Empresariales, División de Desarrollo Productivo y Empresarial, Santiago, Chile: CEPAL. Retrieved 10/25/07 from http://www.eclac.cl/cgi-bin/getProd.asp?xml=/publicaciones/xml/3/28393/P28393.xml&xsl=ddpe/tpl/p9f.xsl&base=/tpl/top-bottom.xsl.

Eisenhardt, K. M. (1989) 'Building theories from case study research,' *Academy of Management Review*, 14(4): 532–550.

Elvira, M. M. and Davila, A. (eds.) (2005) *Managing Human Resources in Latin America: An Agenda for International Leaders*, Oxford, UK: Routledge.

Great Place to Work Institute México (2007). Online. Available HTTP: http://www.greatplacetowork.com.mx/best/lists.php?year=current&idListName=mx&detail=1&order=rank (accessed September 25, 2007).

Pfeffer, J. (1994) *Competitive Advantage through People: Unleashing the Power of the Work Force*, Boston: Harvard Business School Press.

Santiso, J. (2006) *Latin America's Political Economy of the Possible. Beyond Good Revolutionaries and Free-Marketeers*, Cambridge, MA: The MIT Press.

Yin, R. K. (1994) *Case Study Research. Design and Methods,* 2nd edn., Applied Social Research Methods Series, vol. 5,Thousand Oaks, CA: Sage.

# 2 Stakeholder management

## The case of Aracruz Celulose in Brazil

*Asbjørn Osland, Joyce S. Osland,*
*Betania Tanure, and Rodolf Gabrish*

This case study describes a land dispute involving multiple stakeholders and a Brazilian firm, Aracruz Celulose S.A. Stakeholder management theory is used to analyze this case in which unclear property rights constitute an externality that competes with classic value optimization. We term this demand for greater management attention in highly complex settings "situational stakeholder management." We discuss the role of the HR executive and conclude with implications for practitioners and future research.

## Case description

An award-winning Brazilian company, Aracruz Celulose S.A. (hereafter referred to as Aracruz) is the world's leading producer (27 percent of the global supply) of bleached eucalyptus pulp used for paper manufacture. Among others, the company has won awards for sustainability, being one of Brazil's 150 Best Companies to Work For and its most admired forestry product company (www.aracruz.com). Its eucalyptus plantations cover 279,000 hectares, with 154,000 hectares of native forest reserves.

The founder of the company, Erling Lorentzen, was a Norwegian World War II resistance hero who married into the Norwegian royal family and moved to Rio de Janeiro in 1953 (Aftenposten, 2004b). Lorentzen planted the first eucalyptus plantations in November 1967 and founded the company in April 1972. He served as chairman for 37 years.

In a 2000 interview, Lorentzen stated:

> Some of my attraction to the Aracruz project was also that it was developing nature. For me, it's a beautiful forest, and to see the growth of these trees is something that gives me a lot of satisfaction. . . . I was also attracted to Brazil because I felt that I could do a job here. There was a need for things to be done . . . and I saw so many opportunities, so much need for development in Brazil. The misery you saw – and still see – was something that I felt maybe I had to do my little share to alleviate.
>
> (Harvard Business School, 2000)

In that same interview, he made a wide and prescient comment: "To work in Brazil, you have to be very observant. You have to understand what is really going on, not only what appears to be going on, but also the underlying moods, both politically and economically" (Harvard Business School, 2000). Lorentzen also pushed for an independent study, "Towards a Sustainable Paper Cycle," by the International Institute for Environment and Development. This study was the basis for policy development and environmental improvements in the forest products industry (PPI, 1998).

Environmental and social concern at Aracruz has carried forward to the present, witnessed in this statement by Carlos Augusto Lira Aguiar (2005), President and CEO: "In the new business environment, only companies that manage adequately to integrate economic, social and environmental factors in their business planning to the extent necessary to be considered sustainable will have a place in the market – and, indeed, a future."

Nevertheless, Aracruz is still targeted by critics for creating a monoculture of eucalyptus trees ("the green desert") and using harmful chemicals (Lang, 2005). To address such concerns, Aracruz meets with interested stakeholders and has succeeded in responding to certain concerns, discussed in the sustainability report available on the company's website.

One reason for the differing perceptions and interpretations of Aracruz has to do with beliefs about massive agribusiness installations such as Aracruz, which are crucial to Brazil's economy. However, not all observers see this approach as feasible in light of social and environmental sustainability. In particular, the socio-economic sustainability of the neighboring Indians in the Espírito Santo region was the crux of a lengthy property dispute involving squatters, vandalism, pressure tactics by non-governmental organizations (NGOs), and legal battles enacted by multiple stakeholders.

## The context of property rights and the Brazilian landless movement

Property rights in Latin America are problematic where there is no system of title companies and public registries established and supported by the government and the courts. Property rights can be especially problematic for subsistence or small farmers because they often do not hold clear title to the land they use. This may preclude their access to credit given their lack of collateral typically provided by property assets (Yergin and Stanislaw, 1998). Furthermore, land grabs by the rich, the poor, and governments are not uncommon occurrences. Land seizures are a way for poor and landless people to achieve socio-economic and political goals. Individuals and businesses have had their lands expropriated by governments for political reasons. As Everingham (2001: 61) wrote, property is a "contested sociopolitical arena" in Latin America that traces its roots back to colonial rule and legal injustice. Such conflicts hold back shared economic development for the poor, curtail democracy (Lustig and Deutsch, 1998), and can provoke violence.

Brazil has 4 million landless families, represented by the Landless Workers' Movement (MST), who supported President da Silva's election in 2003. Land reform was one of da Silva's platform promises. He spent US$4.45 million on settlements for the landless, but the MST complained this four-fold increase was still not enough (Muello, 2006). In 2004, more than 30,000 families invaded approximately 150 farms, and 12,000 squatter families participated in a protest march in the capital of Brasília in 2005 (Muello, 2006). When the MST did extensive damage to Aracruz forests and laboratory, da Silva deplored the violence and then budgeted $585 million more to achieve his goal of providing land for 400,000 families during his first term in office (Muello, 2006). The MST appears to have raised expectations, enjoys a degree of moral legitimacy and presidential support, and has learned that invasions can pay off.

## The history of the dispute

Aracruz contended that the Indians had not historically lived on the contested land. A chronology of the dispute follows (see www.aracruz.com for more detail):

- 1993: Indians asked FUNAI to increase the reservations.
- 1995: FUNAI suggested they be expanded by 14,200 hectares.
- 1997: The Minister of Justice granted an increase of 2,600 hectares.
- 1998: Aracruz, the Tupinikim and Guarani Indians, FUNAI, and the Federal Public Prosecutor's Office signed an agreement but some Indians seized Aracruz land. The federal court instructed the Indians to depart and they complied. They later agreed to the Minister's decision and Aracruz granted the Indians R$13.5 million in assistance, to be administered over the following 20 years.
- 2002: The Indians wanted to renegotiate; Aracruz agreed to pay them R$1.4 million annually in development assistance and partner with them in its Forestry Partners Program.
- 2005: The Indians asked for approximately 11,000 more hectares for their reservation. Aracruz went to court to stop the expansion and halted its assistance programs. The Indians seized the land and a pulp mill.
- 2006: FUNAI supported the Indians in its recommendations sent to the Ministry of Justice, contradicting Aracruz's extensive documentation that the Indians had not lived on the land in the modern era and that Aracruz was the legal and legitimate owner.
- 2007: The government decided to give the land, valued at US$50 million, to the Indians.

## Pressure on Aracruz Celulose from national NGO stakeholders

The cause of the Indians in Espírito Santo was supported by the MST. Beginning in September 2006, groups of Indians and protesters linked to the MST seized more company property, set fire to more than 200 hectares of forest, blocked roads and intimidated company employees and company sympathizers (Aracruz Celulose, 2007). Between December 12 and 13, 2006, they seized the port terminal operated by Aracruz and Cenibra. The protesters interrupted the operation, intimidating 150 workers. Since 90 percent of Brazilian pulp exports are shipped from this port, Brazil failed to export US$14 million because of this two-day disruption.

In response, on December 13, 2006, 2,000 workers, suppliers, and supporters of Aracruz, including four trade unions, marched in a counter-protest, requesting that Indians and protesters leave the locale and that their right to work be respected. MST protesters destroyed the port's administrative office. On December 14, the port resumed its activities. In addition to the losses caused by two days' stoppage, there was material damage to the infrastructure and pulp estimated at US$2 million.

Yet another group invaded Aracruz land in Espírito Santo, supported by MST and Via Campesina. Two hundred and fifty people linked to the Quilombola movement (descendants of runaway African slaves) seized 18 hectares on July 23, 2007, causing an estimated loss of US$110,430. They were evicted by police on August 12, 2007.

## Pressure and negative publicity from international NGO stakeholders

De'Nadai, Overbeek, and Soares (2005) in a World Rainforest Movement report, financed by SSNC of Sweden and NOVIB-Oxfam Netherlands, were highly critical of Aracruz. The authors stated that Aracruz had expelled thousands of families and destroyed thousands of hectares of Atlantic Forest.

> Over the last 35 years, communities have resisted and reacted to these kinds of violence practiced by the company. Nowadays,with the support of entities and social movements, these communities fight together in the Rede Alerta contrao Deserto Verde (Alert Against the Green Desert Network), combating the exclusive agro-industrial model that Aracruz Celulose and other companies seek to impose on Brazilian territory.
>
> (De'Nadai *et al.,* 2005: 10)

The perspective of the authors was that agribusiness destroys rural society by generating too few jobs and damaging the environment. With the Aracruz case, it is difficult for outsiders to understand whether NGOs are unfairly attacking Aracruz or simply evening up the power discrepancy by supporting poor people in a dispute with a powerful multinational. Different accounts vary widely. Fig (2007), an independent South African environmental sociologist and political economist, reviewed the information available from secondary sources and concluded that the company's stated corporate social responsibility program was inconsistent with its practices.

More bad press for Aracruz occurred when two Indians visited Norway in April 2006 (Aftenposten, 2006a). A national paper (www.aftenposten.no/english/)

carried a story critical of Norway's investment in Aracruz. Its Government Pension Fund – Global, formerly the State Petroleum Fund, had approximately US$5.5 million invested in Aracruz. The founder and owner of 28 percent of Aracruz, Erling Lorentzen, was King Harald's brother-in-law. To avoid further links with the company, the king of Sweden sold his shares earlier that year. While in Norway, the Tupinikim Indian representative, Paulo Henrique Vicente de Oliveira, stated: "Aracruz has taken our land, and destroyed the forest and rivers. In this way they also destroy a part of our life and our culture. Norway must use its influence on Aracruz." He wanted the company to give them 11,009 hectares (27,200 acres) that he claimed had traditionally been owned by the Indians.

In a letter dated March 22, 2006, to the Ministry of Finance, Gro Nystuen, the Chair of the Council on Ethics, the group charged with review of ethical problems in the Government Pension Fund portfolio, declined to review Aracruz's case for the time being: "The Council . . . attaches importance to the Brazilian authorities' engagement in the case and the fact that all stakeholders seem to be involved in the process. The Council will await further developments before considering the need for a more thorough assessment of this case."

## Interview with Aracruz Celulose's Director of Operations

In an interview with the authors, Aracruz's Director of Operations, Walter Lídio Nunes (March 28, 2007), stated that the company had a responsibility to contribute towards the improvement of the quality of life of the communities in which it operates. In the last 40 years, Aracruz has worked in partnership with the neighboring communities on assorted social development initiatives, with the objective of establishing long-term relationships based on mutual respect and improvement of the Indian's quality of life. Aracruz sought a stable solution because it recognized the Indians as important stakeholders. Aracruz has histori- cally assisted the community beyond simply establishing sound operations. It understood that protesters could wreak havoc on operations, so it had to somehow negotiate with protesting Indians with the hope that they would eventually see cooperation as more beneficial than land seizure and sabotage. Aracruz had interacted with protest groups to hear what they had to say.

However, the differences in perspective seemed to be ideological, and neither party was willing to compromise. Still, Aracruz understood that relationship building at a personal level would facilitate communication and believed that protesters could be educated as to why the corporation believed it must manage its operations in a productive and profitable manner. The company's corporate social responsibility program had been shaped in the past through dialogue with the community.

According to Nunes, answering the broader socio-economic development question was even more important than the legal solution for a stable settlement. He discussed the dilemma with representatives of the local and regional communi- ties. He presented Aracruz as an economic and social agent, whose capacity to help in the social field was linked to its success as an economic agent. Should the would-be Indians (referring to the mixed ancestry of some of the protesters) continue to seize property and disrupt operations, the local community would suffer. The socio-economic development question was complex, according to Nunes. In his opinion, Aracruz was an icon, a symbolic example of the success of agribusiness in Brazil. Therefore, it drew the attention of anti-globalization movements such as the MST and the local and international NGOs, such as the Movement of Small Farmers (MPA), Alert Network against the Green Desert, Federation of Organizations for Social and Educational Welfare (FASE), Indigenous Missionary Council (CIMI), Pastoral Commission of the Land (CPT), and Robin Hood. According to Nunes, these movements, in the search for a social utopia based on peasant agriculture, manipulated the Indians and other supporters to fight Aracruz in the land conflict. The lack of socio-economic progress in their communities caused people to join radical movements.

Aracruz wanted to foster community debate involving the public authorities and other stakeholders. General socio-economic development is extremely complex and a long-term process. Governmental and corporate institutions in the area would ideally provide enough training and educational opportunities so that people feel that they have opportunities. The government and NGOs or other voluntary associations could cooperate to provide basic primary health care for the public. The company would attend to the basic health needs of its direct employees and family members. Aracruz could contribute and participate, but the firm would not assume ownership of the problem of indigenous communities as it had in the past.

The Indians and Aracruz had to work together to "develop projects that will offer the communities autonomy and lead to the elimination of their dependency on Aracruz, thus ending any type of paternalistic assistance."

## The government's decision

On August 28, 2007, the Minister of Justice decided in favor of the Indians and ordered Aracruz to turn over 11,000 hectares to expand the reservations. It is worth noting that this amount of land plus the 2,600 hectares ordered in the 1998 agreement totals 13,600 and approximates the 13,300–14,200 hectares FUNAI recommended back in 1995–1997 when the dispute heated up.

When Aracruz heard the long-awaited court decision, it issued this press release two days later:

> The decision of Justice Minister Tarso Genro, favorable to the demarcation of 11,000 hectares of land claimed by indigenous communities in the state of Espírito Santo – almost all of which [sic] from land that is the property of Aracruz – surprised the company, which was in a process of negotiation with FUNAI (the National Indian Bureau) at the invitation of the Ministry itself.
>
> The company regrets that the decision of the Minister does not take into consideration the company's arguments in its response to FUNAI's opinion favoring demarcation. In its response, Aracruz presented arguments and

documentation – including satellite photos, historical records and studies conducted by FUNAI itself – showing the inconsistencies in the FUNAI opinion that they have never been even refuted. "We will continue to seek indispensable legal assurances that there will be no further expansion of the indigenous reservation and we hope that this can be achieved through a process of negotiation, in a manner that avoids prolongation of the dispute, which affects not only the company and the indigenous communities but also the state of Espírito Santo and the country," said Carlos Alberto Roxo, Aracruz's director of Sustainability. "Such legal assurances are indispensable to allow Aracruz to continue producing, ensuring thousands of jobs and generating foreign exchange earnings for Brazil."

(www.aracruz.com, August 28, 2007)

According to one analyst, who preferred to remain anonymous, "Aracruz has 433,000 hectares of land. Eleven thousand [hectares] is not that much. We estimate the land and planted eucalyptus [lost by Aracruz] to be worth around US$50 million. The company is worth more than US$5 billion in market capitalization. So, the impact is negligible."

Nevertheless, Aracruz wants legal assurances that this will be the last annexation of its land. Another unresolved issue is how the company will work with the Indians and other stakeholders, particularly the more radical NGOs, to arrive at a long-term socio-economic solution. The Ministry of Justice decision providing land to the Indians does not guarantee their sustained socio-economic development. The company has not announced its next steps in relation to the stakeholders involved in the land dispute.

## Stakeholder management theory

In the Aracruz case, with its multiple stakeholders, political undercurrents, and conflicting rights, getting to the truth of the matter and finding an acceptable solution is very challenging. The company's best practices reflect operational excellence, but it is difficult to deal with external groups that commit illegal acts such as land and property seizure (Osland and Osland, 2007). In situations like these, companies are forced to switch some of their management attention from profit maximization and internal operations to situational stakeholder management. Aracruz has worked successfully with some external stakeholders for years and espoused concern for the community, as shown on its website. However, they may not have perceived the Indians and the MST as serious stakeholders in the beginning because of the company's legal title to the land and their questions about Indian ancestry. Furthermore, Aracruz has been held responsible for societal conditions by some NGOs and stakeholders who seem to expect Aracruz "to expand their focus on internal operations to use their power to help society" (Osland and Osland, 2007: 446).

This raises the thorny question of whether the purpose of companies is profit maximization or socio-economic responsibility to stakeholders. To consider this question with respect to Aracruz, we turn to the stakeholder management literature.

Jensen (2001) argues that companies should practice enlightened value maximization (or, synonymously, enlightened stakeholder theory) where long-term value maximization of the firm is the goal. Stakeholder management is practiced (hence the term "enlightened"), but long-term value maximization trumps other objectives, such as stakeholder concerns, when they are in competition. Jensen contends that one cannot logically hold several objectives simultaneously; instead, holding long-term value maximization as the primary goal resolves conflicts among competing objectives. As a US$5 billion operation, Aracruz pursued enlightened value maximization. The company focused attention and assets on stakeholders, but value maximization was the dominant goal. Indeed, the company views its contribution to development, employment, and the trade balance as contributions to Brazilian society.

Nevertheless, Aracruz was "distracted" by the Indian problem. Its efforts to appease Indian needs through donations, minor land concessions, and even the Forestry Partners Program proved unsuccessful in the long run, against the backdrop of poorly defined property rights, FUNAI objectives, and political pressure to resolve the landless problem. Poorly defined property was the critical externality. Jensen (2001) recognized that a focus on value maximization is compromised when externalities are present, which was certainly true in this case. Aracruz's assumption of value maximization, while consistent with economic and financial theory as pursued in capitalistic systems, conflicts with the stakeholder approach taken by the Indians (and the MST), who appear more focused on what they perceive as social justice and their perceived claim to the land.

Granovetter (1985) acknowledged that economic firms are embedded within society. Thus, the socio-political context in which Aracruz operates determines how it must balance its efforts between value maximization and responses to stakeholders. Clearly, Aracruz has to focus on value maximization in a capitalistic marketplace, but the muddle over property rights is the externality in which it is embedded. Annexation of its property may simply be part of the cost of business in Brazil. To thrive and increase its value, however, the firm cannot be continually engaged in fending off land seizures and repairing damage by the Indians and, more recently, the Quilombolas.

Jones (1995) tried to synthesize ethics and economics in an instrumental stakeholder theory based on mutual trust and cooperation. Competitive advantage is derived from efficient and effective relationships with many stakeholders formalized through contracts; the firm serves as a nexus for a network of contracts between stakeholders, and the market rewards efficient contracting and punishes poor performers. Rowley (1997) also emphasized the importance of networks in his discussion of stakeholder influences. Thus Aracruz has to compete economically to survive in the market, but its central position in both the local and international networks of relationships has to be based on trust and cooperation. These qualities seem to be lacking in the firm's relations with the Indians and perhaps the Quilombolas. Without clear property rights, capitalism can flounder in its quest for value maximization and trusting relationships.

If the Indians and Quilombolas were simply passive, marginalized neighbors, they would not be stakeholders whose trust and cooperation were essential.

In earlier periods such groups did not aggressively pursue what they now perceive as legitimate property rights. Paolo Freire (1970), a Brazilian, said such marginalized classes constituted a culture of silence. He emphasized participation in the political process and became a threat to the Brazilian military dictatorship and the land-owners opposed to land reform. He eventually had to leave Brazil, but his legacy of activism survived. The Indians and Quilombolas have now had their consciousness raised to the point where they assertively take what they perceive as their property and have the support of large political movements like the MST. Trust and cooperation within the network where Aracruz is embedded depend on more than a legal opinion. Instead, skillful leadership with a human resources focus seems essential for building the positive relations that allow value maximization to proceed. Lira Aguiar, Aracruz's CEO, acknowledges this:

> Our "social license" to operate depends on the quality of the environment, the welfare of the communities in which we are present and the trust of the stakeholders involved – our employees, customers, shareholders and suppliers, among others. Maintaining and expanding the trust of these publics is a crucial challenge for our sustainability strategy.
>
> (Lira Aguiar, 2005)

Firms have traditionally focused on investors, customers, employees, and suppliers, with the established goal of maximizing return to shareholders. Stakeholder theory also includes external parties, but the focus on specific stakeholders and how much management attention they merit is the dilemma for leaders (Freeman, 1984). Mitchell, Agle, and Wood (1997) developed a typology based on managerial perceptions of stakeholder power, legitimacy, and urgency. Over time, Aracruz's perception of the Indians (and perhaps the Quilombolas) has changed with respect to these stakeholder characteristics. The company may not have perceived the Indians as stakeholders meriting attention because the company had purchased the land legally. However, as the Indians invaded and caused significant damage, they increased both power and urgency. The support they acquired from MST and other NGOs and the pressure these groups exerted on their behalf further increased their power, and gave them more legitimacy. FUNAI's proposals also increased their legitimacy, as did the Ministry of Justice ruling. Over the course of the land dispute, the indigenous communities have become a clear stakeholder – powerful, legitimate, with a sense of urgency in their demands.

In view of the fluctuating demands and importance of stakeholder management, we suggest a new term – *situational* stakeholder management. For the most part, companies will focus the majority of their attention on maximizing value, while providing the attention deemed necessary to stakeholders on a regular basis. Occasionally, however, situations arise that demand significantly more focused stakeholder management, as in the Aracruz case. This requires different routines, procedures, and skills, somewhat similar to the different crisis operating mode that some high-tech firms switch into when a product is in trouble. When this occurs at Google, for example, a person is put in charge and given full autonomy to choose the personnel he or she wants on the team and to make decisions in a more autocratic manner than usual in this highly participative organizational culture. However, situational stakeholder management is not best served by an autocratic approach, because these situations are more likely to represent unstructured problems requiring creative solutions that require brainstorming and strong relationships with stakeholders. Nevertheless, situational stakeholder management does require a different mindset and perhaps a temporary special organizational structure to respond appropriately and quickly in the specific cultural context.

## The Brazilian cultural context

There are several cultural factors in this case. High power distance is an important cultural value in Brazil with implications for this case. The traditional definition of high power distance, an acceptance of unequal power distribution (Hofstede, 2001), may determine how the Brazilian managers feel about the demands and illegal behavior of the Indians, a people who previously appeared docile and compliant and historically had little or no power. A common Brazilian manifestation of high power distance is the "ambiguity trait," which permits those who wield power to have some space to maneuver, as explained by Tanure (2005), a Brazilian scholar. In the Aracruz case, ambiguity can be seen in the various views and approaches. Nunes appeared forceful in his view of the errors the company had made and his concern that Aracruz had appeared too compliant. The company went to great lengths to prove its legal right to the land and demanded a court decision, in contrast to the summer 2007 website proclamation that it was willing to consider donating land to resolve the impasse.

Tanure (2004) also discussed flexibility as a Brazilian cultural trait that encompassed both adaptability and creativity. Such traits will be essential for the future situational stakeholder management that the company executives will undertake in relating to the Indians.

The role of HRM in Brazil is another important contextual factor. Research by Tanure (2005) indicates that Brazilian companies and executives do not generally perceive HR as a strategic partner. Using a likert scale in which 1 indicated "fully disagrees" and 7 indicated "fully agrees" that "HR plays the role of a strategic partner," there was a wide gap between the self-assessment of HR professionals and their colleagues and superiors. The average score of HR professionals, their self-assessment, was 6.11. The average score of fellow executives from other areas and senior managers was 3.9. The average score of staff executives was even lower, at 2.78. Company presidents reported an average of 4.14, a more neutral response. While HR professionals see their role as strategic, this view is not shared by their work colleagues, limiting their influence and actions.

This is unfortunate in complex stakeholder situations like Aracruz where HR professionals are more likely than technical colleagues to have training and perspectives that could contribute to creative problem solving and positive relationships with stakeholders. This is clearly a non-programmed decision where standard problem solving may fail managers. The Aracruz HR Director reports to the president, but there are no public data available to describe the director's role in the land dispute controversy or level of influence on the decision making of the executive team. In the Brazilian context, it is particularly important for HR managers to establish relationships with company leaders so that they are willing to heed their counsel.

## Discussion and implications

As Anthony Giddens (1999), former director of the London School of Economics, stated, "Along with ecological risk, expanding inequality is the most serious problem facing world society." Inequality, the basis for the property rights dilemma, compromised Aracruz's pursuit of long-term value maximization and constituted a critical externality that required more management attention to the Indians and MST as stakeholders. Since it was the dominant force in its network of stakeholder influences, it had to resolve the dilemma with the marginalized classes, such as the Indians and Quilombolas, which had become dangerous stakeholders due to episodic property seizure. In addition, the company was embedded in a political context in which the landless problem was very salient and eventually led to a decision against the firm in favor of the Indians. The Indians were aided by both national and international NGOs who used pressure tactics on Aracruz in various countries (Osland and Osland, 2007). Given the complex forces involved, a new form of situational stakeholder management was demanded of the firm.

For HR to be a strategic partner in determining how to manage critical stake-holders, the HR executive would first have to become respected as a partner to the line manager and then possess expertise related to the specific stakeholders, the political context, and the process of situational stakeholder management. Rotating HR personnel through other functions is one way to develop their credibility and networks within the firm; rotating managers from other functions through HR also spreads the skills needed to deal with stakeholders if the HR department is skilled in this area. Developing good relationships and a thorough understanding of current and potential stakeholders are crucial for HR executives.

The ability to guide the process in complex stakeholder situations is also important. This means thinking and planning in advance how such problems should be tackled and who should be involved. More research is needed in this area; perhaps some lessons could be borrowed from the fields of crisis and risk management. HR managers should educate themselves about successful solutions and best practices found in other firms. The following Colombian cases may hold transferable lessons (Ganitsky, 2005; Andonova and Zuleta, 2007).

Indupalma (grower and producer of African palm oil) experienced extremely high levels of violence but managed to resolve the conflict and turn the situation around (Ganitsky, 2005). An adversarial relationship between management and workers resulted in the death of over 70 union leaders (1988–1991), the involvement of guerilla groups, and the murder of the general administrator in 1991. Rather than shut the company down, the owners and directors formed a team of key representatives from the company, union and the Ministry of Work, and three consultants who forged a solution. Workers formed cooperatives and sold their services to Indupalma. Education was a critical factor; the company provided extensive technical, administrative, and personal development training (e.g. literacy and conflict management courses). The workers assumed responsibility and accountability for their own production. Rather than align themselves with the guerillas, they realized that it was more advantageous to partner with Indupalma, who gave them a fair price for their products. The workers benefited by learning new skills and becoming owners of companies and assets, which resulted in more income and security.

The main lessons from Indupalma, according to CEO Ruben Lizarralde Montoya (2004), are the realization that projects benefiting all sectors of society are feasible, as is the creation of wealth and property for workers who had neither. "All this is possible if there is leadership, creativity, trust, communication, participative teamwork and synergy, love for the rural sector and conviction in the capabilities of our people and of the different actors that constitute this alliance" (Lizarralde Montoya, 2004: 6).

Andonova and Zuleta (2007) describe another Colombian case of the Hacienda Gavilanes, where weak property protection afforded by the government led to extreme violence. There, too, management worked with employees to establish a cooperative to enhance the participation of the workers and reduce the seemingly unrelenting violence. The authors stated: "Letting workers earn a share of the profits and make their own judgments about how to perform everyday tasks transforms the workers into decision-makers and owners themselves" (Andonova and Zuleta, 2007: 352).

There are also Brazilian examples of creative solutions to complex stakeholder solutions, including one in close proximity to Aracruz. Linda Murasawa, a Sustainability Specialist, in Equity Research, ABN AMRO Brazil, expressed this opinion:

> In Brazil, the market is changing. The corporations are facing some points, such as, Climate Change, Corporate Governance Practices, Ecological certifications (ISO14001, FSC, etc.), [and] Social responsibility (labor relations, health and safety, diversity, etc.). It is a big new wave movement, but we have a lack of information and in our evaluation, we are trying to ensure a high degree of social responsibility and transparency with respect to peoples' investments.

> Some companies are trying to design [a] new business model using social responsibility plus economic cycle, for example, VCP (Votorantim Pulp and Paper Industry) program . . . This program is successful and it is a first time where you join large company, govern[ment], a bank and the Movement of Landless People (now they have access to credit, they are producers, and they are in the economic cycle).

In the same way, Indian and corporations are taking a place in sustainable business, it is so difficult because it is involving a new mindset, but it is not impossible, and Brazilian companies are facing these problems with responsible solutions.

(Murasawa, 2007)

Thus, VCP (Votorantim Celulose e Papel) (www.vcp.com.br), a competitor and partial owner (12.5 percent of Aracruz stock) of Aracruz, is successfully working with multiple stakeholders and the MST.

These three success stories emphasize economic development, which involves long-term self-sufficiency, personal accountability, and education for economically disadvantaged groups. They reflect a different mindset on the part of workers and employers, new ways of working together, and new skill sets. Economic development is a field of research and practice whose knowledge could be utilized more fully by HR managers in stakeholder management and corporate social responsibility programs. Its proponents realized decades ago that charity and paternalism do not result in long-term development. The solution in the success stories is real economic interdependence, consistent with value optimization of the firm, coupled with an integrated effort by the community, government, and key stakeholders to promote concurrent social development. Community development and the field of international development, which focuses on the socio-economic development of communities in other countries, have also developed a knowledge base that could benefit HR personnel. One of their key lessons is that partnerships create the most successful projects and that projects cannot be imposed on local communities. Self-determination is a critical factor. Other best practices from these three fields of development could inform how HR managers and companies work with stakeholders and result in more creative and viable solutions in the type of stakeholder dialogue needed at Aracruz and elsewhere.

Stakeholder dialogue is one of the most important skills needed by HR managers in situations like this. An adversarial, competitive, close-minded stance resolves nothing, especially when parties are ideologically opposed. Instead, the stance that characterizes stakeholder dialogue (i.e. cooperative, open-minded and empathetic) holds more promise. The requisite skills are willingness to listen to the views of all parties, tolerance of different views, acceptance of criticism, sharing information, searching for common ground, and devising creative, win–win solutions (Kaptein and van Tulder, 2003; Pedersen, 2006). When different nationalities are involved in situational stakeholder management, intercultural competence is also important.

NGOs are capable of using pressure tactics that can harm companies, fairly or unfairly. Willingness to dialogue with NGOs in good faith and a history of good relationships with stakeholders and NGOs can prevent or mitigate destructive conflict in some cases. NGOs in today's business world have to be taken seriously, whether or not their actions are fair. Forming alliances, correcting misinformation, transparency, and aggressive countermeasures are examples of company actions in the face of unfair targeting.

In Brazil, unclear property rights and the political climate constituted an externality that forced managers to switch some of their attention from value maximization to a stakeholder problem that was partly outside their control. This is not the only part of the world where externalities can turn into unexpected problems that companies and HR managers are not prepared to confront. Global warming (e.g. competition for water and energy), poorly respected intellectual property rights, deficient educational systems, and extreme social and political strife are all examples of externalities that could require situational stakeholder management.

More research is needed in the following areas: cases on firms that have successfully dealt with such externalities and multiple stakeholders, the identification of best practices in socio-economic development efforts involving businesses, stakeholder dialogue in global settings, and training methods to prepare HR professionals for situational stakeholder management.

## References

Aftenposten (2006a) *Natives Demand Action from Norway*, April 27. Retrieved on 8/11/06 from http://www.aftenposten.no/english/local/article1296452.ece.

Aftenposten (2004b) *Lorentzen Retires from Aracruz*, May 4. Retrieved on 8/11/06 from http://www.aftenposten.no/english/business/article787137.ece.

Andonova, V. and Zuleta, H. (2007) "The effect of enforcement on human resources practices: A case study in rural Colombia," *International Journal of Manpower* 28(5): 344–353.

De'Nadai, A., Overbeek, W., and Soares, L. A. (2005) "Promises of jobs and destruction of work: The case of Aracruz Celulose in Brazil," Montevideo: World Rainforest Movement.

Everingham, M. (2001) "Agricultural property rights and political change in Nicaragua," *Latin American Politics and Society*, 43(3): 61–93.

Fig, D. (2007) "Questioning CSR in the Brazilian Atlantic Forest: The case of Aracruz Celulose SA," *Third World Quarterly*, 28(4): 831–849.

Freeman, R. E. (1984) *Strategic Management: A Stakeholder Approach*, Boston: Pitman.

Freire, P. (1970) *Pedagogy of the Oppressed,* New York: Continuum.

FUNAI (1994) *The Tupiniquim on the Brazilian Coast*, Report GT783/94, Brasilia: FUNAI.

Ganitsky, J. (2005) "Lecciones Colombianas para afrontar con exito los desafios empresariales: Indupalma y las Cooperativas de Trabajo Asociado (CTA)" [Colombian lessons in successfully fighting business challenges: Indupalma and the Asóciate Cooperative Work (CTA)], *Revista de Empresa* (Business Journal), 11: 96–110.

Giddens, A. (1999) *Globalization*, London: Reith Lecture Series, BBC.

Granovetter, M. (1985) "Economic action and social structure: The problem of embeddedness," *American Journal of Sociology*, 91(3): 481–510.

Harvard Business School (2000) *Erling Lorentzen*, March. Retrieved on 11/06/06 from: http://www.hbs.edu/entrepreneurs/erlinglorentzen.html.

Hofstede, G. (2001) *Culture's Consequences: Competing Values, Behaviors, Institutions, and Organizations across Nations*, 2nd edn., Thousand Oaks, CA: Sage.

International Finance Corporation (2006) *Mission*. Retrieved 11/01/06 from: http://www.ifc.org/about.

Jensen, M. C. (2001) "Value maximization, stakeholder theory, and the corporate objective function," *European Financial Management*, 7(3): 297–317.

Jones, T. (1995) "Instrumental stakeholder theory: A synthesis of ethics and economics," *Academy of Management Review*, 20(2): 404–437.

Kaptein, M. and van Tulder, R. (2003) "Toward effective stakeholder dialogue," *Business and Society Review*, 108(2): 203–224.

Lang, C. (2005) "Brazil: Aracruz – Sustainability or Business as Usual?," *WRM Bulletin*, 99, October. Retrieved on 11/06/06 from: http://chrislang.blogspot.com/2005_10_28_chrislang_archive.html.

Lira Aguiar, C. A. (2005) "Message from the President," *Sustainability Report 2005*, Sao Paulo: Aracruz Celulose. Retrieved on 11/06/06 from: http://www.aracruz.com.br/minisites/ra2005/localaracruz/ra2005/en/rs/index.html.

Lizarralde Montoya, R. D. (2004) *Strengthening Conflict Sensitive Business Practices Indupalma Colombia*, Speech, United Nations, New York, December. Retrieved on 11/06/06 from: http://www.unglobalcompact.org/Issues/conflict_prevention/meetings_and_workshops/gc_symposium_ny2004/MrLizarralde.pdf.

Lustig, N. and Deutsch, R. (1998) *The Inter-American Development Bank and Poverty Reduction: An Overview*, Mimeo POV-101-R, Washington, DC: IADB.

Mitchell, R. K., Agle, B. R., and Wood, D. J. (1997) "Toward a theory of stakeholder identification and salience: Defining the principle of who and what really counts," *Academy of Management Review*, 22(4): 853–886.

Muello, P. (2006) "Dismayed landless Brazilians still back leader," *Mercury News*, October 27. Retrieved on 11/06/06 from: http://www.mercurynews.com/mld/mercurynews/news/world/15862096.htm?source=rss&channel=mercurynews_world.

Murasawa, L. (2007) e-mail message to A. Osland, August 27.

Nunes, W. L. (2007) personal interview by Betania Tanure and Rodolf Gabrish, March 28.

Nystuen, G. (2006) *Letter to the Ministry of Finance*, March 22. Retrieved on 8/25/06 from: http://odin.dep.no/etikkradet/english/documents/099001-110010/dok-bn.html.

Osland, A. and Osland, J. (2007) "Aracruz Celulose: Best practices icon but still at risk," *International Journal of Manpower*, 28(5): 435–450.

Pedersen, E. R. (2006) "Making corporate social responsibility (CSR) operable: How companies translate stakeholder dialogue into practice," *Business and Society Review*, 111(2): 137–163.

PPI (1998) *Brazil: Sustaining the Future*, 40(4): 43, San Francisco: PPI.

*Registry Book of Deeds of the Settlement of Nova Almeida* (1842) Public Archive of Espírito Santo State: Municipal Chamber fund of Nova Almeida.

Rowley, T. J. (1997) "Moving beyond dyadic ties: A network theory of stakeholder influences," *Academic Management Review*, 22(4): 887–910.

Tanure, B. (2004) *Gestaoa Brasileira*, 3rd edn., Sao Paulo: Atlas.

Tanure, B. (2005) "Human resource management in Brazil," in M. M. Elvira, and A. Davila (eds.), *Managing Human Resources in Latin America: An Agenda for International Leaders*, Oxford: Routledge.

Yergin, D. and Stanislaw, J. (1998) *The Commanding Heights: The Battle for the World Economy*, New York: Simon and Schuster.

# 3 The strategic importance of close employment relations in conflict-ridden environments

## Three cases from Colombia[1]

*Veneta Andonova, Roberto Gutierrez, and Luis Felipe Avella*

Emerging markets, including those in Latin America, have received considerable attention recently as more corporations try to adapt their global strategies and tap into the natural resources and young labor markets of these countries. It is now clear that successful strategies to target these attractive markets differ from the Western style of conducting business. Building global capacities in social embeddedness has been proposed as an alternative to the traditional model of operations (London and Hart, 2004). Understanding the social context, building from the bottom up, and sharing resources across organizational boundaries are seen as key activities that guarantee a "license to operate" and add to their competitive advantage. Human resource departments are active participants in this process, since they are frequently in charge of managing the social demands of companies' stakeholders (Austin *et al.*, 2007).

Most human resource management theories, however, have been developed without attention to the specific social, political, and economic forces that shape the Latin American business environment. Factors such as weak governmental enforcement and investment protection, latent class conflict and prejudice in management–worker relations, together with considerable unattended social demands and violence force companies to abandon traditional approaches to human resource management and to consider different priorities. Innovative companies build psychological and economic proximity between workers and managers/owners, sometimes blurring the widely accepted boundaries of these categories.

After studying several Colombian cases, we argue that the more economic interests of workers and managers/owners are shared and the closer they feel psychologically, the less the incentive to violently oppose each other and the less the propensity to allow third-party involvement in conflicts. As a result, the scope and the intensity of conflicts are effectively reduced. We propose this approach as a company-wide strategy for gaining a "license to operate" and building competitive advantage rather than simply as a human resource strategy.

To clarify the effect of management–worker proximity we present our argument in some detail in the next section. We claim that in environments with feeble or no government presence and considerable unattended social demands, employment conflicts tend to escalate into much wider social, political, and economic clashes.

Therefore, attending to employment relationships becomes much more important than traditional theories conceive. We illustrate our argument with three case studies in Colombia and briefly describe the experience of Hacienda Gavilanes, Indupalma, and Hocol. We emphasize the challenges that the Colombian conflict poses for these businesses, and we describe the specific actions undertaken to effectively manage employment relations and to gain a "license to operate." Finally, we present the positive results that have added to the competitive advantage of these organizations.

## Theoretical background

Establishing common economic interests, such as joint ownership and profit sharing, is frequently viewed as a prerequisite for harmonious employment relationships. In their literature review in the fields of economics, entrepreneurship, organizational behavior, and industrial relations, Rousseau and Shperling (2003) define ownership as the right to residual control and three related privileges – profit sharing, information sharing, and decision making regarding the use of the assets. In most of the literature, however, these rights and privileges are assumed to be enforceable in a perfect and costless manner, an assumption that is violated in many developing countries. Furthermore, the assumption obscures the important effect of these rights when they are shared within the employment relationship.

We argue that in circumstances where institutions are weak and where rights are not enforced by the state, companies can obtain a "license to operate" and even build competitive advantage by sharing control rights and ownership-related privileges with employees. This is because in such environments employees can effectively destroy valuable resources for the company with impunity and, unless their economic interest is closely linked to the economic objective of owners and managers, employees may be tempted to use their destructive powers. Moreover, unless a rather strong shared interest exists between company representatives and employees, third parties can become involved in the conflict on either side. The result can lead to an escalation of the conflict to the further detriment of the local social and economic situation. We argue that efforts to bring together the two sides of the employee relation effectively drive away external actors and successfully limit the scope of conflict.

There is some evidence, however, that sharing residual control rights or profits in the employment relationship is not sufficient to change employees' attitudes and, as a consequence, the scope of the potential conflict. The phenomenon of psychological ownership is important for this relationship (Hammer *et al.*, 1981). Psychological ownership is a state of mind in which the individuals feel that the target of ownership is theirs (Pierce *et al.*, 2001; Pierce *et al.*, 2004). Several authors claim that this psychological phenomenon can occur even in the absence of legal ownership (Etzioni, 1991; Rousseau and Shperling, 2003), and that the effect of formal ownership on employee behavior is mediated by psychological ownership (Pierce *et al.*, 1991). Thus, any effort to influence employee behavior, by offering legal ownership or related privileges, should be accompanied by actions that enhance employees' psychological commitment to the firm, for example by delegating more control to employees.

We conceive the implementation of such sharing practices in the wider context of stakeholder interests and see the stakeholder relationships as an essential asset to be managed for the benefit of the company's long-term objectives (Post *et al.*, 2002). Therefore, what we refer to as "sharing" also involves working with communities and entities that employees are linked to and where employees perceive benefits. In this context, many activities commonly labeled social responsibility (for example supporting educational programs and building public infrastructure) can be understood as acts of sharing within the employment relationship.

By applying this rationale to the employment relationship, we identify how challenges of weak enforcement can be managed through human resource policies. Simultaneously, we show how companies' social initiatives have a direct impact on the employment relationship. It appears that giving a leading role to human resource management is instrumental for a company to obtain a "license to operate" and build competitive advantage in a hostile environment. Like researchers on environmental issues (Shrivastava, 1995; Westley and Vredenburg, 1991), we explore how firms gain competitive advantage by attaining social legitimacy.

## Methodology

Case studies provide a wealth of information. In this section we describe the data collection methods and analysis techniques used. When a phenomenon cannot be easily separated from its context, case studies are an appropriate method of empirical inquiry (Yin, 1989). Case comparisons provide answers to "what" and "how" questions, such as: What are the strategies adopted by organizations operating in conflict-ridden environments? How is the practice of human resource management altered?

Three cases were selected for this study because of their potential for answering these questions. They were also chosen because they offer different approaches to bringing workers and managers together. All three take place in rural settings in Colombia where there is a presence of illegal armed actors. The cases depict responses by a medium and a large agricultural company and a medium-size company in an extractive industry.

Almost all the information about these cases was collected for three previous research projects conducted at different periods of time. The Hacienda Gavilanes study was conducted in three stages over four years starting in 2003 (Andonova and Zuleta, 2007); the Indupalma case was documented between 2002 and 2004 (Fernandez *et al.*, 2003a, 2003b, 2003c; Austin *et al.*, 2004); and the Hocol study has been developed since 2003 (Uribe *et al.*, 2007; SEKN, 2006). Each case was triangulated among different sources of data.

The sources of data included archival materials, company documents, unstructured and semi-structured interviews, and other analytical studies. Documents included internal communications, company newsletters, annual reports, social balance reports, industry studies, and newspaper reports. The interviews were between half an hour and three hours long, and in some instances a manager was interviewed several times. A list of top managers and key workers was made at the beginning of each study and it was completed with names that were considered relevant as the studies progressed. Other stakeholders (e.g. industry and community leaders) were also interviewed. For the Hacienda Gavilanes case, 2 top managers and 2 workers were interviewed; for the Indupalma case, 5 top managers, 3 managers from other palm oil companies, 4 cooperative leaders, and 5 community leaders; and for the Hocol case, 10 top managers, 4 managers from other oil companies, 6 workers, and 7 community leaders were interviewed. Finally, visits to regional operations provided important information about the security conditions in which these companies operate and the mechanisms they adopt – sometimes very visible and at other times subtle.

Interview transcripts, summaries, and notes were analyzed by categorizing and comparing emergent concepts and ideas. All the data were compared and contrasted, and partially ordered data displays were used to help in the analysis and reduction process. For example, from the case studies, we listed company strategies, capabilities, and activities. These data displays facilitated both within- and cross-case analysis (Miles and Huberman, 1984). A literature review ran parallel to data analysis in order to theoretically ground the analysis (Glaser and Strauss, 1967; Eisenhardt, 1989). Our data displays and interpretations were updated and refined as we iterated back and forth between existing theory and our findings. The results of our analysis are discussed below.

## The Colombian environment

During the 1990s, the Colombian state underwent a process of downsizing, modernization, and decentralization that resulted in – among other things – a partial or total privatization of state agencies, a move towards provision of public goods and services by private organizations, and the adoption of development models with a stronger role for civil society. Within these elements, some structural characteristics of Colombia stand out: the weakness of the state, a high level of inequality, and the pressing needs of a large portion of its population.

Poverty levels remain high and, despite a decentralized health model – with participatory and solidarity characteristics – and an education system that attempts to articulate the interests of different actors, high measures of inequality are prevalent. The inequalities in income distribution have barely been curbed (e.g. the Gini coefficient during the 2000s has only been reduced from 0.6 to 0.55), living conditions vary greatly between rural and urban settings, and basic utilities are not even universal in the latter (28 percent of townships do not have potable water and 40 percent do not have sewage systems). Additionally, thousands of lives and numerous resources have been wasted in a decades-long conflict.

Wartorn Colombia provides fruitful ground for investigating company strategies, including strategic human resource management, for doing business in a hostile setting. The spacious and rugged territory makes it difficult for the government to gain control and guarantee security. Several guerrilla groups, para-military armies, and persistent drug trafficking have contributed to the ongoing violence through extortion, land expropriation, and human rights abuses. Below we describe the principal illegal armed groups that have been protagonists in the cases we present in the following section.

### *Fuerzas Armadas Revolucionarias de Colombia (FARC)*

In 1964, there were 975 members of the FARC (Armed Revolutionary Forces of Colombia), many of them landless farmers concentrated in rural and poor areas with a scarce government presence. During the 1960s and the 1970s, the FARC slowly expanded to other regions and gained force in small towns, agricultural zones, oil and gold extraction regions, and along the coasts. Expropriation, extortion, and kidnappings ordered by this guerrilla group have posed a serious threat to business in vast areas of the country and to agricultural regions in particular. The number of FARC combatants is currently estimated to be around 17,000–20,000 and they are accused of being associated with drug traffickers.

### *Ejército de Liberación Nacional (ELN)*

The National Liberation Army was founded by a group of intellectuals strongly influenced by the Cuban Revolution. In the 1980s, after internal disagreement, its members developed a strategy to create an impact like that of the FARC. The ELN concentrated on extortion and land expropriation in the Sarare Forest to take advantage of the construction of an oil pipeline between Caño Limon and Coveñas. ELN members are now estimated to be approximately 3,000–5,000.

### *M-19*

This guerrilla group was formed in 1974 by ex-militants of FARC and leftist politicians. During its sixteen-year existence it took part in highly visible acts such as the takeover of the Palace of Justice (the Colombian Constitutional Court) and the Embassy of the Dominican Republic. In 1990, the M-19 negotiated a peace agreement with the Colombian government and former members now participate in the democratic political process; several have been elected to office.

### *Paramilitary groups*

In response to deficient government protection against expropriation and extortion, entrepreneurs – mostly large landowners – have organized private armies, the so-called paramilitaries. Paramilitaries are frequently accused of practicing extortion, having close connections with drug traffickers, and distorting democratic processes by pressuring or backing local and national politicians.

One or several of these illegal armed groups have been active protagonists in the environments where the organizations we describe carry out operations.

Understanding how companies deal with clear and present danger – and how they build competitive advantage in the face of such dangers – can provide clues about how to develop business activity in conflict zones.

## Case studies

### Hacienda Gavilanes

In the area where Hacienda Gavilanes is located, paramilitaries are very active. Spurred by government plans for a peace process, paramilitary leaders are purchasing land from local landowners who are unable to sustain their farms as a result of a decrease in coffee and sugar cane prices. A recently imposed local land tax puts additional strain on landowners, who frequently find themselves forced to sell to the leaders of regional armed groups that are notorious for promoting drug trading and violence.

Hacienda Gavilanes began as a sugar cane farm located in Risaralda, a mountainous region in western Colombia. The farm now has five business units: panela (unrefined brown sugar loaf), pig- and cattle-raising, cold storage and a guava plantation. Until 2005, panela production surpassed other activities in terms of employment and sales, but poor margins forced farm owners to substitute sugar cane for pasture. The pig- and cattle-raising units, together with the cold-storage businesses of Hacienda Gavilanes, are much more profitable, though smaller. The cold-storage unit includes a dairy cattle unit, a slaughterhouse, and eight butchers in Pereira, the nearest big city. In 2006, Hacienda Gavilanes allied with a neighboring farm to develop a guava plantation.

In the 1990s, Hacienda Gavilanes was like any other sugar cane farm in the area. The low margins from sugar cane production forced it to diversify into coffee growing. But the decline in coffee prices and the appearance of new crop pests took their toll on the new business. Unfortunately, sugar cane entered its own crisis and the farm began to incur losses in an economic environment that was unlikely to change. Under these circumstances, the owner of Hacienda Gavilanes decided to restructure the farm's hiring and incentives policy, and encouraged the foundation of a labor cooperative, Cofudeco. Almost immediately, the co-op improved working conditions and increased the farm's profits and security.

Hacienda Gavilanes became a client of the cooperative. The owner no longer pays daily wages directly to the workers, but negotiates compensation for the completion of certain tasks with Cofudeco. This arrangement creates incentives for time-saving innovations, and workers have come up with several proposals for improving the processes.

Moreover, workers have the opportunity to attend courses related to their daily tasks. As a result, not only have they become more productive, but they are now also able to instruct other workers on both Hacienda Gavilanes and other farms. The acquisition of new skills is highly valued by the workers and helps them develop a sense of belonging and psychological ownership. In addition, the members of Cofudeco have access to credit because the cooperative guarantees their personal loans. Access to credit has allowed workers and their families to purchase groceries, home appliances, and motorcycles, and to obtain bank accounts with credit cards. All these benefits increase the cost of abandoning the labor cooperative and strengthen workers' commitment to the farm.

Workers are also given considerable freedom to decide and suggest how to perform different tasks. This arrangement stands in sharp contrast to the widespread feudal relationships in the area. Another local innovation is the ongoing process of shared ownership. Cofudeco is gradually acquiring work tools such as machetes and knives, and it plans to buy a tractor. Apart from capital accumulation and monetary rewards, Cofudeco members receive fringe benefits in the form of literacy programs and improved housing conditions for themselves and their families.

As the Cofudeco manager states, "by offering jobs and social security, the farm has improved its security conditions." In fact, today this is the only farm that does not need a hired guard and one of the few sustainable farms in the area (Andonova and Zuleta, 2007).

### *Indupalma*

In the 1950s, the owners of Grasco – a Colombian company involved in cooking oil production and marketing – decided to invest in a large African palm tree plantation, in Northeastern Colombia, in order to avoid importing raw materials. In 1961, they created Indupalma. To face the enormous technical challenges of turning the jungle into a plantation site, they imported manual labor. As a result, the population in the area increased swiftly and was left without adequate housing. Paternalistic attitudes, extremely hierarchical practices, and regional social and political conditions shaped the tense and complex relations between the company and its workers. A sizable number of workers hired by contractors were not recognized as employees by the company, but at the same time Indupalma provided all health care, housing, electricity, and water services for laborers, who did not view these as additional benefits but as company obligations. In 1971, frictions between union and management increased as a result of the assassination of the company's personnel manager. A dozen top union leaders were accused and found guilty of the crime, and simultaneously union headquarters were destroyed by an anonymous act.

The process that led to the 1977 collective labor agreement took place under dire conditions. The union's first petition was to recognize field workers – those workers hired by contractors – as Indupalma employees. When management refused to include these workers' benefits in the negotiations, workers went on strike. On the third day of the strike, the M-19 guerrilla group kidnapped Indupalma's general manager, Hugo Ferreira Neira. Company negotiators, under instructions to save the general manager at all costs, accepted all six petitions discussed; first and foremost, the legal inclusion of field workers in Indupalma's payroll, taking into account their seniority.

After 1977, an invigorated union obtained substantial benefits for workers in the next seven collective labor agreements (one every two years). Some clauses prevented technological upgrades and, as labor productivity declined, management attributed this to "workers' new relaxed attitude." By the second half of the 1980s, local violence worsened as a new social agent, paramilitary groups, was created to fight guerrillas. Top managers stopped visiting the plant; for years they managed the firm from headquarters in Bogota. Towards the end of the decade, the opening of the economy together with a fall in the international price of palm oil forced the company to undergo structural changes in order to guarantee its survival.

Facing bankruptcy in the first half of the 1990s, Indupalma downsized by subcontracting with cooperatives. One cooperative contract in 1995 was expanded to twenty by 2002. A crisis with the co-ops at the end of 2004 resulted in new contracts with twelve totally different co-ops; the only three that remained were those that owned land. Throughout, the company invested significant resources in training co-op workers at three levels: technical, administrative, and personal. Cooperatives evolved from owning only their labor force, to owning capital goods, and three of them eventually became landowners. A tight control system assured compliance with all employment regulations; it even prevented co-ops from paying any illegal armed force for security services.

The economic turnaround caught the attention of many. Productivity levels went up substantially during the second half of the 1990s and reached a plateau by the beginning of 2000. Indupalma bounced back from near bankruptcy to profitability, and cooperatives became a driver for regional development. Throughout this process the CEO's motto has been "*lo social paga*" (attention to social issues pays off), and he promotes Indupalma's business model as a privately led land reform.

Value has been created for both workers and managers. In the co-ops, increased income tied to performance has been achieved, along with an entrepreneurial spirit and a sense of ownership. Human and regional development is also visible. For the company, changes in cost structure along with productivity increases make all the difference for its survival and competitiveness (Fernandez *et al.*, 2003c).

*Hocol*

Oil companies explore in vast and remote territories, and produce with expensive machinery. As part of the armed conflict in Colombia during 2003, there were 753 attacks against oil infrastructure. None of these attacks affected Hocol's infrastructure. Hocol is recognized as a very well-tuned assembler of technical experts and has a business model that allows it to explore many sites throughout Colombia. Its high mobility, much appreciated in the oil industry, has been instrumental in Hocol's expansion in exploration and in the company becoming the third largest operator in the country; it has been invited to be a partner in different projects with the largest companies in the oil industry; it explored 920,000 hectares in Colombia in 2004, while the second largest private company explored fewer than 300,000 hectares. Strengthened communities and tightly woven relations with them have been crucial for the development of Hocol's business.

In the 1960s and 1970s, communities asked oil companies for basic social infrastructure and Hocol responded by providing resources to build schools and health centers. Until the beginning of the 1990s, Hocol subcontracted organizations that would work with communities where they had operations. Two incidents changed Hocol's approach to communities. In 1991, the oil industry was blamed for a painful drought, which in fact was due to specific weather patterns and cattle-raising practices. Hocol's production was halted by community leaders from a micro-enterprise program they supported and, several days after the strike began, the guerrillas blew up some of the production infrastructure. It was evident to Hocol that the community did not recognize the company as a helpful partner, so it decided to stop subcontracting its social initiatives. From then on, its own foundation – established four years earlier – developed the micro-enterprise program and started an environmental education program that helped community members understand the reasons behind the drought.

Another turning point occurred in 1994: financial difficulties led the company to slash its budget for social initiatives by half. Since the Hocol Foundation had already agreed with the communities to develop projects for twice the resources they had, they decided to keep the plan intact by raising funds within the communities and with the government. This led to the question of why education and health had been Hocol's responsibility. From then on, government organizations were summoned to participate in every program. Social initiatives, worth several million dollars, have been developed by the joint work of different partners: during the 2000s, on average, 46 percent of the funds have come from Hocol, 19 percent from communities, 16 percent from government, and 19 percent from other sources such as multilateral agencies.

As Hocol downsized it kept as core operations its technical analysis teams and its social units. Hocol takes special care in its hiring and subcontracting practices (e.g. the maximum level of local content, technical training, funds for local productive projects, and institutional strengthening programs) within a highly sophisticated control system. More than the HR department, it is the foundation that establishes the close ties with workers and communities. Since the late 1990s, Hocol has worked on every aspect of its competitive context and found social initiatives to be one of its main sources of competitive advantage. Its investments have improved the context for strategy and rivalry, related and supporting industries, and the conditions of its production factors and its demand (Porter and Kramer, 2006). Under conservative estimates, for every dollar the company invests in social issues, Hocol receives 76 cents in return. The company has outstanding results in each aspect of its triple bottom line (Prieto, 2007).

As the relationship between the communities and Hocol evolved, the meaning of community development changed for all parties. The Hocol Foundation opened programs for community development and institutional strengthening. According to a Hocol executive, "the best we can do is to teach people the value of being leaders of their own life." Hocol has learned that it needs long-term relationships with communities. Communication, participation, consensus building, and feedback are all characteristics of these relationships. From their interaction, communities have learned to work together to change their living conditions; not only are they able to solve their internal conflicts, but they are able to create pressure to ensure their rights. In communities where Hocol has moved on, there is evidence that they continue to develop on their own. As Hocol's employees like to state, "oil is a public good that strengthens the social fabric" (Uribe *et al.*, 2007).

## Discussion

The increased importance of company strategies related to what is called "social responsibility" has imposed new demands on human resource departments in Latin America as they are often accountable for managing different demands of their stakeholders. The role of human resource departments is especially important in those circumstances where national and local institutions fail to uphold basic property rights, provide protection, and guarantee peace. In this context, the effective management of employment relationships results in a "license to operate" and supports the construction of sustainable competitive advantage. As Sharma and Vredenburg (1998) discovered for the Canadian oil industry, obtaining a social license and sustainable competitive advantage – in the three selected cases – required company-wide capabilities for stakeholder integration, high-order learning, and continuous innovation.

In addition, doing business in a conflict-ridden environment appears to require a special emphasis on mutual dependence, shared control, and high levels of cooperation. A continuous educational process and high adaptability are instrumental in accomplishing this. Furthermore, technical and administrative training, education in workers' rights and personal growth go a long way. Such policies contribute to effectively decrease distance between owners/managers and workers and support the convergence of interests between the parties in the employment relation, decreasing vulnerability to influences by third parties and subsequent conflict escalation.

The experiences analyzed above have had ups and downs. Subcontracting in the first sixteen years of Indupalma was a source of continuous tensions; since the late 1990s, however, a controlled subcontracting scheme has worked in favor of company profits and the well-being of its stakeholders. This can be found in numerous companies in Colombia: while many use cooperatives to downsize and avoid their responsibility with workers, a few, like Hacienda Gavilanes, have found that a good relationship with workers has made a tremendous difference. The benefits of a direct and supportive relationship with employees was also discovered by Hocol in 1991 when it eliminated most intermediaries involved in its programs for community support. The strategic importance of these programs for Hocol's competitive advantage led the company to move from subcontracting them to directly manage them. Again, company efforts to bring together its own and workers' interests paid off.

Our approach here is not without flaws. Although a historical perspective allows us to derive some general conclusions by contrasting periods when management and workers were far apart with periods when their interests were closely tied, the comparability among cases is somewhat limited by differences in location, size, and industry. Controlling for these factors would undoubtedly improve the precision of our analysis and conclusions, and may be a subject of future research.

## Note

1 We thank Marta Elvira and Anabella Davila for their patience and support. Veneta Andonova thanks Hernando Zuleta and Sebastian Londoño for their comments and suggestions. This research would not have been possible without the patience and generosity of all those interviewed, and the collective research efforts we undertake at the Social Enterprise Knowledge Network (SEKN).

## References

Andonova, V. and Zuleta, H. (2007) "The effect of enforcement on human resources practices," *International Journal of Manpower*, 28: 344–353.

Austin, J. E., Reficco, E., and SEKN (2004) *Social Partnering in Latin America: Lessons Drawn from Collaborations of Businesses and Civil Society Organizations*, Boston: David Rockefeller Center for Latin American Studies, Harvard University.

Austin, J. E., Gutierrez, R., Ogliastri, E., and Reficco, E. (2007) "Capitalizing on convergence," *Stanford Social Innovation Review*, winter: 24–31.

Eisenhardt, K. M. (1989) "Building theories from case study research," *Academy of Management Review*, 14(4): 532–550.

Etzioni, A. (1991) "The socio-economics of property," in F. W. Rudmin (ed.), *To Have Possessions: A Handbook on Ownership and Property*, special issue of *Journal of Social Behavior and Personality*, 6: 465–468.

Fernandez, D., Trujillo, D. M., and Gutierrez, R. (2003a) *Indupalma S.A.: los primeros años, 1961-1977*, Boston: Harvard Business School Publishing SKS005.

Fernandez, D., Trujillo, D. M., and Gutierrez, R. (2003b) *Indupalma S.A.: los años después del secuestro, 1977-1991*, Boston: Harvard Business School Publishing SKS025.

Fernandez, D., Trujillo, D. M., and Gutierrez, R. (2003b) *Indupalma las Cooperativas de Trabajo Asociado, 1991-2002*, Boston: Harvard Business School Publishing SKS026.

Glaser, B. G. and Strauss, A. L. (1967) *The Discovery of Grounded Theory: Strategies for Qualitative Research*, Chicago, IL: Aldine.

Hammer, T.H., Landau, J. C., and Stern, R.N. (1981) "Absenteeism when workers have a voice: The case of employee ownership," *Journal of Applied Psychology*, 66: 561–573.

London, T. and Hart, S. (2004) "Reinventing strategies for emerging markets: Beyond the transnational model," *Journal of International Business Studies*, 35: 350–370.

Miles, M. B. and Huberman, A. M. (1984) *Qualitative Data Analysis*, Beverly Hills, CA: Sage.

Pierce, J. L., Kostova, T., and Dirks, K. T. (2001) "Toward a theory of psychological ownership in organizations," *Academy of Management Review*, 26: 298–310.

Pierce, J. L., O'Driscoll, M. P., and Coghlan, A. (2004) "Work environment structure and psychological ownership: The mediating effects of control," *Journal of Social Psychology*, 144: 507–534.

Pierce, J. L., Rubinfeld, S. A., and Morgan, S. (1991) "Employee ownership: A conceptual model of process and effects," *Academy of Management Review*, 16: 121–144.

Porter, M. E. and Kramer, M. R. (2006) "Strategy & society: The link between competitive advantage and corporate social responsibility," *Harvard Business Review*, December, 84(12): 78–92.

Post, J., Preston, L., and Sachs, S. (2002) "Managing the extended enterprise: The new stakeholder view," *California Management Review*, 45: 6–28.

Prieto, A. (2007) *Medición del beneficio que se recibe por el compromiso social*, Bogota: M.B.A. thesis, Universidad de los Andes.

Rousseau, D. M. and Shperling, Z. (2003) "Pieces of the action: Ownership and the changing employment relationship," *Academy of Management Review*, 28: 553–570.

SEKN (2006) *Effective Management in Social Enterprise: Lessons from Business and Civil Society Organizations in Iberoamerica*. Washington, DC: Inter-American Development Bank & David Rockefeller Center for Latin American Studies, Harvard University.

Sharma, S. and Vredenburg, H. (1998) "Proactive corporate environmental strategy and the development of competitively valuable organizational capabilities," *Strategic Management Journal*, 19: 729–753.

Shrivastava, P. (1995) "Environmental technologies and competitive advantage," *Strategic Management Journal*, summer special issue, 16: 183–200.

Uribe, E. M., Gutierrez, R., and Barragan, A. (2007) *Hocol*, Boston: Harvard Business School Publishing SKS098.

Westley, F. and Vredenburg, H. (1991) "Strategic bridging: the collaboration between environmentalists and business in the marketing of green products," *Journal of Applied Behavioral Science*, 27: 65–91.

Yin, R. K. (1989) *Case Study Research: Design and Methods*, Newbury Park, CA: Sage.

# 4 Stakeholders' perspective and strategic human resource management

## Lessons from a Colombian case study

*Amparo Jiménez and Jose Camilo Davila*

For more than a decade, social responsibility has challenged companies and their managers to introduce social innovations in all their areas of influence. A recent compromise between the expectations of an increasingly vigilant civil society and companies anxious to exhibit a positive social contribution, social responsibility defines new areas of performance related to the environment and local development. At the same time, it calls into question the perspective in which the organization's traditional functions, such as strategic human resource management (SRHM), are considered (Drnevich and Shanley, 2005; Schuler and Jackson, 2005; Paauwe and Boseli, 2003; Vosburgh, 2003).

There is still scant literature in the field making the link between social responsibility and human resource management, despite the fact that "employees" or "the world of work" (along with the environment, consumers, and society or local communities) is one of four primary areas of performance related to social responsibility (Freeman, 1999). Moreover, a number of works take a utilitarian approach in this regard, justifying social responsibility for its potential to attract and retain employees or make the firm more appealing. However, studies reveal that contemporary challenges facing SHRM cannot be effectively tackled through utilitarian approaches that emphasize the application of generic typologies derived from normative perspectives of management science such as resource dependency theory or the resource base view (RBV) theory (Dansereau and Yammarino, 2005).

Approaches must go beyond the traditional perspective of human resource management (HRM) to elucidate the useful theoretical and methodological aspects of resource dependency theory (from the perspective of the management stakeholder) for the purpose of integrating organizational strategy and HRM practices (creating the "fit"), and thus for orienting HRM in a strategic and "critical" perspective. "Critical perspective" refers to the vision the firm holds to successfully develop progressive practices and integrate the principles of resource dependency theory in its SHRM. These progressive practices are likely to embody social responsibility and to have positive social and psychological effects for employees. Further, they can play a role in integrating the marginalized sectors of society and strengthening the social fabric, and can contribute to the collective well-being through employment, training, and localization policies.

This chapter explores the following questions: What role have HRM policies and practices played in the company's organizational success? How are the HRM practices and policies related to principles of stakeholder management (SM)? Are they the result of conflict and compromise, the implementation of a progressive management vision, or a key to strategic positioning? What impact do these practices have on the firm's global performance?

This study is based on the experience of a company in the natural resource exploitation sector that successfully uses such practices to deal with an unstable and turbulent socio-political environment. Three empirical elements are set out that demonstrate the relevance of SM in reconciling economic and social imperatives in SHRM: (1) acceptance of the inherent contradictions between social responsibility and economic imperatives in defining the strategy; (2) implementation of management systems that foster the integration of SHRM, organizational culture, and institutional context; and (3) participation of senior management in the process of defining interesting questions in progressive SHRM practices (skill management in the context of change, employment security, organizational fairness, particularly related to pay, workplace health and safety, and democracy in the workplace).

The chapter consists of four sections. The first section summarizes the principles of corporate social responsibility from the stakeholders' perspective and synthesizes the literature on the main theoretical limitations of HRM approaches linked to the definitions of the term *strategic*. The second section describes the context of the case, the methodology used, and the conceptual framework. Subsequently, the longitudinal data are analyzed, synthesizing the empirical findings on how a Latin American firm was able to strategically orient its HRM policies while integrating SM. Finally, the study summarizes the theoretical lessons related to the advantages of corporate social responsibility for SHRM, and makes recommendations for future research.

## The nature of the term strategy human resource management

Explanatory approaches based on the notion of "fit," "integration," or "alignment" between a firm's strategy and its HRM practices present difficulties with operational variables such as methodological and empirical problems in HRM research (Wright and Sherman, 1999). The principal conceptual problem lies in the limited vision of the notion of "strategy" as it has been adopted by many researchers. Linked to the position of the organization in a competitive environment, this vision has prompted researchers to use well-known, simplistic strategic typologies in order to make the term *strategy* operational (Chadwick and Cappelli, 1999). These typologies emphasize the need to create competitive advantage for the organization from the firm's resources (Barney, 1991; Porter, 1985): human resource management must pay attention to individuals, their rarity, their specific abilities, and the difficulty of replacing them. The vision emphasizes the search for heterogeneity in HRM and the economic rationality of the decision-making process. While these typologies have been widely applied in the SHRM field, their application has often led to limited reasoning concerning HRM systems (debatable notions of interchange, mistaken levels of analysis, and incoherent underlying premises) (Paauwe and Boseli, 2003).

For HRM professionals, the term *strategic human resource management* includes a dynamic relationship between HRM practices, business requirements, and organizational efficiency (Schuler and Jackson, 2005). According to Schuler and Jackson, efficient HRM management demands understanding of the means of integrating an organization's strategic objectives to produce satisfactory results. But understanding strategic objectives requires a vast knowledge of the socio-political environment in which the organization operates. On the one hand, it is the organizational objectives that permit the conceptualization and configuration of HRM's policies and practices, which must be aligned or integrated with these objectives. On the other, it is collaborative relationships between managers and employees that achieve perfect alignment-integration between HRM practices and policies.

Shuler and Jackson (2005) include four components in what they call SHRM: (1) the contribution of systematized HRM practices to the organization's effectiveness; (2) the relationship between strategic organizational objectives and the organization's societal content (vertical integration); (3) coherence between HRM practices and organizational strategy (horizontal integration); and (4) collaborative relationships between HRM professionals and employees, who work together to insure alignment and integration between HRM and organizational efficiency (strategic partners). The first three components constitute the three connotations of the term strategic as defined by Ferris, Hochwarter, Buckley, Harrel-Cook, and Frink (1999), while the concept of "strategic partners" developed by Lawler (2001) appears as a fourth component. We now look more carefully at two of the components which seem to shed light on our results.

Vertical integration exemplifies the second connotation of the term strategy, known as the firm's contingent focus, which concerns the way strategic decisions affect the evolution of HRM practices. Vertical integration emphasizes the firm's strategy as a moderator between HRM practices and the firm's performance. Organizations that have a high degree of integration between strategy and HRM practices will perform better than those that do not. The use of the term strategy connotes a perspective that allows theoreticians to study the effects of the organization's competitive context with regard to its set of HRM practices (Chadwick and Cappelli, 1999). The reflection of strategic decisions in the HRM system is a given, to the extent that management of the competitive environment is conceived as something similar to strategy.

The other component is the term *strategic partnership*, popularized by Lawler (2001) to describe the most advanced HRM model: the structure of the HRM function changing from an "HRM functional" focus toward a "strategic" focus and in the process leaving behind the "staff" and "business associate" models. This evolution is the result of (1) the growth and complexity of the organizations, which are influenced by radical changes in the values of the economy (knowledge and abilities); (2) labor legislation (flexibility in work relations) and the new information and communication technologies (ICT); and (3) increased awareness by organizations of the expectations of other interest groups, shareholders, and employees in the process of defining and implementing strategy and in the organization's profit and social performance. In the strategic partner model, the HR director functions at the same level as other directors and therefore reports directly to senior management. There is no hierarchical or salary difference between HR and other areas of the organization. HRM influences the determinant manner of the formulation and development of business strategy. Its central task is to support the organization's development through staff commitment and management of change.

This study makes an empirical contribution to the vertical integration component of SHRM. It emphasizes the firm's strategy as moderator of the relationship between HRM practices and organizational performance. That is, it seeks to identify empirical aspects that explain how the company under study achieves a high degree of integration between strategy and HRM practices and attains an interesting social performance.

The following section summarizes the principles of SM, in light of this document's stated aim of clarifying theoretical and methodological aspects that are useful and pertinent to SM in order to orient HRM in a strategic perspective.

## The stakeholders' perspective

SM has arisen, since the 1980s, as a modern company management model and theory of organization–environment relations. SM relies on three premises: (1) the organization is continuously threatened by the tension between supporting forces and resistance from other organizational actors in its environment; (2) the degree of attention that various stakeholders require depends on the accumulation of the three attributes of power, legitimacy, and compelling necessity (Mitchell *et al.*, 1997); and (3) organizational strategy is the result of a set of collective forces exercised by all the stakeholders, who seek satisfaction of their objectives and interests. Consequently, the strategic plan's validity depends on suppositions about the types of stakeholders identified and about actions taken during the strategy's planning and implementation period.

Generally, SM's descriptive, instrumental, and normative character helps to produce greater understanding of organization–environment relations (Freeman, 1999). The descriptive character identifies organizational actors in the organization's environment and sphere of interest in order to develop strategies to manage these actors proactively. The instrumental, or relational, character encourages linkage between management practices and attainment of the organization's objectives. For this, social acceptability criteria are established for business and organizational processes (values, policies, and practices) and to track the environment. In this dimension, it can be said that efficient management of stakeholders is an intangible social resource that is essential for reinforcing the firm's ability to create more economic value. Organizations that, among other things, put SM principles into practice prevent conflicts, favor integral performance, increase public confidence, improve media relations, and adapt better to new regulations.

Finally, the normative character acknowledges that the stakeholders are a set of persons or organizational actors who act out of a constellation of legitimate and substantive interests; therefore, this type of management is given a critical mission – to preside over the legitimacy of the company's practices (Carroll, 1989; Evan and Freeman, 1988).

The next two sections describe the contextual elements of the case and the research methodology used as a starting point for this commentary, based on the manner in which the company was able to integrate HRM policies and organizational strategy from SM principles.

## Case context

Cerro Matoso S.A. (CMSA) is a company established under Colombian law, created in 1979 with both foreign and Colombian state participation. Construction and assembly of the plant started in 1980 and the plant began operations in 1982. At the end of 1997 the Colombian state sold its interests in the company, which currently belongs to BHP Billiton, "the largest diversified natural resources group in the world."[1] CMSA is part of BHP Billiton's stainless steel division. The mine and processing plant are located in northern Colombia, in the department (province) of Cordoba on the Caribbean coast.

CMSA's principal activities are mining nickel and producing ferrous nickel. Marketing is done through the home office, BHP Billiton. The mine is considered world class because it is one of the largest lateritic nickel deposits in the world, with more than 400 million tons of mineral and an average grade of 2.2 percent.[2] A second production line built between 1999 and 2001 increased production capacity by 17,554 tons during its first year of operation. Between June 2002 and June 2003, CMSA produced 49,600 tons of nickel for gross earnings of US$199,000,000 and a net profit of US$109,400,600, for which the Colombian government received US$15,557,800 in royalties. In 2003 the company had 836 workers, 770 contractors, and 163 employees of the company-sponsored foundations for total direct employment of 1,769 persons,[3] making it the largest employer in its area of influence (the municipalities of Montelibano, La Apartada, and Puerto Libertador). CMSA has had a labor union since its first year of operation and has signed more than ten collective bargaining agreements over the past 25 years. There was one five-day strike in 1998.

Due to the deposit's characteristics and the lack of technical knowledge on the part of the Colombian workers and consulting companies, nearly 20 years elapsed between the discovery of the mine and the start-up of operations. The first years of production were plagued by major technical problems, beginning with a massive spill in the electric oven in 1985. Coupled with controversy over the large amounts invested in the project, this event aroused considerable public debate. After the first seven years of production, the company initiated an improvement process through the design and implementation of an elaborate control system in which management systems played an important role. These measures sought to insure that all activities that could affect health, safety, the environment, or product quality would comply with company policy, national legislation, and company standards.

CMSA supports three foundations: the Montelibano Educational Foundation (Fundacion Educativa de Montelibano [FEM]), the Panzenu Foundation (Fundacion Panzenu), and the San Isidro Foundation (Fundacion San Isidro). Both FEM and the Panzenu Foundation originated with the Union. FEM was founded in 1981 to provide high-quality, bilingual, primary and secondary education to the workers and their families and, through a quota system, to the larger community (16 percent of the total enrollment). The Panzenu Foundation, which started in 1970, envisioned construction and maintenance of a hospital facility for the purpose of providing quality health services to CMSA's workers and their families. In 1995 the foundation was converted to a service provider (IPS Panzenu) and it currently operates two modern clinics. Even before beginning operations, the company created the San Isidro Foundation as an institution independently supported and financed by CMSA. Its purpose is to improve the quality of life in the communities within the company's area of influence, with the goal of creating a solid and sustainable local economy. In 2002–2003, CMSA invested 1.45 percent of its pre-tax profits in working with the communities, exceeding the corporate goal.

The environment in which CMSA operates is uncertain for several reasons: the company directly and indirectly relates to a large number of organizational actors; these actors have very different characteristics and also continuously interact among themselves; and the effects of these interactions on CMSA are difficult to predict. The result is a highly complex situation.

As an example, the political actors surrounding CMSA include council members and mayors of the three immediate municipalities, regional politicians, regional politicians who participate in national legislative assemblies, and national politicians specializing in natural resources. Government officials at the municipal, departmental, and national levels (ministries and other state agencies) are also involved, and the Catholic Church makes its influence felt through its bishops and parish priests. Within the immediate community are found armed groups (guerrillas and paramilitaries); drug dealers at various stages of their operations (cultivation, processing, internal distribution, and money laundering); peasants displaced by the violence; farmers; local contractors and providers; and the governments of the three immediate municipalities.

Interactions among these actors often become complex. In 2001, for example, paramilitary groups and politicians of the Colombian Caribbean coast (the area where CMSA is located) entered into secret agreements to act in coordination at the national legislative level. The agreements unleashed a national debate when they became public.

Further, these same actors frequently and radically change their characteristics over time, and CMSA must demonstrate great flexibility if it is to generate relational strategies that are appropriate and suited to each actor. Along with the complexity created by the size and diversity of the group of actors involved, this instability produces a highly uncertain environment.

## Methodology

This research into CMSA is an in-depth case study. The company's path over more than two decades (1970–2000) provided the backdrop for the question: What strategic actions did this company's directors take that have enabled the firm to profit and thrive in a turbulent and unstable context? From the analysis of the answers to this question (Davila *et al.*, 2006), the information is revisited in order to answer the questions posed in this paper: What role have HRM policies and practices played in the company's organizational success? How are the HRM practices and policies related to principles of the SM model?

Various triangulation strategies were used to guarantee the validity of the results: (1) the use of three techniques for collecting information (interviews, participatory observation, and document review); (2) triangulation of time (various points in time in the organization); (3) triangulation of the sites (data were collected in diverse places); (4) ongoing comparison of the conclusions derived from raw data and conceptual analysis; and (5) verification of the meaning of atypical cases in relation to the research as a whole.

The researchers carried out 91 interviews – 70 with employees and former employees of CMSA and 21 with representatives of diverse sectors of the community (civic leaders, public officials, and officials of the Catholic Church). Interviews were conducted mainly during seven visits of approximately one week each to the Montelibano plant between January 2003 and January 2004. Also interviewed were three of the company's six former presidents, two outside of the country (in Canada and in Mexico) and one in Bogota; the president and all vice presidents in 2003; two members of the board of directors; and one former minister of mines and energy. Between two and three researchers participated simultaneously in the interviews, which averaged an hour and a half in length and were recorded in their totality. Seventy interviews were transcribed, producing 1,000 pages of text.

The document review included consultant studies done for CMSA (about organizational climate and evaluation of the socio-economic climate, for example); institutional publications (a commemorative publication marking CMSA's 25 years, manuals, policies, financial reports and company balances, the internal magazine, documents pertaining to occupational health, and management reports to the home office); corporate publications and publications about the mining and energy sector in Colombia (reports of the Mines and Energy Minister about competition in the mining sector); and academic documents about issues mentioned in the opening section of this chapter.

### *Analysis of the results*

An initial content analysis of the information yielded six statements revealing the general characteristics that answered the question: What strategic actions did this company's directors take that have enabled the firm to profit and thrive in a turbulent and unstable context? (See Table 4.1.)

*Table 4.1* CMSA actions that allowed the company to survive economically

| | |
|---|---|
| *Statement 1* | CMSA interacted with the surrounding communities, initially adopting a focus of assistance that evolved into a dynamic scheme, open to dialogue and focused on achieving solid results. |
| *Statement 2* | CMSA enjoyed relative discretion with regard to its shareholders due to three factors: the "know how" the organization developed, ignorance of the Colombian environment on the part of the multinationals, and the maturity of CMSA's management systems. |
| *Statement 3* | CMSA managed its profile in a framework of relative organizational austerity, faced with an uncertain and turbulent environment. Initially it did this in a reactive and indiscriminate manner. Later, it developed a proactive policy and differentiated among its various stakeholders. |
| *Statement 4* | An organizational culture evolved in CMSA that was characterized by commitment, solidarity, respect for people and an awareness of the company's history. The culture's development included determinants such as overcoming the difficulties of the early years and the process of "Colombianization." HRM policies and practices helped transmit these organizational values. |
| *Statement 5* | CMSA had to overcome challenges specific to the mining operation and challenges related to Colombia's political, social and economic situation. The company developed innovative strategies and mechanisms that allowed it to adapt to various contexts. |
| *Statement 6* | CMSA's culture is the result of values, practices and customs of both the community and the company's workers, which are not always congruent. The organizational culture shows nuances and fissures that are evident in employee performance. |

A second level of analysis allowed further extraction of the general characteristics mentioned above, which were called "critical issues" that CMSA had to confront. It defined *critical issue* as a set of unresolved problems that required the involvement of individual or collective actors in specific interactions and power dynamics to satisfactorily resolve them (Piotet and Sainsaulieu, 1994). The critical issues synthesized and analyzed as such were the following: (1) handling of changing shareholders that gave rise to conflicts of interest among various actors; (2) handling of the interdependence with the state organizations that gave rise to conflicts in relations with the central government and with governmental agencies; (3) handling of the surrounding communities that gave rise to conflicts related to the protection and security of public health, the conservation of non-renewable resources, evaluation of the environment, and strategies to guarantee the integral security of the company and the persons who worked for it; and (4) organizational performance that allowed the business to have continuity and that gave rise to controversies related to economic performance, indebtedness, increasing competition, and the handling of HR policies and practices (classification and training of officials, labor relations, promotion and career policies, compensation and performance evaluation). (See Table 4.2.)

*Table 4.2* Critical issues related to the integration between organizational strategy and HRM practices

| Critical controversial issues | Stakeholders involved | Results |
|---|---|---|
| **1  Related to the handling of changing shareholders** | | |
| Power conflicts between CMSA and IFI, a partner in the mixed-company phase (1970–1996) | Shareholders (Hanna Mining, IFI, Shell, BHP Billiton); management consultants; decentralized institutes | 1 Negotiations that produced contracts configuring the company as a concession and association<br>2 Privatization |
| Conflicts among partners due to the poor economic performance of the era (1985) | Managers; external consultants; shareholders (Hanna Mining, IFI, Shell, Billiton Overseas, BHP Billiton) | Crisis at CMSA in 1985 caused by the rupture of the electric oven |
| **2  Related to the handling of the interdependence with governmental organizations and decentralized institutions** | | |
| Strongly political negotiations related to the definition of royalties (1985–present) | Regional government; Congress; shareholders; mining ministers; regional politicians | Definition of royalties |
| Poorly developed negotiations to define the normative framework in the mining sector (1989–2001) | Congress; shareholders (Hanna Mining, IFI, Shell, BHP Billiton); mining ministers | Actions that brought about the writing of the first mining code in 1989, the redefinition of six new regulations in 1997, and the adaptation of the code in 2001 |
| Strongly political negotiations to influence the normative framework in the much politicized electricity sector (1997–present) | Congress; shareholders (Hanna Mining, IFI, Shell, BHP Billiton); mining ministers; Corelca | Actions that brought about the signing of the contract to provide electrical energy with Corelca |
| Negotiations centered on defining environmental conservation and protecting public health and safety (after the New Constitution in 2001) | Media; Minister of Health; Minister of the Environment; local community | Environmental study from which the project took off and that led to obtaining an environmental license from the Minister of the Environment authorizing the mining of nickel |
| **3  Related to the handling of the surrounding communities** | | |
| Development of egalitarian relations with the local communities to gain legitimacy in the media (1970–present) | Local community; central and local government; media; foundations (San Isidro, Panzenu, Montelibano Educational) | 1 Actions and negotiations that brought about the creation of the various foundations associated with the company. |

*Continued*

*Table 4.2* Critical issues related to the integration between organizational strategy and HRM practices—Cont'd

| Critical controversial issues | Stakeholders involved | Results |
|---|---|---|
| Development of strategies to obtain security threatened by the ongoing presence of armed groups in the region (1970–present) | Media; general public; foundations (San Isidro, Panzenu, Montelibano Educational); armed groups (paramilitaries) | 2 Investment in the construction of the road between Montelibano and the mine<br>1 Detention and kidnapping of members of the public by illegal groups, 1987–1995.<br>2 Threats of kidnapping and terrorism by illegal groups |

*4   Related to organizational performance*

| Development of technical capacities needed to achieve economic and socio-political objectives (1985–present) | HR vice-presidency; company labor union; employees; Employment Minister | Definition of SHRM practices:<br>1 Ability-based compensation that included housing loans, seniority bonuses and study grants<br>2 Fair career and training opportunities based on merit<br>3 Earnings evaluation<br>4 Development of participation mechanisms, "mobilization" and commitment, and an organizational climate based on egalitarian relations between hierarchy levels<br>5 Security and welfare conditions |

## Notes about the relevance of stakeholder management principles in SHRM

Three principles of stakeholder management emerge from the analysis of CMSA, a company in which management succeeded in strategically orienting HRM in a highly turbulent environment while putting into practice its own approaches as the management stakeholder: (1) acceptance of the inherent contradictions between economic and social imperatives in the company's strategic orientation; (2) implementation of management systems that foster the integration of SHRM, organizational culture, and institutional context; and (3) participation of senior management in the process of defining SHRM practices.

## *Acceptance of the inherent contradictions between economic and social imperatives in the company's strategic orientation*

The creation of economic value is naturally of great concern to the CMSA stakeholders, since they seek to ensure the company's continuity over time. However, the social dimension also represents a fundamental component in the concept of continuity. The case analysis confirms that the socio-political context significantly influenced CMSA's strategic orientation and, consequently, the definition of HRM policies and practices. CMSA successfully reconciles its strategic orientation, the imperatives of economic performance (profitability and continuity), and the satisfaction of social necessities (the expectations of directly and indirectly interested groups). The company achieves this in part through the gradual implementation of partly purposeful HRM policies and practices that are appropriate to the specific conditions of the context in which it exists (Schuler and Jackson, 2005). Such practices concern career development and the multi-skill compensation system; competitive salaries and benefits beyond those required by law; productivity bonuses reflecting company performance; control systems and earnings evaluation; health and security at work; and mechanisms for communication and participation.

Economic efficiency and social equality are, then, two objectives simultaneously pursued by the company and by the social actors of the immediate community, although in different proportions. Faced with the broad expectations of Colombian society with respect to large mining projects during the 1970s and 1980s, for example, CMSA built equitable relations with the socio-political actors (communities, general public, and government) and effective relations with economic actors (shareholders, providers, and employees). The term *equitable relations* alludes to the permanently tense relations between the organization and the surrounding society, in which the environment's social actors maintain legitimate expectations with regard to the company. These expectations are both socio-economic and ethical.

Socio-economically, CMSA's collective work in association with the three non-profit foundations showed that the company could operate without creating excessive social costs (environmental contamination, product safety, workplace safety, and health). As noted above, even before beginning operations the company created the San Isidro Foundation, which seeks to improve the quality of life of the communities affected by the company's operations and to create a solid and sustainable local economy. The Panzenu Foundation was founded in 1970 as a precondition of the initial contract between the government and Hanna Mining to offer health services to CMSA workers and their families, and in 2003 was operating two modern clinics. The Montelibano Educational Foundation, which was created in 1981, provides high-quality, bilingual primary and secondary education to the workers and their families. As mentioned, in 2002–2003 CMSA invested 1.45 percent of its pre-tax profits in the socio-economic development of the regional community, surpassing corporate goals.

With regard to ethics, CMSA has adopted practices that conform to legal requirements and promote social equality. In particular, the company has shown respect for the individual and collective rights of the persons with whom it maintains relations. (It does not discriminate against persons, it offers loyalty in financial transactions, and it shows commitment to regional development.) CMSA has always been very respectful of its workers, particularly of their right to association.[4] This attitude is reflected in (1) the diligent manner in which collective agreements are planned, prepared, and executed; (2) the existence and proper functioning of a worker–employer parity committee that jointly resolves day-to-day conflicts; and (3) the company's interest in the workers' general health and well-being. This goodwill on the part of CMSA is based on economic reasoning: "Labor costs are very low, comprising between 12 and 13 percent of total production costs of a pound of ferronickel produced at the plant; because of this, if CMSA wants to cut expenses, the company does not look to salaries."[5]

CMSA's ability to understand the characteristics of its business and its specific context and to respond appropriately to the apparently contradictory demands of economic and social imperatives has allowed it to overcome difficult conditions that have at times threatened its survival. These include (1) the process of "Colombianization"[6] of the 1980s; (2) the lack of financial resources and technical knowledge in the first years of operation; (3) the region's persistent insecurity due to the presence of paramilitary groups; and (4) the possibility of terrorist actions against the electrical infrastructure and the politicization of the electricity sector on which CMSA depends. These difficult conditions are addressed in the following sections.

### *Implementation of management systems that foster the integration of SHRM, organizational culture, and institutional context*

In the case analyzed, the social dimension took form through technical knowledge, employee commitment to and solidarity with the company, and the capacity for teamwork that the employees developed, all characteristics that influenced the company's global performance. Because of the lack of technical knowledge and experience in mining, 20 years went by between the discovery of the mine and the start-up of operations. The company's first years of operation were marked by serious technical problems that culminated in the rupture of the electric oven in 1985, which caused a four-month halt in operations and related financial losses. This situation, and the fact that CMSA was at the center of a huge public political controversy, placed the company's viability at risk. As a result of these circumstances, in 1985 the company decided to give priority to the process rather than to reaching established production goals. Operational stability, then, came about through collective effort and action that arose in the organization because of a need to understand and control the production process. This effort directly committed a core group of Colombians that included the vice-president for operations, 28 professionals (at the supervisor level or higher), and at least 100 rank-and-file employees (workers, supervisors, and managers).

Once operations had reached an acceptable degree of stability, the company committed to a program of continual improvement that involved putting in place a sophisticated control system in which management systems played a vital role. These management systems were adopted to guarantee the workers' safety and well-being as well as product quality. The quality of the product was assured through strict policies adopted by the company and through evolving industry legislation.

CMSA's organizational strategy and management systems developed out of a strong culture that emerged in the context of ongoing evaluation by economic and socio-political actors in Colombian society. The difficult circumstances that threatened the company's stability and the manner in which the company confronted these difficulties helped shape a sense of belonging, commitment to the organization, and a strong spirit of solidarity among the employees. The employees' physical safety became a priority in response to the risks of the mining and mineral processing business.

The implementation of management systems in the 1980s and the central role these acquired in the company have contributed decisively to promoting and internalizing physical security values day to day. Throughout its history CMSA has built an organizational culture that is characterized by commitment, solidarity, and concern for physical safety in the workplace and the environment, and an awareness of its past:

> There is one thing that brought us together that has not happened to other companies; CMSA was at the point of bankruptcy and the government tried to close it in 1985. When one is in a company where the oven has ruptured and they are trying to close you down, surviving the shipwreck produces great solidarity.[7]

An isolated geographic location and human resource policies and practices had together created a relatively favorable work environment, contributing to the sense of belonging, commitment, and solidarity mentioned and to the internalizing of the value of physical security. The work environment was in part the result of complex negotiations held every five years with a mature and focused labor union, during which the threat of a strike loomed, with its accompanying latent threat of shutting down the plant. Autonomous decisions by CMSA also played a role. The company incorporated HRM policies and practices related to the following:

1  compensation: CMSA offers a very competitive salary that guarantees the workers purchasing power and that is not necessarily linked to the company's results; extralegal benefits include housing and vehicle loans, seniority premiums, study grants for the workers and their children, and a substantial annual bonus that is based on CMSA's earnings;[8]
2  training and development: the employee is paid for what he knows and not for what he does;
3  systems for motivation and commitment: the company focuses on creating an organizational climate based on informal, respectful, and open relationships between hierarchical levels.

Decisions related to HRM policies and practices are applied, then, congruent to the organizational culture that has been generated over time: (1) social responsibility associated with concern about the environment; (2) solid confidence in dialogue with the stakeholders; and (3) a feeling of continuity maintained over the long term and anchored in the history and nature of the business (exploitation of natural resources). Investment in community development has been a fundamental component of the company's strategy, as one of the company's directors states:

> We invest in the community and thereby gain a license to operate. The people appreciate it and that generates an atmosphere with conditions suitable to pursuing our business. This strategy constitutes an ongoing challenge for each company.[9]

### Participation of senior management in the process of defining SHRM practices

With the arrival of Billiton Overseas as a shareholder in 1979, CMSA became a public corporation. In January 1981, the company appointed as its second president (1981–1987) a Colombian engineer who had been involved in the planning and development of the project since 1971, when the company was a public–private joint venture. This president's personal convictions and his persistence in dedicating time and effort to managing relations with the immediate community oriented CMSA's policies toward helping the community take an active role in its own development. Long term, the company was attempting, in the words of its president, "to teach the community to fish instead of giving the community a fish."[10] In practice, public relations between the company and the community have been a complex and demanding process, full of ups and downs. The concerns of this president (a pioneer for that era, at least in Colombia) were instrumental in elevating the concept of sustainable development that has characterized CMSA from the beginning. Sustainable development is one of the fundamental issues on which the company has focused and that currently makes up part of corporate strategy.

In another area, the second president decided, in 1982, to "Colombianize" the company and to delegate comprehensive authority in the company's operations to Colombian managers and operators. The learning process was very demanding, but within two years operation passed into the hands of Colombians, where it remains to this day. This president's leadership is evident again in this decision, which has proved critical to CMSA's future. However, all was not rosy during the "Colombianization" process: from 1982 to 1987, material spills created considerable financial loss and rates of production that were 75 percent of annual goals. These problems were the result of the technical complexity of the process and the personnel's lack of specific knowledge in the sector.

The vice-president for operations, a Colombian engineer who would later become CMSA's fourth president (1988–1993), was instrumental in the decision to focus on stabilizing the process rather than on complying with established production goals. His knowledge of the thermodynamic and physiochemical characteristics of the process was key to his ability to lead and orient the collective action of a broad group of professional and operating personnel who, as mentioned previously, made possible establishment of the production process in 1988.

CMSA's sixth president (1994–1997) played a definitive role in two primary issues that required the company's attention at that time. The first was implementation of an ongoing improvement program rooted in organizational control systems and management systems. This program would later be converted into organizational training that has allowed CMSA to develop a competitive advantage based on the efficiency and excellence of its mining and ferronickel production process. The second was start-up of a development program for employees in which "the worker earns for what he knows and not for what he is doing."[11] This program arose as an alternative to the former automatic job reclassification system proposed by the union.

Finally, CMSA's seventh president (1997–2004) initiated a low-cost strategy consistent with the nature of the company's product – a commodity that does not lend itself to a principal strategy of differentiation. This new strategy was implemented through economies of scale resulting from construction of a second production line (1999–2001) that allowed costs to be lowered to protect against the price volatility of nickel and generate greater profits. In the words of this president, "Within the large strategic objective of staying competitive, doubling the production capacity of ferronickel was an essential step to dilute the high fixed costs in a greater volume and thus reduce unit costs, seeking to be competitive."[12] Greater production volume achieved unclogging of the first production line in 1999 and, with the production of the second line, allowed CMSA to enjoy some of the lowest production costs in the sector and, in 2001, to enter the Japanese and Chinese markets for the first time.[13]

The case of CMSA shows, then, how the influence and leadership that these directors exercised at different times and with issues of primary importance contributed to creating the conditions for a strategic HRM dynamic and for integration between the organizational culture and the institutional context.

## Useful methodological aspects of the SM that facilitate SHRM

This study reflected on the question: Which theoretical and methodological aspects of the SM model facilitate a strategic HRM orientation in a company that operates in an environment of great uncertainty? Table 4.3 synthesizes empirical elements related to the relevance of SM in the orientation of SHRM policies.

First, in relation to the HRM's normative focus, which is concerned with identifying variables and applying generic typologies that stem from strategic-economic thought, the descriptive, instrumental, and normative character of SM allows for a more refined and adjusted understanding of the relationship between organizational strategy, HRM policies and practices, and organizational performance (Freeman, 1999). At the descriptive level, this study provides clarity in the debate that seeks to answer the question: Which stakeholders are involved in the critical SHRM issues of an organization? It demonstrates the importance of identifying critical issues in the context of power relationships to determine the degree of implication of each of the parties involved in the process of defining HRM policies and practices. This approach provides precise information not only

*Table 4.3* Useful methodological aspects of SM that facilitate SHRM research

| Management stakeholder dimensions | Levels of analysis | Central proposition | SM applications in CMSA |
|---|---|---|---|
| Descriptive | Rational level: Identify the actors who make up the SHRM environment of the organization and its sphere of interest | The organization is a constellation of cooperative and competing interests, all of which are of intrinsic value to it | 1 Participation of senior management was necessary and definitive in strategic planning and in the development of SHRM policies and practices<br>2 Participates in the identification of who is a stakeholder, their interests and degree of involvement, the meaning of the intervention, and the specificity of the context |
| Instrumental, or relational | Process level:<br>1 Develop processes for social acceptability of the business (values, policies and practices) and to track the environment<br>2 Establish proactive relations with the stakeholder(s) | Organizations that practice the principles of SM are relatively more competent in financial performance | 1 Actions that integrate SHRM, organizational culture, and the institutional context<br>2 Constantly adjust HRM as a strategic partnership on the organization's critical issues |
| Normative | Ethical level:<br>Give management a critical mission to declare the legitimacy of the company's HRM practices and develop social legitimacy criteria | The stakeholders are persons or groups with legitimate interests; these interests are ends in themselves and are not means to serve shareholder interests | 1 Accept the inherent contradictions between social and economic imperatives<br>2 Recognize that global success is evaluated by diverse stakeholder groups based on criteria of financial profitability and social responsibility |

about who is influenced by these decision processes, but also about the interests, the meaning of the interventions and the specificity of the institutional context in which the different interests intervene. This information becomes essential during the planning and validation period of the organizational strategic plan, as well as when putting into place SHRM policies and practices.

Second, when the analysis of controversial HRM issues arises, the instrumental, or relational, character of SM supplies the elements needed to capture those details of the organizational reality that foster relations between management practice and the pursuit of organizational goals. More specifically, taking into account the company's socio-political environment at the various points in time of project management (threatening environmental conditions that put at risk the security of persons and the infrastructure, conditions related to geographic localization, management of cultural differences) allowed the organization to constantly adjust HRM practices (career opportunities, training system, performance control system, participation mechanisms, industrial security) to the nature of organizational "strategy" and organizational controversies.

Third, to accept the normative character of SM – that is, the principle by which all stakeholders are organizational actors who act out of legitimate and concrete interests – means recognizing that (1) a company's global performance is evaluated by the diverse actors of the institutional environment, based not only on financial profitability but also on societal effects and the legitimacy of the company in its social milieu; (2) the attributes that help to characterize the categories of stakeholders (power, legitimacy, urgency) are static and ideal; in reality it is the management of controversies around HRM in specific contexts of power that determine the dynamic between organizational strategy and HRM policies and practices; and (3) company–stakeholder relations are immersed in dimensions that oscillate between cooperation and conflict and that over time change the time, content, and actions of the same organizations, and the actions of new and old groups of stakeholders.

Finally, the study shows that vertical integration that is interested in how strategic decisions affect the evolution of the system of HRM practice constitutes the most coherent orientation with the SM perspective (contingent focus). It can be expected, then, that organizations that put SM principles into practice have a high degree of integration between organizational strategy and HRM practices and that, consequently, they achieve performance levels superior to those that do not practice SM principles.

With regard to the evolution of HRM's role, it can be said that models three (agent of change) and four (strategic partner), described by Lawler (2001), are not the representations of HRM that are most theoretically and methodologically linked with the notion of "organizational actor" that underlies the idea of "stakeholder" – that is, the idea that actors that were involved in defining and implementing HRM practices and policies were capable of producing vertical integration at various levels. HR's main task was to support development of the organization through the people's commitment, led by an HRM convinced that its function was related to change and continuous learning. In this view,

(1) fair career opportunities, (2) merit training systems, (3) profit control systems, (4) development of participation and "mobilization" mechanisms, and (5) safety and welfare conditions in the workplace constitute strategic practices in the case studied.

## Conclusion

The case study reported here makes important contributions in what can be termed the conception of SM as a link to connect HRM practices and policies with the orientation of the organizational strategy in Latin America. We demonstrate the importance of identifying critical issues in the context of power relationships to determine the degree of implication of each of the parties involved in the process of defining HRM policies and practices. We make evident that considering the company's socio-political environment at the different points in time permits the organization to continuously adjust HRM practices to the nature of organizational "strategy" and organizational controversies. We reveal the necessity of recognizing the cooperation–conflict relationships with different stakeholders that over time change the time, content, and actions of the same organizations, and the actions of new and old groups of stakeholders. Finally, certain of the study's limitations emerge. In particular, this study is based on the empirical results of just one case. Generalization of the conclusions is limited. Nevertheless, the scope of the results can be broadened with other cases from organizations that operate in the same industrial sector and in unstable and turbulent environments in other Latin American countries that face similar conditions. These could further illuminate the specific research pathways opened in this study. For example, to what extent do the HRMs of multinationals play a determinant role in the search for equilibrium among the local forces of the host country's environment and the global forces of the multinational's environment?

## Notes

1 BHP Billiton (2003) *Our Resources at Work,* BHP Billiton PLC Annual Report 2003, p. 2.
2 BHP Billiton (2002) *Operations Performance Report Financial Year 2002. Health, Safety, Environment, Quality and Community*, p. 1.
3 Econometría (2000) *Evaluación de los impactos socioeconómicos de complejo minero industrial de ferroníquel de Cerro Matoso S.A. 1980–1999, 2000–2020*, Medellin, Colombia: Impresiones Rojo., p. 16.
4 Interview with labor consultant, no. 92, August 2006, p. 2.
5 Ibid., p. 41.
6 "Colombianization" refers to the process by which the company's operation was gradually assumed by Colombian directors, professionals, and workers during the period 1982–1987.
7 Interview with director, no. 12, May 6, 2003, p. 3.

8  This bonus was awarded exclusive of the collective bargaining agreement. It is linked to the following factors: general productivity, the price of nickel, accident rate, attendance, and the absence of capricious work suspensions. These factors are combined in a mathematical formula, and the result indicates the amount that each employee will receive as an annual bonus.

9  Interview, no. 20, June 10, 2003.

10  Interview with former president, no. 33, July 16, 2003.

11  Interview with manager, no. 22, June 10, 2003, p. 17.

12  CMSA (2001: 5–6).

13  CMSA (2001: 5–6). Company balance sheet.

## References

Barney, J. (1991) "Firm resources and sustained competitive advantage," *Journal of Management*, 17: 99–120.

Carroll, A. B. (1989) "Management ethics in the workplace: An investigation," *Management Quarterly*, 30(3): 40–45.

Cerro Matoso S.A. (2002) *Informe y balance social 2001*, Bogotá: Impresos Ltda.

Chadwick, C. and Cappelli, P. (1999) "Alternatives to generic strategy typologies in strategic human resource management," *Research in Personnel and Human Resources Management. Strategy Human Resources Management in the Twenty-First Century*, Supplement 4, JAI Press Inc., pp. 1–30.

Dansereau, F. and Yammarino, F. (2005) "Multi-level issues in strategy and methods," *Research in Multi-level Issues*, 4, Elsevier JAI.

Dávila, J. C., Dávila, C., Jiménez, A., Milanés, L. M., and Rubio, M. I. (2006) *Cerro Matoso S.A. (CMSA): Sustainability of a Mining Company in Latin America's Turbulent Environment (1970–2003)*, Monografías de Administración no. 90, Bogotá: Universidad de Los Andes.

Delery, J. E. and Doty, D. H. (1996) "Modes of theorizing in strategic human resource management: Tests of universalistic, contingency, and configurational performance predictions," *Academy of Management Journal*, 39: 802–835.

Drnevich, P. and Shanley, M. (2005) "Multi-level issues for strategic management research: Implications for creating value and competitive advantage," in *Research in Multi-level Issues*, 4, Elsevier JAI, pp. 117–162.

Evan, W. M. and Freeman, R. E. (1988) "A stakeholder theory of the modern corporation: Kantian capitalism," in T. Beauchamp and N. Bowie (eds.), *Ethical Theory and Business*, Englewood Cliffs, NJ: Prentice Hall.

Evans, P. and Genadry, N. (1999) "A duality-based prospective for strategic human resources management," *Research in Personnel and Human Resources Management. Strategy Human Resources Management in the Twenty-First Century*, Supplement 4, JAI Press Inc., pp. 367–397.

Ferris, G., Hochwarter, W., Buckley, M., Harrel-Cook, G., and Frink, D. (1999) "Human resources management: Some new directions," *Journal of Management*, 25(3): 385–415.

Freeman, R. E. (1999) "Divergent stakeholder theory," *Academy of Management Review*, 24(2): 233–236.

Jiménez, A. (2002) *Stakeholders: Una Forma Innovadora de Gobernabilidad de Empresa. Análisis de un Caso Colombiano,* Bogotá: Ediciones Uniandes.

Lawler III, E. E. (2001) "Cómo incrementar la productividad y rentabilidad de su empresa," Congreso "Dirección estratégica de recursos humanos y capital humano," Seminarium, Bogotá.

Lawler, E. and Mohrman, S. (2003) *Creating a Strategic Human Resources Organization. An Assessment of Trends and New Directions*, Stanford, CA: Stanford University Press.

MacDuffie, J. P. (1995) "Human resources bundles and manufacturing performance: Organizational logic and flexible production systems in the world auto industry," *Industrial and Labor Relations Review*, 48: 197–221.

Mitchell, R., Agle, B., and Wood, D. J. (1997) "Toward a theory of stakeholder identification and salience: Defining the principle of who and what really counts," *Academy of Management Review*, 22(4): 853–886.

Paauwe, J. and Boseli, P. (2003) "Challenging 'strategic HR' and the relevance of the institutional setting," *Human Resource Management Journal*, 13(3): 56–70.

Piotet, F. and Sainsaulieu, R. (1994) *Méthodes pour une sociologie de l'entreprise*, Paris: Presses de la Fondation Nationale des Sciences Politiques.

Porter, M. (1985) *Competitive Advantage: Creating and Sustaining Superior Performance*, New York: The Free Press.

Schuler, R. S. and Jackson, S. E. (2005) "A quarter-century review of human resource management in the U.S.: The growth in importance of the international perspective," *Management Review*, 16(1): 11–35.

Ulrich, D. (1999) "Integrating practice and theory: Towards a more unified view of HR," *Research in Personnel and Human Resources Management. Strategy Human Resources Management in the Twenty-First Century*, Supplement 4, JAI Press Inc., pp. 53–74.

Vosburgh, R. (2003) "The state of the human resources profession in 2003," *Human Resources Planning*, 26(1): 18–22.

Wright, P. and Sherman, W. S. (1999) "Failing to find fit in strategic human resource management: Theoretical and empirical problems," *Research in Personnel and Human Resources Management, Strategy Human Resources Management in the Twenty-First Century*, Supplement 4, JAI Press Inc., pp. 53–74.

# 5 Learning best human resource management practices from Spanish multinationals in Latin America

## A case study of Telefónica

*Lourdes Casanova*

This chapter will examine Telefónica's historical development in Latin America and identify key aspects of its human resource management (HRM) practices that have contributed to its success in the region. The company's human resources policies and practices have played a key role in its ability to dominate the region's telecommunications sector through several major economic crises and in the face of pressure from powerful American competitors.

I have been conducting field work on Telefónica since 1997. I have visited and interviewed several dozen executives at both executive and operational levels in Spain and Latin America. Over the span of a decade, I have observed at close quarters how Telefónica has built up a dominant position in several Latin American countries and emerged as a major global telecoms player. Besides conceiving and executing an ambitious strategy of global expansion, effective human resource management lies at the core of Telefónica's success.

## A Spanish success story in Latin America

Prior to becoming a full European Union member in 1986, Spain expressed a wish to become Europe's bridge to Latin America. This statement was viewed with some skepticism by other European countries. European multinationals had been in the region for decades, while Spanish companies had little international experience. Twenty years later Spain has become the most important European investor in the region, second only to the US.[1] Telefónica in telecommunications, Banco Bilbao Vizcaya Argentaria (BBVA) and Banco Santander in banking, Endesa, Iberdrola, and Unión Fenosa in public utilities, and Repsol YPF in oil and gas have become the biggest companies in the region in their respective sectors. These seven firms, which represent 60 percent of the total capitalization of the Madrid stock market, have generated about 70 percent of the foreign direct investment (FDI) that Spain has invested in Latin America since 1990.

Spanish companies have found in Latin America a natural market for their products and services. Companies that expand in natural markets have an inherent competitive advantage. I define natural markets as those in which participants share a common history, language, religion, or enjoy a geographic proximity.

Information and communication move more easily into and within a natural market because of these shared commonalities. For example, the average Spaniard is likely to know more about a given Latin American country than his North American counterpart despite the North American's greater geographic proximity. The affinities that give Spanish firms an edge run deep. North Americans tend to be more direct in communications and have clearer delineations between life inside and outside of the office. Latin Americans, however, place greater emphasis on personal contacts.

Spanish investments in Latin America have been driven not only by natural market affinities but also by a favorable international climate and by emerging investment opportunities resulting from privatization processes initiated in the region's main economies. A direct consequence of these forces has been a "reinvasion" of the region by Spanish firms. Spain is again enjoying a greater presence throughout Latin America than any other European player and is the largest investor in the region after the United States.

Movement of both financial assets and human resources into the region represented a turning point and contributed crucially to the internationalization of the Spanish economy. In view of this exceptional investment cycle, it is possible to speak of a "golden decade" for Spanish investors in the region as Spain's economy for the first time in recent history became a net exporter of capital. Cumulative investment in Latin America by Spanish firms through 2006 amounted to more than US$124 billion; 73 percent of that total was directed to Argentina, Brazil, Chile, and Mexico.

Investment by Spanish firms has transformed some of the most important sectors in Latin America, such as energy and utilities, financial services, and telecommunications. Spanish companies have become dominant players and have dramatically altered the supply, quality, and cost of services throughout the region.

For example, in the banking sector Grupo Santander and BBVA have enjoyed great success in Latin America. Grupo Santander has become the leading financial services group in Latin America. The group currently maintains a network of more than 4,000 offices in the region, with a 9 percent market share and nearly 13 million customers. BBVA entered the Latin American market in 1995 and as of 2006 it was active in fourteen countries in the region, with more than 61,604 employees, or 65 percent of its worldwide workforce.

These Spanish leaders have used Latin America as a platform to become global. Even after the Argentine crisis in 2001, their commitment to the region has been renewed. Santander, Telefónica, Repsol YPF, and Endesa announced in 2006 investments of more than US$20 billlion in Latin America.

## Human resource management in globalization

Human resource management is a key strategic issue for all firms because the cumulative actions of the organization's employees influence to a large extent the successful execution of the firm's strategy, the degree of satisfaction of its customers, the effectiveness of its processes, and its profitability. Every firm operates in the context of multiple stakeholder groups – such as customers, owners, employees, society, and other organizations. Schuler, Jackson, and Luo (2004) note that an organization's approach to managing human resources is central to its success. Every organization has to satisfy multiple stakeholders and consequently its human resource management practices cannot be designed solely to meet the concerns of any one group such as employees or shareholders. The organizations that are most effective at managing people develop human resource management systems that meet the needs of all key stakeholders.

Managing the multiple stakeholder groups while at the same time responding to the global pressures in talent attraction, development, and retention makes human resource management a constant challenge for firms operating in any market. These challenges are accentuated when firms move out from their home markets into faraway new markets with very different sets of stakeholder groups. Telefónica was one of the first Spanish companies to enter Latin America and faced many of these challenges in a foreign market. However, Telefónica's leadership was especially adept at using its human resource strategy to lay the foundations of its success in Latin America and show the way for other Spanish (and European) companies which followed in later years. Telefónica provides valuable lessons in how a firm can effectively use its human resource management approach to successfully satisfy a complex set of stakeholder groups during a process of internationalization.

Of many theoretical perspectives relevant to human resource management (Schuler *et al.*, 2004) those most relevant for understanding Telefónica's success include Human Capital Theory (Becker, 1964), Organizational Learning Theory (Kogut, 1988), and Selection Theory (Boudreau and Rynes, 1985).

## Telefónica today

Originally a state-owned enterprise, Telefónica has been fully privatized since 1997 and has become a global telecommunications leader with a customer base of nearly 200 million and a presence in Europe, Africa, Asia, and Latin America. The company is an integrated, multi-service operator offering fixed-line, mobile, internet, and cable services in its home market and the largest player in the Spanish- and Portuguese-speaking markets in the world. As of 2006 Telefónica was ranked one of the top five telecom service providers in the world in terms of market capitalization and it is listed on the main stock markets, with over 1.6 million direct shareholders. Telefónica is today the most international telecom company in the world and the most profitable.

In Spain, the Telefónica group has more than eighty years of experience, providing services to 16 million fixed-line customers, nearly 4.5 million data and internet access customers, and more than 20 million mobile subscribers as of 2006. In Europe, Telefónica operates in the United Kingdom, Ireland, Germany, and the Czech Republic. As of mid-2006, the company counted more than 33 million mobile subscribers and 4 million fixed-line customers in Europe outside of Spain.

Telefónica's largest market is in Latin America, where it enjoys a customer base of 110 million (56 percent of the total), a market share in the telecommunications sector of 28 percent, 35 percent of the income (US$38 billion), and 34 percent of the operating income before depreciation and amortization (OIBDA). The company has been in the region since 1990 and it can boast of cumulative investments in infrastructure and acquisitions in excess of US$5 billion. Telefónica is the leading operator in Brazil, Argentina, Chile, and Peru and has substantial operations in Colombia, Ecuador, El Salvador, Guatemala, Mexico, Nicaragua, Panama, Puerto Rico, Uruguay, and Venezuela.

Telefónica's global expansion can be described in three phases: its initial forays into international markets, its early emergence as a true multinational, and its current status as a global leader and a strong and vibrant player across a variety of cultures and continents.

### Phase I: internationalization, 1990–1996

In 1990, under the leadership of Chairman Cándido Velázquez, Telefónica began its Latin American expansion through the purchase of a controlling stake in Chile's fixed-line operator, Compañía de Telecomunicaciones de Chile (CTC) and followed this acquisition with control of Telefónica de Argentina, one of the two fixed-line operators carved out of the former Argentine state-run telephone monopoly, ENTel. In 1991, Telefónica participated in a GTE-led consortium that purchased CANTV, the national telecommunications company of Venezuela. In 1994, Telefónica acquired a 31.5 percent stake in Telefónica de Perú. The company's Latin American strategy later came to fruition when it used its Chilean and Argentine subsidiaries in a successful bid for control of Brazil's Companhia Riograndese de Telecomunicações (CRT). In 1990 the first Latin American companies were listed on the New York Stock Exchange; they were each Telefónica subsidiaries: CTC from Chile, Telefónica de Argentina, and Telefónica de Perú.

For Telefónica, Latin America was a natural market where the company's technology was urgently needed. Telefónica had consistently followed an entry strategy based on the acquisition of voting stakes and management control of the companies in which it participated. Furthermore, Telefónica's decision to invest in Latin America was motivated by a strong belief in the market potential, reflected in the low levels of penetration of telecom services in relation to gross domestic product (GDP) per capita levels.

In the early period of Telefónica's expansion the company's managers were telecommunication engineers from the best engineering schools in Spain. Typically, the best students in the graduating classes were recruited. Telefónica was the most important company in Spain (it still is) and attracting the best talent was easy. Furthermore, these initial management teams often lacked members with professional experience in international arenas. Management courses and MBAs became much more common towards the second half of the 1990s. The elite then had more of an engineering orientation than a business background.

Note that such profiles were the norm for members of European management teams in general – even among the ranks of senior managing directors. Countries like France and Germany with long-established histories of multinational corporations frequently recruited their top managers from its elite institutions that historically specialized in turning out graduates in mathematics, engineering, and science. Though rigorously trained and generally considered among the "best and the brightest," until quite recently European top management were not necessarily management experts by academic training.

The principal human resource management program Telefónica created for its entry into Latin America was an all-volunteer program. Key management positions throughout the region would be staffed by expatriate Spanish managers. The initial notion was that these overseas assignments would be for short periods of time. However, in many cases expatriate managers ended up staying abroad for longer periods, sometimes for as long as eight to ten years.

The lack of Latin American professional experience was compensated for by eagerness to succeed in their new jobs. The company's expatriate managers were well suited to tackle the initial challenges facing Telefónica upon its entry into Latin American markets. Remember too that in the beginning of the 1990s Telefónica de España started downsizing and went from 74,500 workers in 1990, with a productivity of 167 lines per employee, to 41,000 at the end of the decade and 490 fixed lines per employee, the highest productivity ratio in Europe and one of the highest in the world. During the privatization of the Spanish telecommunication sector, Telefónica's management teams demonstrated a capacity to handle the development of networks and the movement of important human, technological, and financial resources in short periods of time in order to implement large investment plans to expand and update the company's network infrastructures, which had previously been underdeveloped and characterized by significant unsatisfied demand. During the replication of these processes in Latin America, many industry observers noted that "*la tecnología de la zanja*" (ditch-digging technology) was extremely useful and successful in satisfying the urgent need for fixed-line expansion, especially given the high level of unsatisfied demand in these countries.

As a condition of Telefónica's takeover of its newly acquired Latin American subsidiaries, local governments imposed a number of performance targets such as improvements in network capacity, a reduction of "down" times, an increase in access to services, and reductions in customer wait-times for new service activation.

Because of their recent experiences in successfully achieving similar goals and objectives laid out by government regulators in Spain, many of Telefónica's managers who had been dispatched to Latin America were ideal candidates to handle similar challenges and achieve similarly successful results.

Furthermore, this group of initial managers had experience handling changes in corporate culture. They had worked through Telefónica's initial privatization processes in Spain when the company had to shift from a group of civil servant-minded employees to a customer-oriented, market-driven organization. Due to the privatization of markets in Chile, Argentina, and Peru, employees and mid-level local managers in Telefónica's newly acquired Latin American companies would face similar changes in corporate culture. Again, the recent experiences of Telefónica's expatriate Spanish managers could serve as a good and useful model for corporate change.

Telefónica's expatriate management team did achieve several noteworthy performance successes in Latin America, such as introducing a measurable degree of rigor into the management practices of its newly acquired local subsidiaries. They were able to improve the technical capacity and performance of the company's networks by improving the network infrastructures. Furthermore, they were able to improve customer service and build a larger customer base by reducing consumer waiting times for obtaining telecommunication services. This also helped to create a cadre of managers and leaders within Telefónica whose talents developed through challenging international assignments (Black *et al.*, 1999).

### Phase II: making a multinational, 1996–2000

In 1996 Telefónica entered its second development phase when the company achieved full privatization and came under the leadership of a new Chairman, Juan Villalonga. Villalonga saw Latin America as a unique opportunity for growth and to create an international culture within the company. At an internal level, in 1998 the company shortened its name from Telefónica de España to Telefónica to reflect its international status. It also reorganized into eight independent subsidiaries and one corporate center.

The Corporate Headquarters (Telefónica) would now focus on decisions concerning the optimization of the group as a whole, the functional articulation of the company, and the management orientation of its business units, while Telefónica de España would manage the company's domestic Spanish telecommunications businesses (except for mobile, data, and media services) and Telefónica Internacional would oversee activities in Latin America. A third subsidiary, Telefónica Intercontinental, was created in 1997 to participate in locations other than the Americas. Its primary objective was to replicate the company's Latin American successes in other countries, primarily in Europe and the Mediterranean basin (see Figure 5.1 for the organizational structure of the company during this period).

However, Villalonga's first big move toward multinational status occurred with the decision to expand the company's Latin American presence by moving into Brazil – the biggest economy in the region and the eighth biggest in the world.

In July 1998 Telefónica acquired for US$6 billion the fixed-line operator Telesp, the fixed-line operator for Sao Paulo, Brazil's largest state, whose population of 35 million was nearly equal to the total population of Spain, and the mobile operators Tele Sudeste Celular and Tele Leste Celular after the monolith Telebras was carved up by Brazilian regulators and put up for sale on the open market. During the privatization of Telebras, Telefónica dispatched one hundred of its best

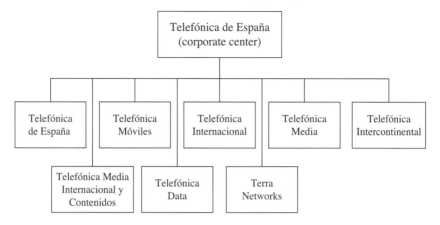

*Figure 5.1* Telefónica organizational structure (2000–2006)
Source: www.telefónica.com in 2005.

managers to Brazil and was the only company to pay for the financial particulars on all of Telebras's constituent companies that were for sale.

One of Telefónica's first management moves following its entry into the Brazilian market was to appoint Fernando Xavier Ferreira, President of Telebras since 1995, and President of the Board of Directors of Telesp. Ferreira's appointment signaled two things. First, Brazil should not be regarded or treated as simply another Latin American country. Brazil has a different language than the other countries in the region, and the sheer size of Brazil requires it to be considered as distinct. Second, Brazil's uniqueness required the company to actively recruit and retain talent with both local and international expertise and experience.

Towards the end of the 1990s, Telefónica was in the midst of a noteworthy change in its corporate structure and culture. The expansion into Brazil, the successful start-up of internet and mobile services, and the rapid acquisition and integration of numerous foreign subsidiaries fostered an entrepreneurial spirit among the company's managers and employees. Telefónica began by reorganizing its holdings and by developing a structure that enabled it to provide each business area with its own legal identity. Telefónica, as the parent company, became the corporate nucleus for the main subsidiaries, and these subsidiaries in turn acted as the heads of each separate business line.

In order to achieve his ambitious multinational goals, Villalonga began hiring managers with a new profile for its Latin American interests. Seeing a great deal of value in local knowledge and know-how, the company looked toward local talent to fulfill the management functions once primarily allocated to Spanish nationals. The genesis of these hiring practices lies in the realization that much of the local talent qualified for senior-level management positions enjoyed two significant advantages over expatriate Spanish managers. First, as Latin Americans local talent would be in a better position to understand the needs and demands of both a Latin American workforce and customer base because they would naturally be better suited to understand the complexities and idiosyncrasies of working in their "native" environment.

Second, Latin American elites go to study in the United States and often stay to work for multinationals. Consequently, many Latin American management personnel were at that time more internationally oriented than their Spanish counterparts.[2] The combined educational and work experience of Latin American management talent tends to go a long way in producing managers with excellent communication skills and team leaders. In terms of human resource management policies, the best-practice contributions made by the company's Latin American management teams, such as equality opportunities and systems of meritocracy, have come to benefit the company as a whole. From a theoretical perspective, this can be understood from the perspectives of Selection Theory (the success of the firm is determined by the multiplicity of choices available to it) and Organizational Learning Theory (effective learning processes within the firm increase its chances of success). Table 5.1 outlines the HR strategy and key success factors in each stage of Telefónica's internationalization. Telefónica, as a leader, was able to attract the best talent available to it at each stage – whether it was technical talent in the early years or more local expertise in later years of international growth. However, as the firm progressed on its journey of internationalization, it had to invest in the learning and development of these managers to create a global company with one strong culture and globally integrated processes. Hence Telefónica started investing significantly in supporting organizational learning.

At the same time, Villalonga saw the importance of complementing the manager's engineering profiles with management skills and started recruiting MBA graduates from local and international business schools and training programs with international management schools. All this resulted in a change in corporate culture to a more agile international company.

### Phase III: becoming a global leader, 2000 onwards

In July of 2000 César Alierta assumed the chairmanship of Telefónica. It was clear from the start of Alierta's tenure that Telefónica's management teams faced a fresh set of challenges. Their main concern was how to incorporate and manage the scope of acquisitions made under Villalonga while simultaneously managing the company's competitive position in a marketplace with a decidedly bearish face.

In late 2001 companies throughout Latin America suffered when Argentina's economy collapsed. Many companies, including Telefónica, suffered reductions in their share price because of its wide exposure in the region and a general economic panic over the future stability of the region as a whole. These facts led Alierta and his teams to rethink their strategies and curtail their investment policies. They began to shift their interests north to the more stable Mexican economy. By the end of 2002, Telefónica had acquired five Mexican companies.[3]

*Table 5.1* Telefónica expansion phases, HR policies, and key success drivers

| Expansion phase | HR strategy | Key success drivers |
|---|---|---|
| Phase I: Internationalization 1990–1996 | "Volunteer technical expatriate" • Volunteers with strong technical skills (best graduates of telecom and engineering schools) • No previous international experience as few in the firm had relevant experience | • Excellent technical skills useful to serve the needs of foreign markets • Common culture and language (natural market) reduced negative impact on lack of prior international experience |
| Phase II: Making a multinational 1996–2000 | "Local managers" • Need for local managers • Need for management skills in addition to technical skills • Need to manage change in culture | • Local management and know-how in Brazil and Latin America • Local Latin American managers had more international experience • Recruitment at international business schools • Investment in executive development • Restructuring business |
| Phase III: Becoming a global leader 2000 onwards | "Professionalized" • Global managers for a multi-domestic company • Balance local and global needs • International mindset of managers | • Creation of Corporate University • Integrating the company processes • Relocation system for short periods • Learning and development program for young high potentials |

The rationale behind these acquisitions was to maintain the company's geographic expansion in the two most important economies in Latin America, Brazil, and Mexico. In April of 2003, Telefónica partnered with Portugal Telecom under a joint venture to form the mobile operator Vivo. By 2006 the company had become the largest mobile phone service provider in Brazil and South America, with over 30 million users.[4] Telefónica continued its expansion throughout the region. In March 2004, the company announced the acquisition of BellSouth's Latin American assets. For Telefónica, BellSouth was the ideal target company in terms of both the operational and geographic complementarities. With the acquisition of all the subsidiaries of BellSouth, Telefónica obtained in a single transaction a leadership position in Argentina, Chile, and Peru and gained entry into six new Latin American countries: Venezuela, Panama, Nicaragua, Uruguay, Colombia, and Ecuador. Furthermore, the deal enabled Telefónica to become the single wireless player operating in all key markets (present as number one or number two in most Latin American countries), achieving significant economies of scale and becoming the clear leader in innovation and technology in the region. The post-merger acquisition process was seamless and very fast. Over the years Telefónica had acquired an enormous "know-how" in the integration of companies. However, most American managers left Telefónica and were replaced by local Latin Americans.

In the last quarter of 2005, Telefónica purchased the British mobile operator O2 in an effort to expand its European operations by replicating its successes in Latin America. With significant market presence in both Germany and the United Kingdom – 34.1 percent and 59.4 percent respectively – the Telefónica–O2 deal greatly added to the company's worldwide presence.

As Alierta's tenure progressed so did his notions about how the company should be organized and managed. Alierta asserted that Telefónica should behave as a "multi-domestic company," a company comprised of individual companies fully in touch with its respective local workforce and customer base. Alierta's paradigm shift proved especially appropriate to handle multiple "local" issues: government regulation, customer service best practices, branding and product/service identification. While the multi-domestic structure gave Telefónica the ability to respond to local stakeholder groups, it soon started facing pressure to increase the amount of organizational learning across the different country operations. From an Organizational Learning Theory perspective, Telefónica needed to increase its ability to capture the learning from prior experiences and to integrate it effectively to satisfy the needs of global stakeholder groups. This lead to the next shift in the company's strategy: structure and human resource management.

Since 2005 the company has moved away from the organizational profile previously employed, one based largely on core business units (see Figure 5.1), to an organizational profile increasingly based on the company's geographic presence. Telefónica's present corporate structure, furthermore, tends to facilitate operational streamlining by emphasizing organizational coordination at the center (see Figure 5.2).

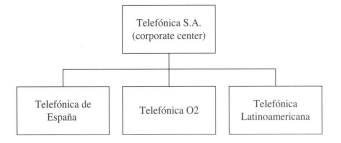

*Figure 5.2* Telefónica organizational structure (from 2006 onwards)
Source: www.telefónica.com in 2007.

The company's Corporate Headquarters (Telefónica S.A.) is responsible for global strategy, corporate policies, and the management of common activities and the coordination of the activities among its various business units. Telefónica de España is the corporate umbrella under which all fixed-line, mobile, and broadband telephony services in Spain are offered; its business units are: Telefónica Móviles España, Telefónica Empresas, Telefónica Soluciones, and Terra's Spanish operations. Telefónica O2 provides fixed-line, mobile, and broadband telephony services in the United Kingdom, Ireland, Germany, and the Czech Republic; its business units are Cesky Telecom and Telefónica Deutschland. Telefónica Internacional provides fixed-line, mobile, and broadband telephony services through much of the Western Hemisphere.

Alierta's shift toward a more centralized, geographically centered organizational structure resulted in a shift in the company's corporate culture as well. In November 2004, Telefónica held its first annual management convention in Madrid. Key managers from each company in the Telefónica group gathered in order to establish specific goals and objectives and to set work guidelines for the entire group of Telefónica companies. The establishment (and continuation) of these meetings exemplifies two key elements of Alierta's new management vision for Telefónica: horizontality and centralization.

Alierta determined that in order to fully integrate the Telefónica network of companies the overall management structure of the group would have to be rethought and revised. In terms of overall organizational structure, Alierta moved to geographical areas instead of traditional business lines in view of the current context of fixed-mobile convergence. Additionally, Alierta's vision for the company's management was holistic or horizontal rather than hierarchical or vertical. He believed that in a modern multinational managers need to be prepared (in terms of both willingness and competencies) to move into any managerial position in any location throughout the entire company. Alierta not only wanted his managers to employ best practice to increase efficiencies while reducing costs; he also wanted well-rounded, internationally-minded managers with global perspectives. He wanted his managers to be able to go anywhere at anytime and achieve any task and make the old concept of an expatriate manager obsolete.

Under Alierta's leadership, Telefónica adopted a six-pillar global competencies model reflecting the company's cultural shift toward horizontality and centralization and enumerating the company's essential employment philosophy. This model is applied to all employees in all operations in all countries where the company does business. The competencies used for both seeking out new talent and developing the professional skills of its existing workforce are:

1   making a commitment to better understanding and anticipating the needs of the company's customers and delivering quality solutions with high added value;
2   participating in the wider aspects of the company environment in order to adapt to new situations and driving changes;
3   employing transparent communication and relationships in order to foster a better work environment;
4   cooperating across the whole organization to achieve common goals;
5   adopting a commitment to each employee's personal and professional development;
6   contributing to profits by efficiently managing resources and driving business results.

In order to set the company's employment philosophies in motion and make them active and real elements of Telefónica's corporate culture, the company provides a variety of ways and means for its employees to grow both professionally and personally. From the Corporate Headquarters down, the entire Telefónica group utilizes the best resources available to ensure that its employees have ample opportunities to attain their goals and assume greater responsibilities.

Telefónica's Relocation Special Program is designed to provide training mechanisms to make it easier for employees to acquire the skills required to be successful at jobs different from the ones they usually perform. It is specifically geared toward "high-potential" managers by providing short-term assignments outside of their usual geographic regions. For example, a native Colombian manager in the company's Latin American division of Telefónica Móviles might undertake a six- to eight-month assignment in the Madrid offices of Telefónica's mobile division in order to build greater ties and synergies between the two business units as well as share his practical experiences in best practice with his European colleagues.

For young professionals who demonstrate a high degree of potential for professional growth and greater responsibility within the company, Telefónica established its Corporate Program for Promising Young Employees ("*jóvenes con alto potencial,*" in Spanish [JAP]). JAP was designed to continually meet the professional challenges faced by young employees through rotations and specific training programs designed for their needs. The rotation and training activities are further augmented by an in-house mentoring program in which a senior executive can provide practical, experienced-based guidance relative to career development.

In its continual quest for one of the best-trained workforces in the world, early in Alierta's tenure, Telefónica implemented electronic training programs based around what is referred to as "cooperative learning." These types of programs are all developed and run around six central features:

1   Interactivity: The participation and interaction of all participants is key to the program's overall success.
2   Facilitation: Trainers are not regarded as guardians of information, but rather as someone whose primary role is to facilitate the interaction among program participants.
3   Accessibility: The systems employed must provide access to training materials without requiring participants to be in specific locations or adhere to fixed timetables.
4   Adaptability: All training programs must be adaptable to the real work-related needs of each group of employees.
5   Flexibility: The programs must be able to undergo quick responses that guarantee the acquisition of knowledge.
6   Employability: Training programs must facilitate the training of employees so that they are able to react in the face of a variety of challenges and augment their value to the company.

Telefónica utilizes a learning management system called Red Teledidáctica (RTD). RTD improves an employee's employability through three modalities: self-study, technical courses, and videoconferences. Self-study is available to employees through the internet. This type of training consists of a wide catalogue of computer-assisted teaching courses in which employees can choose those courses that interest them. They install the course materials on their computer and study them when they wish and at the pace they set themselves.

Tutored courses in RTD involve the presence of an instructor who provides students with learning support, orientation, and supervision during their learning. In accordance with the conditions of existing collective bargaining agreements, if the instructor rates the employee's performance positively the employee's participation in the course will be included in the employee's performance record.

With respect to the company's videoconferencing network Telfonet, formative or informative sessions on current topics of interest are regularly offered through the network. These sessions are taught by experts in their respective fields, and employees who attend these courses have the chance to engage in real-time question and answer sessions.

At the same time the number of management programs has grown exponentially. Telefónica's Latin American subsidiaries organized training courses with the best Latin American schools, while the Corporate Headquarters partnered with the best international schools for the top managers. The idea was to learn, to empower, and at the same time to share knowledge and create networks and a sense of belonging to the company. All these efforts resulted in the creation of

Telefónica's Corporate University in Barcelona, launched in December 2005. The idea was to invest between US$150 million and US$200 million in the next ten years and to have about 6,000 executives from all over the world taking courses each year.

In September 2006, Telefónica realized another element of Alierta's vision. For decades Telefónica's headquarters in Madrid had been scattered in different offices and buildings throughout the city and the surrounding area. In line with the company's decision to consolidate management, Telefónica inaugurated its new headquarters in a suburb north of Madrid. Las Tablas is a centralized office complex that will eventually accommodate approximately 30 percent of Telefónica's employees in Spain, or slightly more than 14,000 people.

## Conclusions

Telefónica's expansion in Latin America over the last sixteen years provides an interesting backdrop to the evolution of its HRM practices as the company evolves from a national public-sector company to a major global multinational. Each phase of Telefónica's growth and internationalization can be understood from a particular theoretical perspective.

The first phase of Telefónica's growth was driven by a traditional expatriate approach to HRM. Given the cultural proximity between the Spanish and Latin cultures, it was easy for Spanish managers to move into management positions in Latin America. The technical skills of the managers were also well suited to the needs of the Latin companies, which were in acute need of upgrading of their infrastructures and services. The expatriate managers were chosen from a volunteer program and were asked to stay for a few years in Latin America. However, given the cultural proximities between the two cultures, many of them ended up staying for much longer periods, often as long as eight to ten years – providing valuable management continuity for the future expansion of Telefónica in the region. From a Selection Theory perspective, Telefónica emphasized positive selection by choosing the best set of managers for its Latin American operations and this helped to increase the success of the company during this first phase of internationalization.

The second phase of Telefónica's growth in Latin America was marked by a serious effort towards internationalization of the profiles of the managers as well as recognition of the value of the local talent. This was natural given the changing nature of the company. Telefónica was no longer a Spanish company – it had evolved into a multinational with operations in multiple countries. Management skills were needed to complement technical skills. The company started hiring MBAs and offering management education programs to its key managers. Local talent was also hired and groomed for key positions in the international operations. This was seen as an important part of being able to successfully assimilate into the local business contexts. From a Human Capital Theory perspective, Telefónica emphasized the development of human capital as its operations spread in multiple countries and it faced the challenges of satisfying multiple sets of stakeholder groups in different countries.

The third phase witnesses a rapid localization of the international operations of the company. The company's HRM practices are professionalized and best-in-class processes established in accordance with the global nature of the firm. This was also aligned with the firm's move into newer markets (such as the UK) where the earlier strategy of moving expatriates would no longer work and also where strong local talent was available. The importance of executive education is highlighted with the establishment of a centralized corporate university; eLearning (by a special subsidiary called Educaterra) is used for lifelong learning, and short programs to exchange knowledge and best practice from across the far-flung corners of the firm are emphasized. From an Organizational Learning Theory perspective, Telefónica's actions in this period can be seen as aiding the consolidation of its learning experiences within and across its operations in different countries.

## Notes

1  Spain has been the most important investor in Argentina and Chile.
2  According to the Graduate Management Admission Council, about 1,000 Mexicans and a similar number of Brazilians have attended MBA programs in the United States every year since 1996.
3  Norcel, Cedetel, Bajacel, Movitel, and Pegaso.
4  www.vivo.com.

## References

Anderson, J. (2002) "Telefónica's Balancing Act," *Institutional Investor Magazine*, March: 40–47.
Arahuetes, A. and Casilda, R. (2004) "Spain," in Ž Vodušek (ed.), *Foreign Direct Investment in Latin America: The Role of European Investors: An Update,* SOE/IDB Working Paper Series, No 5, Paris.
Becker, G. S. (1964) *Human Capital*, New York: National Bureau of Economic Research.
Black, J. S., Gregersen, H. B., Mendenhall, M. E., and Stroh, L. (1999) *Globalizing People through International Assignments*, Reading, MA: Addison-Wesley.
Boudreau, J. W. and Rynes, S. L. (1985) "Role of recruitment in staffing utility analysis," *Journal of Applied Psychology*, 70(2): 345–366.
Casanova, L. (1999) *Telefónica: The Making of a Multinational*, case study, Paris: INSEAD.
Casanova, L. (2002) "Lazos de familia: Las inversiones españolas en Iberoamérica," *Foreign Affairs en Español*, 2(2): 67–85.
Casanova, L. (2003) *Endesa: The Making of a Multinational*, case study, Paris: INSEAD.
Casanova, L. (2004) "East Asian, European, and North American multinational firm strategies in Latin America," *Business and Politics*, 6(1). Online. Available HTTP: http://www.bepress.com/bap/vol6/iss1/art6.
Kogut, B. (1988) "Joint ventures: Theoretical and empirical perspectives," *Strategic Management Journal*, 9: 319–332.
Schuler, R. S., Jackson, S. E., and Luo, Y. (2004) *Managing Human Resources in Cross-Border Alliances*, Routledge.

# 6 Consistency of business strategy, post-acquisition integration, and management of people

## Developing an HRM best practice

*Betania Tanure and Roberto Gonzalez-Duarte*

This paper analyzes why and how human resource management (HRM) may take on a strategic role within merger and acquisition (M&As) processes. The success of these deals depends to a large extent on the successful management of people-related issues. For HRM to effectively become a strategic partner in these arrangements, we argue that HRM should take part during the negotiations and not merely during the integration phase. Second, HRM needs to formulate people management policies that are consistent with the determining reason for the acquisition and the integration strategy adopted.

The determining factors of an acquisition directly influence the choice of method to use in integrating the acquired organization. In turn, this choice impacts HRM. The success of an acquisition is due in great part to the extent to which the integration strategy and the management of people are intrinsically consistent with each other. In order to ensure this consistency, the acquiring company may use a different integration strategy and, hence, a different strategy for the management of people. We contend that the ability to integrate the acquiring and acquired companies in accordance with the business strategy of the acquiring company is an actual HRM best practice.

In order to discuss how intrinsically consistent strategies are fundamental to the success of an acquisition at the post-acquisition integration phase, we discuss the acquisition of two banks – a Brazilian bank and a subsidiary of an Italian bank – by ABN AMRO, a Dutch bank. Since these two acquisitions were motivated by different reasons, the post-acquisition integration strategies and the management of people differed for each. Despite these differences, the management of people was consistent in each case with the acquisition strategy and the reason that determined the post-acquisition integration strategy. This consistency was a key factor in the creation of value by ABN AMRO. Above all, this consistency has demonstrated that radical change processes may leverage HRM towards a more strategic role in organizations.

This paper is structured as follows. In the next section, we broadly discuss the issue of post-acquisition strategy and, in particular, the main HRM challenges – transfer of strategic capabilities and organizational change and learning – during the integration process. Subsequently, we present the case of the acquisition of the Brazilian banks Real and Sudameris by the Dutch bank ABN AMRO, emphasizing how great care was taken with each acquisition to add new competencies while, at the same time, creating one single culture. Thus, we discuss how radical change processes, such as M&As, may impel the HRM toward a more strategic role. Finally, in the last section, we raise some implications for managers and suggest some future avenues for further research on the topic.

## Post-acquisition integration in M&As: business strategy and HRM issues

Value creation is the rationale behind an acquisition decision. This decision is based on the assumption that the acquired company will contribute to either the strategic or the financial improvement of the acquiring company (Schweiger *et al.*, 1994; von Krogh *et al.*, 1994). The combination of the acquired and acquiring companies' value chains will result in a synergy that is expected to create value.

> If the value chain is a major mechanism by which firms create value, then we can argue that in strategy-driven M&As, value obtained by capturing synergies can ensue only when the value chains of two firms are reconfigured in ways that create value for, or improve competitive advantages of, the combined firm.
>
> (Schweiger *et al.*, 1994: 23)

The synergy that is expected to result from the acquisition will depend on the integration strategy adopted by the acquiring company and the compatibility of management styles. It also presumes a transfer of strategic capabilities. These capabilities represent potential. However, once transferred, they must be applied so that they can lead to a competitive advantage. The challenge is not only to acquire these capabilities, but also to preserve, transfer, and apply them in order to improve the competitive advantage (Haspeslagh and Farquhar, 1994; Haspeslagh and Jemison, 1991).

Therefore, the first factor normally considered before deciding whether to make an acquisition is strategic. However, it has been shown that organizational factors also should be taken into account because real value is created only during the post-acquisition phase. As Haspeslagh and Jemison (1991: 164) say, "although the strategic fit of an acquisition is the basis of the potential for value creation, it is managing the acquisition well that underlies actual value creation."

The results of this process – the transfer of strategic capabilities – depend on how HR issues are managed within the acquired company. Carrying out people-related changes is probably the most challenging issue during the integration phase (Ulrich *et al.*, 1989; Paine and Power, 1984). However, this is a challenge that has not received the same level of attention from the acquiring top managers (Nahavandi and Malekzadeh, 1994; Schweiger and Weber, 1989). According to Tanure *et al.* (2007), HRM can help the acquiring company to integrate the acquired organization and to transfer the strategic capabilities, so as to ensure a consistency between business strategy and post-acquisition integration. Tanure *et al.* (2007) have proposed a model – named "fours sides" – that may be helpful in understanding why and how this consistency may be ensured.

The first stage is called execution. It refers to the main tasks exercised by HRM. This stage is focused on action and must be bound to the business strategy. There must be consistency, but the execution itself cannot guarantee internal or external consistency, which illustrates the importance of binding execution to the business strategy. Besides, consistency is essential to the other phases. Nevertheless, it is very common to find this bond absent in Brazilian organizations.

The second stage, called construction, is essential because it is based upon internal consistency, which is related to concepts like adequacy and performance. At this stage, HRM principles are adjusted in order to ensure an internal coherence so that the company strategy can be accepted as correct. The constructor role, based on the internal adjustment and focused on the internal coherence of HRM elements, is central to creation of the company's infrastructure. However, Brazilian organizations have faced some difficulties when trying to formulate principles, which require a major investment in infrastructure.

The third stage is called realignment. It enables HRM to become compatible with changes in the external environment. It must focus on reconfiguration and the change in management approach so that each strategy can be effectively implemented. Here, HRM takes a "changing partner" role, which includes a partnership between production-line managers and human resource (HR) profes-sionals. There is an external adjustment at stake, so that the contingency theory becomes compatible with the competitive environment. The realignment process can only occur if HRM is bound to a strategy that reflects the industry and the competitive environment. Hence, HRM must be trusted partners who are involved in the business strategy and are aware of external changes that will lead the realignment process.

Finally, direction, which is the fourth stage, has functional capability development as its main activity. At this stage, strategic and HR factors are deeply intermeshed and cannot be separated. This phase is focused on people and organizational capability development so that the organization can be successful in a constantly changing world. HRM must constructively manage the tension created by opposite forces (dualities) and function like a sailboat, moving along opposite forces and trying to create an organizational context in which those forces may enhance development, instead of serving as sources of conflict. However, only 9 percent of the presidents interviewed consider HRM to have an important role in shaping the business's future.

It may be noted that if a company has been able to establish solid HR principles at the second stage – in which the main HRM principles must be internally adequate and consistent – and at stage three – in which HRM becomes a partner for change and carries out a realignment process that brings more compatibility with the external environment – it will be better able to map and find the best solution for creating a management model for its people and culture during a time of, perhaps, radical change.

The focus on people-related factors is one of the most important elements in the successful execution of an acquisition strategy. This can be verified in a report of an international M&A research study carried out by McKinsey & Company, in which the four main success factors were related to people and cultural shock. The same conclusion was reached by a research study that was undertaken in Brazil, in which 64 percent of interviewees chose people and cultural differences as the critical aspects during an acquisition process.

Therefore, HRM can significantly contribute to the entire acquisition process. The most important contribution throughout the acquisition planning phase would be an investigation of all transaction-related aspects, including an evaluation of the acquired company's culture. Cultural evaluation is an essential aspect, as cultural shocks due to cultural differences are one of the main sources of difficulty after the transaction has been completed. This evaluation must be undertaken with the understanding that each company should see and understand its own culture.

HRM must also consider two important due diligence dimensions of HR. One involves prevention and is focused on responsibilities, such as complaints, duties related to pension funds, and all causes of anything that may impact on an acquisition process. The other dimension is related to talent recognition, which is essential to the long-term success of an acquisition.

Before finalizing the agreement, the acquiring company must have all essential components from its HR implementation model installed and must have selected an integration manager and a transition team to deal with conflict of interest issues, ambiguities, and the typical questions that result from a radical change process. It is necessary to articulate acquisition strategy, the general conditions of both companies, and the need for people's cultural integration so that notions such as adequacy and consistency can permeate the whole process.

During the post-acquisition phase, HRM is responsible for ensuring that there is an accurate focus on the acquired company's people and leadership issues. It must ensure that integration teams are ready to deal with intercultural complexity; recognize and manage post-acquisition symptoms, such as feelings of loss, uncertainty, and despair; and be aware of talent and key-people retention, so that the acquisition process can enjoy long-term success.

Despite the relevance of people management in M&A processes, this issue has been disregarded in many Brazilian M&A processes. In a research study carried out by Barros (2003), almost 63 percent of M&As were said to have failed due to problems related to the management of people. HRM is not normally included in the *due diligence* process because, in general, companies focus on the analysis of quantitative, hard aspects of the business. The involvement of the HR department in the due diligence process occurred only occasionally.

In practical terms, we observe that HRM influence during the acquisition process is inconsistent. In a research study carried out by McKinsey & Company (Tanure *et al.*, 2007), 55 percent of Brazilian CEOs of acquiring companies said that the cultural and people integration process occurs naturally and so there is no need for a more specific HRM action.

One reason that could explain the low participation of HRM in Brazilian M&A processes is the perception of this function within companies. A study carried out by Tanure (2005) has revealed that, although HR managers self-assessed themselves as strategic partners, their fellow executives, mainly from the finance and accounting areas, do not share this view. This difference is due to the fact that some functional areas do not perceive the true contribution of HRM to the performance of the organization.

Thus, there is a vicious cycle in which HR managers do not take part in the due diligence processes. Without doing so, they cannot effectively exercise one of the crucial roles of this HRM area, namely to help the transfer of strategic capabilities, organizational learning, and organizational change processes. Therefore if they are absent from these processes they cannot, as a consequence, contribute to the value creation process – that is, to the performance of the acquiring company. This only reinforces the perception held by managers in other functional areas.

However, as value creation in M&As depends on the successful management of people-related issues, these operations open an avenue for HRM to effectively become a strategic partner and, hence, to end this vicious cycle. There are three conditions to satisfy before this can happen. First, HRM should take part in the process from its earliest phase (i.e. from the due diligence period). This will depend on consistency between top management's statements that people are actually an organization's best asset and top management's practice (Tanure, 2005). Second, HRM will play a more prominent role only if it formulates people management policies that are intrinsically consistent with the determining reason for the acquisition and integration strategy chosen. Third, people management policies designed by HRM should, in fact, leverage the value creation process.

In order to understand how M&As (i.e. radical change processes) may redefine HRM's role and, as a consequence, change the perception of HRM relative to its contribution to the performance of the company by other functional areas, we present the ABN AMRO case in the following section. The Dutch bank first acquired one of the largest Brazilian banks and later the Brazilian subsidiary of an Italian bank. These acquisitions have raised common, but different, challenges concerning the management of people. In both acquisitions, the successful integration of the acquired bank by the acquiring one was determined by the consistency among three factors – the determining reason for the acquisition; the integration strategy adopted; and the HRM policies for the management of people. More importantly, the HRM function in both deals undertook a seminal role in preserving the value of the acquired bank.

## The ABN AMRO case

ABN AMRO, which stems from the merger in 1991 of Banco ABN with AMRO Bank, acquired Banco Real in March, 1998. The bank had been founded in Belo Horizonte, Minas Gerais, in 1925. The Banco Real group operated mainly as a commercial bank, but also included insurance and real estate loan companies, subsidiaries in the IT industry and a small travel agency. The commercial bank's activities were focused mainly on short-term commercial loan operations and transactional services for corporate and private clients.

The impact of the acquisition on the Banco Real staff was enormous. The feeling of being "abandoned by the Great Father" – Dr. Aloysio Faria – was shared by all. However, top executives, particularly the CEO, focused on making former Real employees feel that they had not been the losers or that ABN AMRO employees had been the winners. Fábio Barbosa remarks, "I always say that we bought your bank because you have been successful."

With the caution that accompanies respect – one of the values of ABN AMRO – an integration plan was drawn up. "There was great cooperation throughout the due diligence process, and it persisted after the sale became effective. This was due to two main factors: minimum overlap between the two banks and the feeling of relief because it was ABN AMRO that had been the acquirer," says an ABN AMRO executive. Fábio Barbosa says that he was less surprised, because "Banco Real carries the typical traits of the Brazilian company: centralization, paternalism, and loyalty to people while dramatically avoiding conflict with superiors." However, awareness of such differences – mainly on the part of the chairman, Floris Deckers, and the CEO, Fábio Barbosa – and the understanding that organizational culture is the main factor that can lead to unsuccessful merger and acquisition processes rallied the top executives around this issue.

In 2002, ABN AMRO acquired another bank, Sudameris. Just as had happened in the case of the Real acquisition, Sudameris had some competencies that were distinct from those of Banco Real–ABN AMRO. Sudameris mainly added premium clients, as well as SME (small and medium-size enterprise) clients, to the client base of Real. Two teams were sent to Sudameris soon after the acquisition. According to one interviewee, "the synergy team comprised five to six people from ABN. Its main objective was to manage the bank, eliminate any inefficiencies that could be found, make the most obvious changes and enhance synergies, so as to reduce overhead and increase scale." At the same time, there was an integration team that dealt with "watching and learning," thus taking advantage of the good things at Sudameris. The job performed by both groups demanded a certain alignment with each other, but there were many times when their interests were at odds. The challenge, then, was to ensure the synergy while at the same time taking advantage of opportunities. Another challenge was to bring together the good practices found in the acquired company and to implement the acquirer's practices in the acquired company. Therefore, unlike the acquisition of Real, ABN AMRO absorbed Sudameris and adopted its best practices. The Sudameris acquisition has not been consolidated yet and what is important to note is that the strategic goal of this latest acquisition differed from the one that led to the Real acquisition. This has decisively influenced the cultural integration process.

According to the acquired banks' employees, the success of the integration process was due to some key aspects, such as the integration team's posture and attitudes; the quality of the consultant; a true concern for the acquired bank's professionals; the team's modesty and a willingness to learn, teach, and exchange processes; the will to make HR policies right, taking advantage of the acquired banks' know-how and respecting cultural differences; all of which was clearly represented by Fábio Barbosa's coherent posture and action.

However, the process of change didn't happen quickly. According to employees of Sudameris and Real, the process took place gradually. It was necessary to identify all people who took part in the integration team, so that they could welcome and support the acquired banks' personnel. Subsequently, there was a monitoring and helping process that lasted for about six months. According to Celso Antunes, ABN products and services chief executive, "it takes time until people start believing and trusting the new bank's organization and staff. The most important issue is the acquiring bank's respect towards the acquired one."

ABN AMRO was very careful during terminations. There was a great concern for continuity, and the organization itself was able to establish a comfortable environment. According to ABN's business supervisor, Marcelo Cujailo, "all fired people were taken to a re-assignment location center and Sudameris's staff was treated just like the Real one. HRM was concerned with people's competency, not their origin." Besides, everyone received feedback and the number of re-assignments was very high.

The organization's president, Fábio Barbosa, gave the integration process its essential feature, demonstrating the active and consistent role that a key manager must adopt. His first challenge was to integrate and engage more than 30,000 employess. According to Fábio, an inside-out movement was implemented, focusing on people and trying to familiarize them with the organization, the market and society. "The big issue," Fábio adds, "is that this process can only be consistent if it comes from within." Most of the acquired banks' employees recognized that Fábio's leadership style was a big part of the success of the integration. According to them, Fábio is a great leader and one who is modest, consistent, and brave, teaching all to not regard him as an idol. He liked to hear what people had to say about him, was very well assisted, and taught his team how to assist others. He had a great deal of ability and gained much pleasure from talking to people, radiating confidence and making everyone feel a part of the process. Fábio's attitudes and postures on issues were consistent and recognized as such by all. Respect, ethics, consistency between discourse and practice, and a desire to build an organization in which people could fulfill themselves and help to make a better society were Fábio's achievements, and everyone within the organization, as well as the stakeholders, recognized that. Therefore, Fábio Barbosa's actions and personality were a great part of the success of the integration process. According to Fábio himself, the success was also due to respectful behavior towards the acquired banks' culture and, at the same time, a willingness to share values and experiences, consistent leadership exercised daily, the investment in employees, clients, and suppliers' education and commitment. Consequently, the bank was able to achieve sustainable results, with the approval of more than 90 percent of employees as well as pride and commitment.

# Discussion of the case

Tanure (2005) has pointed out that the matter of strategic partnering has been one of the great concerns of HR managers in Brazil. The author's investigation of the perception of HRM by other functional areas as a strategic partner revealed that there is a gap between the assessment made by corporate managers and the assessment by HR area professionals. While the latter self-assessed themselves as strategic partners, the former do not assess them as such. This gap will not be reduced if corporate managers do not identify the contribution of HRM to the performance of the organization. However, the role of HRM will not change if CEOs and top management do not effectively acknowledge the relevance of people to their organizations. The consistency between the discourse and practice of CEOs about this is thus a *sine qua non* if HRM is to play a more strategic role within radical change processes, particularly M&As.

In the acquisition of both banks – Real and Sudameris – by ABN AMRO, it was possible to identify traditional difficulties related to post-acquisition integration, such as cultural differences between the acquiring and the acquired company, fear, insecurity, trauma, feelings of loss, and so on. Nevertheless, instead of becoming potential sources of value destruction, they were carefully managed by ABN AMRO managers in order not to affect the value of the acquired banks. The successful integration of both banks may be attributed to two main features: (1) the consistency among the reasons leading to the acquisition, the strategy of integration, and the management of people; (2) the consistency between what the top management, who led the process, said and did to support this.

The coherence between the discourse and the practice of both the CEO, Fábio Barbosa, and the chairman, Floris Deckers, of ABN AMRO was critical in guaranteeing that the reasons for each acquisition, the strategy of integration, and the management of people were intrinsically consistent with each other. This consistency had two overall effects. One was the ability of ABN AMRO to cope with challenges that an acquisition normally raises and, in particular, those of HR. The other was to leverage the role of the HR area throughout the entire process. This last effect was especially meaningful because, unlike what normally occurs within Brazilian companies (Barros, 2003; Duarte, 2001), HRM was, in fact, a strategic partner in both acquisition processes, contributing to the performance of ABN AMRO (i.e. it prevented value from being destroyed by taking part throughout the process and by carefully managing people-related issues).

Integration success also reflected solid ABN AMRO HR principles, which significantly contributed to the acquisition success. There was a bond between HRM and business strategy, which enabled HR managers to fully exercise a constructive role. Therefore, "phase 1" is essential to the existence of "phase 2," which can have an important role in enabling the company's internal coherence and business strategy consistency during an acquisition process. This was reflected in the coherence between Fábio Barbosa's discourse and practice in the successful integration strategy and in the acquired banks' employee's positive evaluation of the entire process. HRM also acted as a true partner for change, as expected, on "phase 3," being involved in the business strategy, adjusting itself to the new external environment and helping opposite forces to enhance employee and organizational development, which also demonstrates the importance of "phase 4" within the process. Hence, when the four "phases" are present in a company and equally relevant, HRM can perform a major role in helping to transfer the company's strategic capabilities and making the integration process successful.

Although there was a common axis driving these processes, they varied from one case to the other. The common axis was determined by the president of ABN AMRO, who established some key principles with which to guide the activities of these processes. One was to be aware of the relevance of cultural differences – national and organizational. The other was to set up the principles of the new organizational culture. These principles guided the action of all those managers who were involved in the process of integrating Bank Real and then Bank Sudameris. This was particularly important in communicating how people from the acquired company should be dealt with.

At the same time, the post-acquisition integration strategies differed in each case, leading to distinct differences in the management of people. In the case of the acquisition of Real, ABN AMRO initially adopted the *plurality* strategy, followed by the *bending* strategy. In the acquisition of Sudameris, the Dutch bank adopted the *assimilation* strategy. Different post-acquisition integration strategies may produce different effects in the management of people.

Therefore the ABN AMRO case demonstrates that a major challenge in acquisition processes that adopt different integration strategies is to match the reason that determines the acquisition, the integration strategy, and the management of people. In this sense, the team or executive leading the post-acquisition process should establish the most appropriate policies, including those for HRM, so that each integration strategy effectively results in value creation. In other words, we contend that there is not a unique path in the management of people during the period following acquisitions. On the contrary, we argue that the competency of ABN AMRO in matching post-acquisition integration, which is eventually determined by the reasons for the acquisition, and management of people constitutes best practice by bank as a whole and, in particular, HRM.

## Final remarks

The case discussed has illustrated that HRM may effectively contribute to the performance of a company and, in consequence, modify the perceptions of this function held by other corporate managers. As Tanure (2005) argued, a basic condition for that role to be fully executed is its integration in the business strategy and the power system. This process of integration and support is personalized in the role of the president, mainly in a hierarchical and relational culture, such as Brazilian culture. The ABN AMRO case has shown that, in processes of radical change such as acquisitions, the president as well as the top management of the acquiring company have a critical role in establishing, by means of consistency between discourse and practice, that people constitute a key asset of the company, thereby opening avenues for HRM to assume a strategic role within companies.

As argued by Tanure *et al.* (2007) and confirmed in the ABN AMRO case, HRM practices within the organization may enact radical change processes, such as M&As. It is essential that HRM act as a partner for change within the organization, having its functions bound consistently to the business strategy and aligned with the internal infrastructure and the company's external environment, so that it can develop employee and organizational capabilities. Nevertheless, the research carried out among Brazilian companies showed that, in practice, HRM does not have a strategic and consistent role within companies. This reinforces the belief that M&As may have an important role in changing this situation.

These opening avenues have implications for HR managers. Due to the gap between the perception of HRM's strategic relevance that is held by HR managers and that held by other corporate managers, there is no alternative for HR managers but to realign (Tanure *et al.*, 2007) HR's policies and practices with the general strategy of the company. The M&A process is a fine example of this sort of realignment. Further, if a company acquires several other companies, differences in objectives may force HRM to realign its practices according to the objective and the integration strategy of each deal.

Although radical change processes, such as M&As, may be levers for HRM to play a more strategic role within Brazilian companies, this may not happen so easily. On the contrary, although many CEOs of Brazilian companies assert that "people are the best organizational asset," Tanure argues that the facts show an ambivalence (i.e. an inconsistency between the discourse and practice of these CEOs). Some organizations heed the statement of the importance of people in the discourse, but do not follow it consistently in practice. In turn, other organizations have articulated the principle in speeches, but do not go beyond it. In such ambivalent circumstances, HRM may find it difficult to realign its policies and practices with the overall strategy of the organization in processes of radical change. If it does not do so, the vicious cycle discussed above will possibly remain.

Therefore, even though the HR managers should seek to take a more active and strategic role, contributing effectively to the performance of the organization so that the HR function can be perceived differently by other corporate managers, their action is, in effect, determined by the consistency between the discourse and practice of CEOs regarding the true importance of people within organizations. Any mismatch between this discourse and practice is likely to affect the role played by HRM within the organizations. The ABN AMRO case has shown that the top management, particularly the CEO, played a critical role in guaranteeing consistency between discourse and practice concerning the relevance of people in both deals. This opened up the possibility for HR managers to play a more strategic role. This single case obviously does not reflect the reality of most Brazilian companies. Nonetheless, it is a sign that M&As, as well as other radical change processes, may be levers with which to turn HR into a strategic partner.

Furthermore, this article has a critical theoretical implication. Although the literature on post-acquisition management and integration acknowledges that value creation resulting from an acquisition depends on the integration strategy chosen, it does not relate this strategy to the role of HRM. In turn, the literature on HRM does not take into account how the management of people following an acquisition is related to post-acquisition integration. Therefore, we have attempted to link both streams of literature, claiming that HRM and post-acquisition integration research are actually complementary.

## References

Barros, B. T. (2001) *Fusões, Aquisições e Parcerias*, São Paulo: Atlas.

Barros, B. T. (2003) *Fusões e Aquisições no Brasil: Entendendo as Razões dos Sucessos e Fracassos*, São Paulo: Atlas.

Datta, D. K. (1991) "Organizational fit and acquisition performance: effects of post-acquisition integration," *Strategic Management Journal*, 12: 281–297.

David, K. and Singh, H. (1994) "Sources of acquisition cultural risk," in G. von Krogh, A. Sinatra, and H. Singh (eds.), *The Management of Corporate Acquisitions: International Perspectives*, London: Macmillan Press.

Davis, R. E. (1968) "Compatibility in corporate marriages," *Harvard Business Review*, July–August: 86–93.

Deiser, R. (1994) "Post-acquisition management: A process of strategic and organizational learning," in G. von Krogh, A. Sinatra, and H. Singh (eds.), *The Management of Corporate Acquisitions: International Perspectives*, London: Macmillan Press.

Duarte, R. G. (2001) "Cross-Border Acquisitions and the Change of Domestic Management Practices – The Case of Brazil," unpublished Ph.D. thesis, Cambridge, UK: University of Cambridge.

Ghoshal, S. and Tanure, B. (2004) *Estratégia e Festão Empresarial*, Rio de Janeiro: Elsevier.

Haspeslagh, P. C. and Farquhar, A. B. (1994) "The acquisition integration process: A contingent framework," in G. von Krogh, A. Sinatra, and H. Singh (eds.), *The Management of Corporate Acquisitions: International Perspectives*, London: Macmillan Press.

Haspeslagh, P. C. and Jemison, D. B. (1991) *Managing Acquisitions: Creating Value through Corporate Renewal*, New York: The Free Press.

Kay, I. T. and Shelton, M. (2000) "The people problems in mergers," *McKinsey Quarterly*, 4: 29–37.

Kitching, J. (1967) "Why do mergers miscarry?," *Harvard Business Review*, November–December: 84–101.

KPMG (2001) *Merger & Acquisition in Brazil: An Analysis of the 90's*, São Paulo: KPMG.

Krüger, W. and Müller-Stewens, G. (1994) "Matching acquisition policy and integration style," in G. von Krogh, A. Sinatra, and H. Singh (eds.), *The Management of Corporate Acquisitions: International Perspectives*, London: Macmillan Press.

Lindgren, U. (1982) *Foreign Acquisitions: Management of the Integration Process*, Stockholm: IIB/EFI.

Lindgren, U. and Spangberg, K. (1981) "Management of the post-acquisition process in diversified MNCs," in L. Otterberck (ed.), *The Management of Headquarters–Subsidiary Relationships in Multinational Corporations*, Aldershot: Gower.

Lorange, P. (1994) "Preparing for value creation in a complex merger among firms in similar business: Synergy generation and distribution issues," in G. von Krogh, A. Sinatra, and H. Singh (eds.), *The Management of Corporate Acquisitions: International Perspectives*, London: Macmillan Press.

Markides, C. and Oyon, D. (1998) "International acquisitions: Do they create value for shareholders?," *European Management Journal*, 16(2): 125–135.

Marks, M. L. and Mirvis, P. H. (1992) "Rebuilding after the merger: dealing 'with survivor sickness,'" *Organizational Dynamics*, 21(2): 18–32.

Nahavandi, A. and Malekzadeh, A.R. (1994) "Successful mergers through acculturation," in G. von Krogh, A. Sinatra, and H. Singh (eds.), *The Management of Corporate Acquisitions: International Perspectives*, London: Macmillan Press.

Paine, F. T. and Power, D. J. (1984) "Merger strategy: An examination of Drucker's five rules for successful acquisitions," *Strategic Management Journal*, 5: 99–110.

Salter, M. S. and Weinhold, W. A. (1978) "Diversification via acquisition: Creating value," *Harvard Business Review*, July–August: 166–176.

Schweiger, D. M. and Weber, Y. (1989) "Strategies for managing human resources during mergers and acquisitions: An empirical investigation," *Human Resource Planning*, 12(2): 69–86.

Schweiger, D. M., Csizar, E. N., and Napier, N. K. (1994) "A strategic approach to implementing mergers and acquisitions," in G. von Krogh, A. Sinatra, and H. Singh (eds.), *The Management of Corporate Acquisitions: International Perspectives*, London: Macmillan Press.

Schweiger, D. M., Ivancevich, J. M., and Power, F. R. (1987) "Executive actions for managing human resources before and after acquisition," *Academy of Management Executive*, 1(2): 127–138.

Searby, F. W. (1969) "Control postmerger change," *Harvard Business Review*, 4(13): 154–155.

Sinatra, A. and Dubini, P. (1994) "Predicting success after the acquisition: The creation of a corporate profile," in G. von Krogh, A. Sinatra, and H. Singh (eds.), *The Management of Corporate Acquisitions: International Perspectives*, London: Macmillan Press.

Tanure, B. (2005) "Human resource management in Brazil," in M. M. Elvira and A. Davila (eds.), *Managing Human Resources in Latin America*, London: Routledge, (pp. 111–127).

Tanure, B., Evans, P., and Pucik, V. (2007) *Gestão de Pessoas no Brasil: Virtudes e Pecados Capitais*, Rio de Janeiro: Elsevier.

Ulrich, D., Cody, T., La Fasto, F., and Rucci, T. (1989) "Human resources at Baxter Healthcare Corporation merger: A strategic partner role," *Human Resource Planning*, 12(2): 87–103.

United Nations Conference on Trade and Development (UNCTAD) (1999) *World Investment Report 1999*, New York: United Nations.

United Nations Conference on Trade and Development (UNCTAD) (2000) *World Investment Report 2000*, New York: United Nations.

Vicari, S. (1994) "Acquisitions as experimentation," in G. von Krogh, A. Sinatra, and H. Singh (eds.), *The Management of Corporate Acquisitions: International Perspectives*, London: Macmillan Press.

von Krogh, G. (1994) "Implementing strategy in a newly acquired firm," in G. von Krogh, A. Sinatra, and H. Singh (eds.), *The Management of Corporate Acquisitions: International Perspectives*, London: Macmillan Press.

von Krogh, G., Sinatra, A., and Singh, H. (eds.) (1994) *The Management of Corporate Acquisitions: International Perspectives*, London: Macmillan Press.

Walsh, J. P. (1988) "Top management turnover following mergers and acquisitions," *Strategic Management Journal*, 9: 173–183.

# 7 Human resource practices and business performance
## Grupo San Nicolás

*Francisco A. Leguizamon, John C. Ickis, and Enrique Ogliastri*

A heightened awareness exists among Latin American executives of the fact that human resource practices are related to business performance, but the question remains as to which practices matter and how they interact to improve a company's competitive position. How can management simultaneously achieve its financial goals and satisfy the needs of its employees? Which management styles are most effective at ensuring these results? Executives and academics looking for answers to these questions might look to the Grupo San Nicolás, a small pharmaceutical company in El Salvador that was named "Best Employer in Central America" in 2005 and "Best Medium-Size Employer in Latin America" in 2006 (AméricaEconomía, 2005, 2006).

Three strategic paradigms of human resource management (Delery and Doty, 1996) have been applied in this work to interpret the empirical evidence in the Grupo San Nicolás case: the universality of its best practices (Pfeffer, 1994), the need for "contingent" adjustment to the business strategy of the enterprise (Gomez-Mejia and Balkin, 1992), and the theory of the "configurations of factors" that appear most appropriate (Doty and Glick, 1994).

Our inquiry is organized in three parts. In the first, we shall examine those human resource practices of the Grupo San Nicolás that may be considered to be universally applicable and which, if adopted by an organization, might increase the quality of human capital and its potential for creating economic value. Second, we look at those practices that appear to have been adopted in response to the special circumstances faced by the Grupo San Nicolás in the business environment of El Salvador. These practices, which we refer to as "contingent," probably do not have universal applicability, but were effective in meeting the unique challenges of that environment. Finally, we shall describe how these universal and contingent practices have constituted, for San Nicolás, a configuration of factors that are closely interrelated with one another and with company strategy.

A review of human resource practices over the course of this company's history suggests that four factors account for their high performance. First, some of their HR practices, such as training and development, are generally recognized as leading to increased employee productivity. Second, company management has been careful to adapt each new practice to the San Nicolás culture and to the volatile social, political, and economic environment of El Salvador. Third, there appears to have been an understanding by company management of the interrelated nature of the practices adopted: they are not isolated but rather form part of a coherent whole that leverages performance. Fourth, the mutual reinforcement of these practices, supported by a set of shared values and guiding principles, has served as an inspiration in the life of the organization. In this chapter we shall examine the company's HR practices, their interplay with the environment, and the results achieved, as recounted by company executives, middle managers, line operators, and outside observers.

Data on the Grupo San Nicolás were obtained by the authors through interviews with the executive director, Glorybell Silhy, with seven middle managers,[1] and with five employees at the operating level. Secondary sources, including AméricaEconomía and company materials, were also consulted.

## San Nicolás: principles, mission, and vision

The Grupo San Nicolás began operations in 1965 when Dr. Victor Silhy, then a recent graduate in pharmacology, opened his first drugstore in the city of San Salvador and established Laboratorios Suizos (Swiss Laboratories) for the production of pharmaceuticals and cosmetics. The company he founded, Victor Silhy & Cia., began with two employees. By 2004 the number had grown to 577, working in 18 drugstores and three distribution warehouses for Laboratorios Suizos in Guatemala, Nicaragua, and the Dominican Republic. Throughout the company's history, management has remained true to three fundamental principles: justice, reflected in the fair treatment of every member of the organization, even in the most difficult of times; honesty, expressed in every action of every employee; and dignity, through assurance that the moral values and physical integrity of every person who joined the company would at all times be respected. These principles, together with the personal philosophy and style of the founder and CEO, appear to have exercised a powerful influence on the company's human resource practices.

The mission statement of the company and its guiding principles, developed in 1992 with the assistance of the founder's daughter, Glorybell Silhy, upon her return from university studies in the US, appear to have provided an ambitious but attainable standard for obtaining employee commitment: "achieving the satisfaction of our clients through the manufacture and sale of quality pharmaceutical and cosmetic products." The long-term goals also appear to have been a cohesive force: "achieve a sustained annual growth in production of 30 percent, export 60 percent of our products, and maintain majority ownership of a distributor in each Central American country; innovate with aggressive, attractive, and profitable marketing programs, carried out through continuous training and access to real-time information on inventory levels, processes, prices, and markets."

In 2004, the Grupo San Nicolás was one of the major locally-owned companies in the Salvadorian pharmaceutical and cosmetics industry, having garnered 58 percent of the market for hair dyes.[2] The company's return on equity had increased from 19 percent in 2001 to 22 percent in 2002 and 29 percent in 2003.

Its sales revenues had increased by 600 percent in 12 years. With 577 employees and 18 drugstores among the 2,000 drugstores in El Salvador, it had gained 12 percent of the pharmaceuticals market. Its success has contributed to the image of El Salvador as a friendly place for international business.

### *"Universal" HR practices*

The AméricaEconomía survey of "Best Employer in Latin America" takes into account such factors as commitment, defined as the employees' willingness to "go the extra mile" in adapting themselves to the needs of their employer, and also their sense of belonging to the organization and satisfaction on the job. The survey also explores the effectiveness of an organization in creating a workplace that has the commitment of its employees, both intellectually and emotionally. Three common features are shared by the companies ranked among the 25 best employers in Latin America:[3]

1   *Employees are connected with the business*: The best employers focus upon results and set a clear direction. Consequently, employees fully understand the goals and objectives of the company and what is expected of them. They are totally committed to contributing to their company's business success.
2   *Successful companies have created a virtuous circle of collaboration and alignment*: There is frequent and frank communication among the leaders, managers, and employees of the company on its future direction. This continuous dialogue ensures that the business strategy is well articulated and well understood. This makes it easier to design and implement HR policies and practices that support and facilitate the strategy.
3   *Employees are intrinsically motivated*: Employee commitment, as defined by a desire to work in the company, to praise it, and to work hard to make it succeed, appears as a common factor among the 25 best employers, which had a commitment level of 88 percent, as compared to other companies in the survey, which did not surpass 73 percent.

Beyond these standard survey measures, our interviews with the Grupo San Nicolás reveal the adoption of several universally recognized HR practices: lead by example; treat people with dignity; train them on the job; provide services to them as internal clients; and use economic incentives. All of these contributed to company performance.

Dr. Silhy has led by example. The first days were challenging ones for Dr. Silhy: the company was starting out as a neighborhood drugstore tended by just three employees and there were three competing drugstores less than a block away. He could frequently be seen tending personally to clients, setting an example for his employees that possibly accounts for the company's initial success. Ana Silvia Saldaña, now assistant manager but then a salesperson, remembers how he would stand at the door and ask departing customers how they felt about the service that they had received. In weekly meetings with employees, he emphasized how important it was to provide friendly service to clients. With Dr. Silhy and his salespeople providing service of this quality, the San Nicolás drugstores soon became preferred over the others.

Dignified treatment of employees, known as "collaborators," translates into loyalty and commitment to company goals. In 2005, 20 percent had more than 10 years' continuous employment in the company.

There is on-the-job training. During its first years, the laboratory was located in the home of Dr. Silhy's parents, where the first products were processed manually with the help of a few employees who had been trained in production operations.

The company takes care of the internal client – the employees within. With time, cooperation among the various departments in San Nicolás became a regular practice. The HR Manager, Carmen Palacios, recalled the initial challenge: how to avoid friction between the sales and credit departments, or between purchasing and production? This was achieved by adopting the philosophy of providing service to the client within the company, that is, the employee.

The first competition for best service to the client within was held in 1998. The winning employees and departments, chosen by a company-wide survey, were rewarded with a cash bonus. Even this initiative, however, did not completely eliminate inter-departmental friction, and the programs of service to the internal client continued. These efforts eventually paid off when collaborators were allowed to set their own goals. "When we set a goal of our own, we fight to achieve it, and this is what led to the success of the internal client program. The key was getting people to set their own goals, which bit by bit they are achieving," said Glorybell Silhy.

Another universal practice adopted by the company in the human resource area has been the implementation of a system of economic incentives, consisting of cash awards for punctuality, attendance, productivity, collaboration, meeting quotas, showing initiative, demonstrating feelings of belonging, making effective use of time, and using available resources wisely. The evaluation system for awarding the incentives is a 100-point scale in which points are assigned for each of these criteria. The collaborator with the highest score in each department receives the cash prize and becomes eligible to compete for a company-wide prize. This incentive system has had the effect of raising company standards.

### *"Contingent" practices*

Adoption of the universal human resource practices described above was cited by the managers interviewed as having produced satisfaction, personal growth, and commitment among members of the Grupo San Nicolás organization. Other practices, which we describe below as "contingent," were also widely mentioned, often with emotion, by salespeople and collaborators at the operating level.

Contingent practices are those that are adopted in response to particular events or conditions. In a context of war, violence, poverty, and natural disasters, contingent practices assume heightened importance. Such practices might include demonstrating solidarity with employees in the face of calamity, offering flexible work schedules for personal security, developing entrepreneurial capabilities, and even organizing group reading sessions.

There is solidarity in times of crisis. The civil war in the 1980s was "a difficult time, but we were never without the support of company management," recalled Emperatriz de Escobar, Head of Sales, Cosmetics. There were occasions on which it was too dangerous to open the business, according to Ana Silvia Saldaña. She recalled, "when we closed the drugstore at night, Don Victor and his wife would often pick us up and take us home in his car. These are the little things that we shall never forget. This is a family, and all of us feel that we are a part of it."

On October 10, 1986, the Salvadorian capital was jolted by a violent earthquake that cost 1,400 lives. Following the quake, there was neither electricity nor telephone communication. One of the San Nicolás drugstores was damaged by a landslide and had to be closed. Instead of laying off the employees who worked in that store, management let them take their vacations for two years in advance, maintaining their current salary levels. As Ana Silvia Saldaña recalled, "When they learned of the decision, the employees showed up for work at Laboratorios Suizos. It was their way of reciprocating, of giving back to their company in a time of crisis."

The managers formed a team that visited the employees house by house, evaluating the damage caused by the earthquake and ascertaining their needs. The results of those evaluations were used by the company to allocate resources for reconstruction, clothes, food, or other forms of assistance," commented Luis Velazquez, Plant Manager. "This was a genuine demonstration of solidarity. They didn't have to do it, but they did, and we shall never forget it."

The company offers benefits beyond legal requirements. Though the provision of medical and insurance benefits beyond legal requirements may be considered a universal HR practice, the Grupo San Nicolás has provided an unusual array of benefits that take into account the shortages and difficulties faced by families in El Salvador. These benefits include home and auto financing; discounts on groceries, appliances, and auto parts at selected retail outlets; financing plans for the purchase of cellular phones; and free laboratory and optical exams. At the company drugstores, they receive discounts of 10–20 percent on pharmaceuticals and 20–30 percent on cosmetics. Other benefits include scholarships of up to 50 percent of the cost of tuition for continued study and flexible schedules so that employees are able to attend classes. "Our work is to provide benefits for our collaborators so that they are happy in our company," said Carmen Palacios. "We are always looking for new ways to provide for their welfare."

The company established flexible work schedules during the civil war. Public transportation was unreliable and violent incidents were occurring throughout the country. A curfew was imposed by the military during much of the conflict. Once the peace accords were signed and calm was restored, the regular work schedule was reintroduced.

With the end of the civil war in 1992, the company faced new opportunities and challenges. That year Laboratorios Suizos moved to a new building from its original site in the home of Dr. Silhy's parents. The Grupo San Nicolás was now a medium-sized company, which, over the years, had become the preferred company of Salvadorian consumers. But as the political climate improved, and as El Salvador and other Central American countries adopted liberal economic policies, competition became more intense. The Grupo San Nicolás responded to the challenge by setting a goal to transform the organization into a leading Salvadorian company with regional coverage. Through an in-company program called training for expansion, San Nicolás opened 14 additional drugstores throughout the country between 1993 and 2004, making it the largest-selling drugstore chain in El Salvador. In 2004, with 18 drugstores, it had gained a 12 percent market share. In the same period, the Group opened wholly owned distributorships in Guatemala, Honduras, Nicaragua, and the Dominican Republic. In Costa Rica, its products were sold to retail outlets by independent distributors.

The development of entrepreneurial skills among its collaborators prepared the company for expansion. In 2003, the company initiated a program for the development of 30 entrepreneurial behaviors or competencies, known as Empretec, with the support of the Ministry of Industry.[4] The Empretec workshop, which lasts eight days, concludes with a performance improvement plan or PMR (from the Spanish) that each participant must commit himself or herself to carry out in his or her department. All 23 people from the Grupo San Nicolás who participated in the workshop in 2003 developed their PMRs, and one of the San Nicolás participants was awarded a prize for the best performance in the implementation of the plan at the end of the year.

A novel idea occurred to Glorybell Silhy one morning in June 2002. She had recently been inspired after reading a book about overcoming obstacles, and she decided to share these ideas with the sales force. She read some passages from the book to them, after which they discussed how the underlying ideas might be applied to their own lives. This uplifting experience culminated in the tradition that came to be known as the Monday readings, which soon spread to other departments. The readings were scheduled each Monday at 7:30 a.m. for plant and warehouse personnel, at 8:00 a.m. for beauty counselors, and on Saturdays for salespeople. Though very simple, Silhy believed that this practice of Monday readings created a bond among members of the San Nicolás family that transcended the employment relationship. The collaborators interpreted the Monday readings as a genuine desire on the part of management to share ideas and examples of personal development that had a direct application to their private lives. Shortly afterward, these readings were sent by email to all drugstores and distributorships. Management believed that the Monday readings created an improved work environment among all parts of the organization and that this produced better business results.

Another practice, called "the creation of a collaborative work environment" (*creación de un ambiente de colaboración en el trabajo*) was begun on a regular basis with the organization of a workshop attended by people from several departments. The workshop was carried out in two stages: First, participants learned the importance of a positive work environment and agreed that improvement of the current environment would depend upon every member of the organization treating every other as "the most important person in the company." After conducting critical self-evaluations, each department made a presentation of those things that should be improved. In the second stage, each department prepared a survey for its internal clients to grade the quality of the services provided, identifying weaknesses and opportunities for improvement. Two weeks later, there was a meeting of everyone in the company in which each department shared the client evaluations that it had received and the commitments that it had assumed. This list of commitments was posted as a visible reminder of these self-imposed goals for improvement.

For personnel in the Sales Department, the company has pursued the practice of monthly assignment of product. This program, by which each salesperson receives a personal supply of the company's pharmaceuticals or cosmetics each month, encourages the salesperson to use company products, experience their quality, and speak to their clients with authority about the products' attributes.

The growth and stability that were achieved as these practices were being put into effect convinced Dr. Silhy to institutionalize many of the benefits that had been granted to employees. Thus the Special Loan Fund was created, providing a safety net for employees in cases of emergency or special need. This fund, administered by the Department of Human Resources, is made available at reduced rates of interest, with the interest reinvested in the fund. Employees may place their savings in the fund and earn interest at the lending rate.

The company also provides meal subsidies in the form of coupons valued at 40–50 percent of the cost of lunch in the company cafeteria, the exact percentage depending upon overall company financial results for the period. Other benefits include private medical and hospital insurance and dental service for a subsidized annual fee of around $5 per family member. The company also offers group life insurance. In case of death of the spouse, parents, or children, the company provides for funeral expenses. This is a unique packet that is not at all common in Latin America.

Although there is congruence between the universal and contingent HR practices, it should be clear from the above description that the contingent practices are unique to the Grupo San Nicolás and that they originate in the values of the founder. This has had a profound impact upon the role and functions of HR in the company. "We are not a typical HR department that is charged by management with controlling employees in defense of the owners' interests. We don't fit that profile," said Carmen Palacios. "Instead, we are always looking to develop new practices that not only provide benefits for our collaborators and keep their motivation levels high, but also achieve a strong sense of commitment that contributes to their own prosperity and to that of the company." This has been possible in today's environment of fierce competition and free trade just as it was during the Salvadorian civil war, and in times of natural catastrophe. Beginning with the company's founder, Dr. Victor Silhy, the relations of owners with members of the organization have been guided by principles that include dignified treatment, meritocracy as a basis for compensation and promotion, solidarity in time of disaster, and, above all, honesty, practiced consistently throughout the life of the organization.

## Human resource strategy, trajectory, and practice

The ranking of the Grupo San Nicolás as the best employer in Latin America cannot be fully explained by a single human resource practice or any combination of practices. By simply imitating these practices, it is doubtful that another company could achieve the same results. It is, instead, the internal consistency of these practices, the timing of their adoption, their congruence with strategy in the different stages of the company's development, and the implementation of a unique leadership style that help explain the results achieved in this medium-size Salvadorian company. The relationships identified among the practices, strategy, and environment of the company are shown in Table 7.1. The first and second columns describe the five stages in the historical development of the Grupo San Nicolás and the basic strategy adopted to deal with the changing environment at each stage. The human resource management practice that was used by the company is shown in the third column, and the most clearly identifiable results appear in the fourth.

Competing by providing attention to the client was the first strategic response of the company, dating back to when Victor Silhy installed his first drugstore in his parents' home within one block of three competitors. By setting a clear standard of client attention for his first employees to follow, and by coaching them continuously until they were able to provide the same quality of attention, he was able to gain the preference and loyalty of his customers.

By taking advantage of opportunities, Victor Silhy kept one step ahead of competitors and was able to grow his enterprise. In 1967, he sensed a business opportunity when he learned of an abandoned lot of cosmetics in a local customs house, and he bought the entire lot. When he put the cosmetics up for sale in his drugstore, the demand was immediate. As the inventory declined, he wrote to the home office in Europe and offered to distribute their brand in El Salvador.

*Table 7.1* Congruence among practices, strategy, and the historic trajectory of Grupo San Nicolás

| Environment | Strategy | HR practices | Results |
|---|---|---|---|
| Intense rivalry (ongoing) | Personalized attention to clients | Lead by example | Loyalty; sales growth |
| Products salvaged (1967) | Marketing; representation | Development of entrepreneurship | Growth with profitability |
| Import substitution (1970–1992) | Produce, expand | Training provided to outside collaborators | Continued growth with profitability |
| Civil war (1980–1992) Earthquake (Oct. 1986) | Establish accessible prices; survival | Sense of family solidarity | Survival/ commitment |
| Increasing demand (since 1992) | Regionalization/ expansion | Training/education | Growth/ profitability |

He was made the company's exclusive representative and thus began a long and profitable business relationship. The development of this same entrepreneurial spirit among his collaborators would constitute a practice that was later formalized through the Empretec program.

The company produces as well as distributes. In 1969, while on his honeymoon in Europe, Don Victor visited several pharmaceutical laboratories and obtained exclusive representation for their products in El Salvador. Upon his return, he found that the governmental policy of import substitution, with high tariff barriers, favored locally produced drugs over imports. Not discouraged, he created his second business, Laboratorios Suizos, S.A., for the production of pharmaceutical and cosmetic products.

Grupo San Nicolás offers discounts on its products. During the early 1990s, at the height of the civil war, the Grupo San Nicolás continued to grow with the opening of two additional drugstores in San Salvador. Aware of the hardships facing the Salvadorian population, Victor Silhy began to offer discounts on essential medicines, which was unheard of in the industry at that time. "No one was giving discounts then, something that is today a common practice in the industry," recalled Ana Silvia Saldaña. "In that time of crisis, Don Victor asked us to strengthen our commitment to 'low prices, variety, and friendly service,' adding that 'those three elements were the keys to our being successful, while other companies were closing their doors.'"

The unique leadership style of Victor Silhy combines a concern for personal growth and autonomy with the more traditional aspects of benevolent paternalism. Throughout the company history there have been numerous examples of assistance provided to employees by the family in times of difficulty. Collaborators recall many experiences in which Don Victor personally helped the person or the family in need. Those stories have a mythical quality and have been effective in generating powerful commitment and a sense of solidarity among the employees. As one employee said, "It confirms for everyone, those of us who have received direct assistance as well as those who have not, that we can count on our company." It may confirm as well that paternalism is a useful form of leadership in Latin America (Martinez, 2005).

Personnel turnover has been less than 1 percent throughout the company's history. "We see our organization as something more than a company," commented Ana Silvia Saldaña. "It is perhaps for this reason that those who come to work here never want to leave, and stay until retirement. The few times that I have seen a collaborator leave, it has been to start up his or her own business or to live abroad. And I can remember several cases of those who asked to return, several years after leaving the company." When possible, space was made for them.[5]

This unique leadership style has been reinforced by the use of symbols and metaphors to obtain the commitment of organization members. The logo of the company, known as the San Nicolás trophy, is an owl, signifying wisdom, dedication, and sacrifice. The owl is seated upon three pillars, representing knowledge, resources, and human capital. The human pillar is considered to be the most important by the Silhys, because they recognize that the success of the company rests upon its dedication and the effort of people.

One general practice that might be overlooked, precisely because it appears obvious, is the repeated application of common sense. For the management of the Grupo San Nicolás, concern for employee welfare made both business and ethical sense. "Sometimes I have been asked whether our human resource practices translate into financial results and I can assure you that they do," says Glorybell Silhy:

> Our people are our principal resource; it is they who achieve results in a fiercely competitive market. When I came back to work in the company after graduating from MIT, some thought that I would bring innovative business proposals and that I would make big changes. But that was not the case. I've found that in business, much of success comes from applying common sense, and the relationship between motivated employees and good business results is no more than that, just common sense. That formula, applied by my father, has brought this company to where it is today, and it is what will guide us in the future.

Moreover, she added, "we use ethical common sense to define the role that our business should play in society. Companies cannot isolate themselves; they must contribute to the welfare of the societies where they operate and where they make their profits. And being concerned with employee welfare is one way of doing this."

## Summary and conclusion

The lessons of the Grupo San Nicolás may be summarized as follows:

- Even in violent and uncertain environments, amidst poverty, it is possible to build successful companies that demonstrate world-class human resource management.
- Best universal practices are not enough to ensure business success; contingent actions are needed to go the extra mile.
- Contingent HR practices, based on common sense, were much more appreciated by employees than universal practices, for the circumstances in which they were applied.
- A company does not need to be large to have the best HR practices.
- The best HR practices are those that send an unequivocal message that people are at the center of the business strategy.
- Successful HR management is grounded in values and supported by leadership that is able to express these values over the life of a business.
- Culture is a precious resource that must be embraced and strengthened with honest work in a positive and creative way.

This case is of particular interest because it exhibits good HR practices that produce solid business results in a complex and turbulent environment.

The experience of the Grupo San Nicolás appears to demonstrate that, in practice, elements of the three human resource theories or paradigms work in combination. As was seen in this case, these elements may include some of universal relevance, as these are clearly superior for application in a diversity of environments and circumstances.

"Contingent" practices – those specific to company strategy and the environment of El Salvador – have have also been examined in this study. Among these, the personalized attention to peoples' needs in dangerous and sometimes tragic circumstances stands out. Benevolent paternalism is a part of the Salvadorian and Latin American culture, which may be distinguished from cultures in other regions of the world by three essential characteristics: the primacy of close family and small group relations; acceptance of power distance (magnitude of the difference in influence, authority, and privilege between members of a society); and tolerance of uncertainty (Ogliastri *et al.*, 1999). The leadership exercised by Dr. Silhy in the Groupo San Nicolás is clearly a product of these three cultural traits, to the point of becoming a key competitive factor in the business. What makes the Grupo San Nicolás unique is that its HR practices are consistent with these cultural traits, and they provide simultaneous attention to personal growth and development.

In the context of regional integration, economic liberalization, and more intense global competition, it appears likely that the combination of these paradigms will persist in the Grupo San Nicolás for one very pragmatic reason: they work. The fundamental values of the company and the practices we have seen in support of these values are really nothing more than a combination of the common sense and intelligence of universal practices, blended with the judicious use of contingent elements that are grounded in the cultural environment. This is easily stated, but very difficult to imitate.

## Notes

1 Extensive and in-depth interviews were held with Ms. Silhy and with Ana Silvia Saldaña, Assistant manager; and Carmen Palacios, Manager of Human Resources. Also interviewed were the Plant Manager of Laboratorios Suizos, the Financial Manager, a Country Director, the Sales Manager (Cosmetics) and the representative of the Group in Costa Rica.
2 As measured by A. C. Nielsen & Fasani, San Nicolás Marketing Consultants, February 2004.
3 The prize focused on best practices like specific incentives, training, open communications, incentives for teamwork, visibility, formal processes for leadership development, respectful evaluation of employees, career development plans, specific strategic goals, promotion of diversity and work/family balance (América Economía, 2006).
4 Empretec was financed, in part, by the Inter-American Development Bank (IDB) and carried out in El Salvador by a private foundation, FUNDEMAS (Ickis and Vazquez, 2004).
5 Interviewees cited several specific cases where returning employees were accommodated in the organization, and one case where it was not possible to do so.

# References

AméricaEconomía (2005) *Los mejores empleadores en America Latina* [Best employers in Latin America], Santiago.

AméricaEconomía (2006) *Los mejores empleadores en America Latina* [Best employers in Latin America], Santiago.

Delery, J. and Doty, D. H. (1996) "Modes of theorizing in strategic human resource management: Tests on universalistic, contingency, and configurational performance predictions," *Academy of Management Journal*, 39(4): 802–835.

Doty, D. H. and Glick, W. H. (1994) "Typologies as a unique form of theory building: Toward improved understanding and modeling," *Academy of Management Review*, 19: 230–251.

Gomez-Mejia, L. R. and Balkin, D. B. (1992) *Compensation, Organizational Strategy, and Firm Performance*, Cincinnati: South-Western.

Ickis, J. and Vazquez, N. (2004) *FUNDEMAS*, INCAE Business School Case Study, Alajuela, Costa Rica: INCAE.

Martinez, P. (2005) "Paternalism as a positive form of leadership in the Latin American context," in M. M. Elvira and A. Davila (eds.), *Managing Human Resources in Latin America*, Oxford, UK: Routledge.

Ogliastri, E., McMillen, C., Altschul, C., Arias, M. E., Bustamaute, C. de, Dávila, C., Dorfman, P., de la Coletta, M. F., Fimmen, C., Ickis, J. and Martínez, S. (1999) "Cultura y liderazgo organizacional en diez países de America Latina: El estudio Globe," [Culture and organizational leadership in 10 Latin American countries: the Globe Study], *Academia. Revista Latinoamericana de Administracion*, 22: 29–57.

Pfeffer, J. (1994) *Competitive Advantage through People: Unleashing the Power of the Work Force*, Boston: Harvard Business School Press.

# 8 HRM systems in Mexico

## The case of Novo Nordisk

*Jacobo Ramirez and Laura Zapata-Cantú[1]*

The term human resource management (HRM) system was coined in the USA (e.g. Pfeffer and Veiga, 1999) and denotes a bundle of HRM practices (Macduffie, 1995) or systems (Bamberger and Meshoulam, 2000) that are linked with higher performance and employee commitment, which, in turn, leads to higher profits for firms (e.g. Huselid, 1995). However, empirical studies of HRM systems have largely been limited to the Western context of relatively stable institutional economic, political, and social environments. Little empirical research on Latin America has been conducted, with the exception of studies presented in two special journal issues (Elvira and Davila, 2005a; Davila and Elvira, 2007) and a book on Latin America (Elvira and Davila, 2005b).

We aim to contribute to the academic discourse on HRM systems in Latin America by presenting the case of the Danish pharmaceutical company Novo Nordisk. This firm was ranked as one of the top 100 best places to work in Latin America in 2007. We will focus on its Mexican operation, which ranked 27th in the Best Place to Work in Mexico according to the Great Place to Work Institute México; the list was published in the Mexican business magazine *Mundo Ejecutivo* (Vargas-Hernández, 2007). The analysis of multinational corporations (MNCs) with operations in Latin America is important as they seem to have become familiar with the idiosyncrasies found in the region when implementing their HRM systems. According to the 100 best places to work in Latin America, 95 percent of the firms in the 2007 ranking are either US- or European-based firms that have invested in the region as a foreign direct investment (FDI) (Great Place to Work Institute México, 2007). This result could have different interpretations. First, it could be seen as supportive of a universalistic HR argument (e.g. Terpstra and Rozell, 1993). Researchers in this direction go as far as to claim that all organizations, regardless of size, industry, or business strategy, should adopt so-called "best practices" (Bamberger and Meshoulam, 2000: 175). This implies that one HRM model should be applied to all firms (Wood and Albanese, 1995). Second, the best places to work ranking could be interpreted to suggest that FDI in Latin America has understood the relevant contextual factors when implementing strategies in the region. However, the academic literature presents limited empirical research in this direction. Therefore, no conclusive evidence can be presented on the approach that MNCs have utilized when implementing HRM systems in Latin America. In our analysis of HRM systems, we aim to understand which HRM practices foreign firms are implementing in Mexico and how they are implementing them. Our analysis is based on neo-institutional theory (Scott, 1995), which sheds light on the influence of the systems and idiosyncrasies surrounding organizations in emerging economies such as Mexico (Hoskisson, *et al.*, 2000). The results of this research could help both national and international firms to understand the impact of national context on the operation of HRM systems in Latin America. This perspective will set the context in which the case is analyzed. Implications for practitioners and academics are presented as concluding remarks.

## HRM systems

A number of studies linking HRM practices to firms' performance (e.g. Huselid, 1995) have focused on two levels of analysis: (1) organizational – return on investment; or (2) individual – employees' workplace satisfaction. However, researchers do not agree on a consistent measure of performance at these two levels of analysis (e.g. Legge, 2005). In this chapter, we will consider the term "firms' performance" based on the employees' satisfaction in their workplace. In particular, we will relate the Best Place to Work in Mexico, as judged by Great Place to Work Institute México, to firms' performance. The dimensions that this Institute uses for assessing the firms are: (1) credibility – open communication and accessibility; (2) respect – individuals and professional work creating a work–life balance; (3) justice – fairness in recognition, objectivity in the hiring and promotions process, non-discrimination practices; (4) pride – sense of pride in the company, colleagues, the company's products, and its position in the market and community; and (5) camaraderie – relationship with other people, friendly environment, sense of teamwork and/or family (Great Place to Work Institute México, 2007). Researchers argue that these dimensions are linked to firms' performance at the two levels of analysis: financial and higher levels of commitment among employees (Xiao and Tsui, 2007). Additionally, we propose that these dimensions are closely related to the HR employee relations subsystem of the configuration of high-performance human resource practices proposed by Bamberger and Meshoulam (2000) (see Table 8.1).

Taking into consideration the notion of HRM systems and contextual factors, it is also important to emphasize the cross-national aspect of MNCs (divergence) in this study. Research in this agenda has shown both successful case studies of companies operating in Latin America and the complexity of implementing HR practices in different national settings (for a review, see Elvira and Davila, 2005b). Abramo and Montero (2000, in Cavalcanti, 2002: 10) suggest "the reality is that Latin American nations still have precarious human capital policies and are still struggling to develop a better educated workforce." In this context, MNCs face different barriers that slow their ability to implement high-performance HRM systems. Thus it is important to further investigate which HR practices work in Latin America and why they work. HRM systems in different national

*Table 8.1* Configuration of high-performance human resource management practices

| HR subsystem | Dimension | |
| --- | --- | --- |
| | Resource and control-based HR practices | Sample HR practices |
| People flow | Staffing<br>Training<br>Mobility (internal & external)<br>Job security | • Selective training<br>• More extensive, general skills training and development<br>• Broad career paths<br>• Guarantee of job security |
| Appraisal and rewards | Appraisal<br>Rewards | • Long-term, results-oriented appraisal<br>• Extensive, open-ended rewards |
| Employment relation | Job design<br>Participation | • Broad job description, flexible job assignments<br>• Encouragement of participation, and teamwork |

*Source:* Adapted from Bamberger and Meshoulam (2000: 66–67).

settings should be considered within a number of the major societal institutions and organizational context factors (e.g. industrial sector, level of technology, etc.). This view suggests that the specific bundle of HR practices would vary by sector and business strategy and cultural settings (Ramirez and Fornerino, 2007).

The following sections present a specific analysis of the nationality influence in management between Mexico and Denmark and a discussion of the influence of contextual factors on the "best" HR practices. These two analyses seek to support theoretically the analysis of Novo Nordisk in Mexico.

## Contextual factors: Mexico and Denmark

Institutional theory emphasizes the influence of systems surrounding organizations that shape social and organizational behavior (Hoskisson *et al.*, 2000: 252). Mexican and Danish economic development, labor legislation, and societal features as well as some cultural dimensions – power-distance, egalitarianism – present major distinctions (e.g. House *et al.*, 2004). Based on these differences we expect that HRM systems will be approached differently in these countries. The following section presents the most salient economic, social, and organizational cultural factors that might shape HR management (Gomez and Sanchez, 2005).

### *Economic development*

Mexico has implemented fundamental reforms in different aspects of its economy and policy since the late 1980s. It has become the fourteenth largest export economy in the world, with US $214.2 billion in 2005 (UNCTAD, 2005). Additionally, Mexico has signed a free trade agreement with the European Union (EU) and, as a result, could become more attractive for FDI. According to the Mexican

Ministry of Economy (2005), Denmark invested US $0.3 billion in FDI from 1994 to 1999, which increased to US $1 billion from 2000 to 2005. These figures represent a 211.9 percent increase in FDI.

Denmark is a stable economy in which the government plays an important role. For example, Denmark's general government expenditure on infrastructure investment and maintenance as a share of gross domestic product (GDP) stood at 56.3 percent in 2004 (EIU, 2005). In contrast, the Mexican government spent about 1.2 percent of GDP in 2003 (World Bank, 2005). These figures show the importance of FDI in Mexico for its economic development. On the other side of the spectrum, the role of Denmark needs to be properly understood; for example, a striking feature is its business environment and the stability, transparency, and efficiency of the political systems (Co-Industri, 2007). These features are often neglected but are some of the most important conditions for the overall attractiveness of a country's business environment. It is the political system, after all, which sets the legal and institutional context within which business is conducted (EIU, 2005).

### Social factors

Denmark is characterized by a high level of social welfare (Schramm-Nielsen, 2000). Employees (the overall organizational structure in both public and private organizations) are insured against unemployment, sickness, and retirement, and employees have five weeks' paid holidays from the first year of work. To some observers "Denmark is an over regulated society and Danes tend to abide by the rules. Life in Denmark obviously becomes less risky and less unpredictable" (Schramm-Nielsen, 2000: 9).

The Danes have been proud of what they consider a unique labor market model. Employers and trade unions have long had a centralized system of negotiations to determine pay and working conditions. One of the characteristics of Danish labor relations is the philosophy of democratization of the workplace (Haug, 2004). "It encompasses the participation of all employees in the decision-making process, from the individual workers on the shop floor, through various cooperation committees or work councils, to the board of directors, and even outside of the organization" (Haug, 2004: 135). Researchers support this democratic view by presenting Denmark as a high egalitarianism and low power-distance society (House *et al.*, 2004). In the Danish model, known as "flexi-security," there are few restrictions on companies' hiring and firing of workers. However, the state provides generous financial support to people who are out of work while simultaneously providing motivation for the jobless to actively seek work.

Mexico presents some management particularities such as high power-distance and low levels of egalitarianism (House *et al.*, 2004), which are reflected in Mexican labor law. Mexican labor law is based on Article 123 of the Federal Constitution. This law provides worker and employee rights that insure against sickness and retirement; employees have one week's paid holiday from the first year of work and can form unions and other associations. However, there is no insurance against unemployment. There is some overt employer hostility toward unions, but managerial paternalism is a characteristic feature of labor relations. In addition to wages, unions emphasize controlling hiring, job tenure, union security, work standards, and a wide range of fringe benefits. Economic disputes are usually settled after government participation in negotiations without strikes or mass demonstrations.

### Organizational culture

Culture operates not only at the national level but also at the organizational level (Martin, 1992). The relationship between culture and HRM can be understood "in terms of the symbolism and meaning that they communicate and/or group members ascribe to (or interpret from) arrangements and practices" (Alvesson and Kärreman, 2007: 712). Ryan, Wiechmann and Hemingway argue that organizations with a "strong" corporate culture help implement "global" staffing practices "because individuals throughout the globe have a shared understanding of what is important in the organization" (2003: 88). In the same line of argument, Alvesson's and Kärreman's findings suggest that the "success of the HRM system depends less on the quality or rationality of the HRM arrangements, and more on their sheer quantity and intensity and the backup of supportive ideologies" (2007: 721). It seems that HR practices support the creation of an organizational identity that employees tend to endorse. Sun and colleagues argue that high-performance HR practices foster a high-quality employment relationship, which enhances a high-quality relationship among employees, mutuality and reciprocity (2007: 571). These features in Mexico can be interpreted as "solidarity and sense of community" (Davila and Elvira, 2007: 389), which build an environment that enhances personal networks and the psychological contract (Michailova and Worm, 2003; Elvira and Davila, 2005a). These patterns of relationships follow Bamberger and Meshoulam's (2000: 134) employees' relation subsystem, "relating to those strategic managerial activities aimed at establishing, enforcing, and reinforcing the psychological contract between employer and employees and thus shaping both the tangible work environment and the less tangible normative base (i.e. culture) of the organization." Employees come to understand, interpret, and eventually internalize the terms of their employment relationships and work-related "psychological contract" (Davila and Elvira, 2007).

We have presented the high-performance HR system, which we related to the model of the Great Place to Work Institute México. We have also presented the contextual settings in Mexico and Denmark, and discussed organizational culture, which tends to shape employees' behavior. The following section presents the methods used for this research.

### Methods

This study uses a grounded theory approach (Bartusch and Lindgren, 1999) to examine the implementation of the Novo Nordisk management style in Mexico. We used an exploratory and qualitative research design that relies on external contextual information, firm documentation, and in-depth interviews with the

HR manager and employees at different levels of the organization. Novo Nordisk's description was developed by taking the firm as the main unit of analysis. The case study (Yin, 1989) protocol was constructed from contextual information about the firm's industry and Mexican contextual factors. We conducted formal interviews and "hung around" (Dingwall, 1997) for informal talks with staff at different levels in Mexico City and in Bagsværd, Denmark. The formal semi-structured interviews took place from May to September, 2007, were audio-recorded and lasted between 90 and 120 minutes. The interviews were transcribed verbatim and all information shared by the two authors to subsequently generate the full write-ups on each case. We followed Alvesson and Kärreman's (2007) interpretative approach for the case description and interpretation, in which we tried "to go beyond the surface and look for something less obvious, or less easily revealed in a quick coding process." In the following section, we present the findings of this study.

## Findings

Novo Nordisk is a healthcare company and a world leader in diabetes care. The company has the broadest diabetes product portfolio in the industry, including the most advanced products within the area of insulin delivery systems. Table 8.2 presents a general description of Novo Nordisk.

*Table 8.2* Description of Novo Nordisk

| Factors | |
| --- | --- |
| Industrial sector | Healthcare company that manufactures and markets pharmaceutical products |
| Size | 23,600 full-time employees in 79 countries, and markets its products in 179 countries. Approximately 53 percent of employees are located in Denmark, 47 percent in the rest of the world (North America: 2,846; Japan and Oceania: 980; International Operations, includes Latin America: 4,188; Europe: 2,944; Denmark: 12,214): 17.4 percent within research and development, 35.6 percent in production and production administration, 29.6 percent in international sales and marketing, and 17.4 percent in administration. |
| Human resources | The firm has developed its tailored "Novo Nordisk Way of Management," which is based on 11 management principles. Please refer to the appendix for further details. |
| Surroundings and atmosphere | Corporate People and Organization is located in a four-floor building called House of People outside Copenhagen. The workplace is spacious and clean. There are no private offices, except for the department's director. The atmosphere is open and pleasant. Each level of the building has in the center of the floor a glass phone-cabin. The coffee area has fresh fruit, water, and tea. There are no soft-drink vending machines in the building. |

*Source*: Adapted from Novo Nordisk (2006).

Novo Nordisk has developed its "Novo Nordisk Way of Management"[2] (NNWoM), a management framework for how the company does business. It consists of three elements: the Vision, the Charter, and a set of global company policies (Novo Nordisk, 2006: 4). According to one manager in Denmark, "The Novo Nordisk Way of Management is a system that combines modern value-based management with traditional control. In short, it is like the 'bible' for the firm."

The Novo Nordisk Charter describes the company's values, which underscore its commitment to the Triple Bottom Line (socially responsible, environmentally sound, and economically viable), Sustainable Development, and its Fundamentals, which consist of 11 Management Principles and Values. Table 8.3 presents the firm's values. According to a manager in Mexico, "The Charter for companies in the Novo Group and the Novo Nordisk Way of Management established a new way of thinking and working across the company."

Novo Nordisk's internationalization strategy seeks to expand its market to Latin America and other emerging economies. In 2004, Novo Nordisk established in Mexico its first sales force. The firm's outlook is presented in Table 8.4. Mexico represents a potentially large market for the firm. Mexico is ranked ninth worldwide for people with diabetes, a disease that is responsible for 13 out every 100 deaths in the country (Federación Mexicana de Diabetes, A.C., Instituto Nacional de Salud Pública, 2007). Novo Nordisk's global campaign Changing Diabetes has been implemented in Mexico. The employees have given talks and visited schools in Mexico in order to raise public awareness about diabetes. One of the interviewees in Mexico stated, "we started a campaign in an elementary

*Table 8.3* Novo Nordisk's values

| Values | Statements |
|---|---|
| Accountable | Each of us shall be accountable – to the company, ourselves, and society – for the quality of our efforts, for contributing to our goals and for developing our culture and shared values. |
| Ambitious | We shall set the highest standard in everything we do and reach challenging goals. |
| Responsible | We shall conduct our business in a socially and environmentally responsible way and contribute to the enrichment of the communities in which we operate. |
| Engaged with stakeholders | We shall seek an active dialogue with our stakeholders to help us develop and strengthen our businesses. |
| Open and honest | Our business practices shall be open and honest to protect the integrity of the Novo Group companies and of each employee. |
| Ready for change | We must foresee change and use it to our advantage. Innovation is key to our business and therefore we will encourage a learning culture for the continuous development and improved employability of our people. |

*Source:* Novo Nordisk (2006).

*Table 8.4* Description of Novo Nordisk Mexico

| Factors | |
| --- | --- |
| Industrial sector | Commercialization and distribution of pharmaceutical products. It plans to open a manufacturing plant in Mexico City in 2007. |
| Size | 100 full-time employees: 28 employees on the Mexican site who give service to the Central American and Caribbean operations; 4 employees in R&D and 6 employees who work on the manufacturing plant project; 12 percent of employees in Mexico are foreigners. |
| Human resources | The firm has implemented "Novo Nordisk Way of Management" in accordance with Mexican labor legislation. The Department has four employees: Recruitment, Selection and Career Development, Operational Personnel Management, Communication and General Service. |
| Surroundings and atmosphere | The corporate building is located in an exclusive area of Mexico City – Lomas de Chapultepec. The workplace is spacious and clean. The HR manager has a private office. The atmosphere is open and pleasant. The coffee place has fresh fruit, water, and tea. There are no soft-drink vending machines in the building. |

school in which we are teaching the children and their parents healthy eating habits." While this type of activity is voluntary, it has been popular among the employees in Mexico according to the HR manager. To some extent, it reflects the employees' *pride* in working at Novo Nordisk in Mexico, which is rooted in the firm's organizational culture. It seems that the employees have assimilated Novo Nordisk's organizational culture, which shapes their behavior. One of our interviewees put it this way: "The bottom line is that we need to change the way people think and behave. This is reflected within the firm and in our daily life."

The firm's values described in Novo Nordisk's Charter appear to be consistent with HR practices. We experienced this congruence in our visits to the firm in Mexico and Denmark. The interpretation of our text suggests that Novo Nordisk's values are based on universal values, such as trust, respect for human dignity, integrity, and fairness, among others. These basic values are not negotiated or modified in the firm's operations around the world. As a manager in Denmark explained: "If an employee does not subscribe to the firm's values, it means that this is not the workplace for him/her." It seems that Novo Nordisk's values are consistent in Denmark and Mexico. For example, we were offered either coffee or water, not soft drinks (sugar-based drinks), during the interviews. Also, we saw that there was a plate with fresh fruit in the coffee area. One of the employees interviewed in Mexico stated:

> We have a dietitian who gives seminars and lectures on eating habits; these practices have changed my whole life. For example, my son talks about not eating too much sugar and diabetes.

The challenge in Mexico is to change the work culture. According to the HR manager in Mexico:

> I think it is a mistake to argue that international firms must align their internal operations to the national culture where they locate their subsidiaries. I think that we can learn from other cultures, in this case from Denmark which has achieved higher standards of development than Mexico. Our challenge is to make people understand the main principles of the firm such as honesty, openness, among others. In this way, employees can learn the organizational model. We have not and will not change this model in Mexico, but we want the employees to understand it.

It seems that Novo Nordisk in Mexico considers the dimensions of credibility, respect, and justice in setting the organizational culture. These types of dimensions are considered by the Great Place to Work Institute México for its ranking.

## Human resource systems

The results of our interviews are presented in Table 8.5 following the theoretical development of the Bamberger and Meshoulam (2000) high-performance HR practices model.

*Table 8.5* Configuration of high-performance HR practices in Novo Nordisk Mexico

| | Dimension | |
|---|---|---|
| HR subsystem | *Resource and control-based HR practices* | *Novo Nordisk Mexico operation of the HR practices* |
| People flow | Staffing<br>Training<br>Mobility<br>  (internal & external)<br>Job security | ▪ Online psychological test<br>▪ Panel interview based on competencies<br>▪ Employees are responsible for their career development<br>▪ Zero discrimination<br>▪ Opportunities for worldwide mobility within the firm |
| Appraisal and rewards | Appraisal<br>Rewards | ▪ Based on Balanced Score Card<br>▪ Productivity bonus given to all employees without hierarchical distinction |
| Employment relation | Job design<br>Participation | ▪ Job design based on competencies<br>▪ Encourage participation in decision-making process<br>▪ Based on Novo Nordisk Way of Management |

*Source:* Adapted from Bamberger and Meshoulam (2000: 66–67).

### HR subsystem: people flow

In terms of the people flow subsystem, Novo Nordisk in Mexico has adapted the recruitment and selection processes according to the Mexican national context. Hiring employees for the Mexican subsidiary was challenging because Novo Nordisk products were not well known. The HR manager stated: "This is a reality. We are new in the Mexican market. We are very small in comparison to our competition, e.g. Sanofi Aventis and Eli Lilly. It was not easy for some of the employees to understand the firm's philosophy: Novo Nordisk's Way of Management." The staff who started the operations in Mexico had experience working in other pharmaceutical firms but never in European firms and particularly never in Danish firms. In the first year of operation Novo Nordisk in Mexico experienced an employee turnover rate similar to the average for the Mexican pharmaceutical market. This could be an interpretation of the learning and development of the people flow subsystem. The recruitment and selection coordinator explained: "We followed the guidelines of the global recruitment process and then we designed our local recruitment procedures." Novo Nordisk aligns the recruitment and selection process strictly to the competence level required in the vacancy. The recruitment and selection coordinator explained that "Novo Nordisk's philosophy is completely different from other companies where I have worked (USA and Mexico). Now, I have to make sure that there is no discrimination in any of our HR subsystems." This philosophy supports the organizational culture that the firm tries to build around the world. According to the interviewees, although Mexican labor laws protect employees against discriminatory practices, factors such as age, gender, and marital status (especially for women), still determine hiring decisions.

The interviews indicate that employee personal networks (word of mouth) are one of the basic sources for the recruitment process. Novo Nordisk in Mexico has established a bonus system to reward employees who recommend a candidate. This policy motivates employees, not only for the monetary bonus, but also for the credibility that the firm gives to the employee recommendations in the recruitment process. The recruitment and selection coordinator stated: "Novo is a very open organization. This openness helps us to learn from each other and the environment."

In the selection process, the firm assesses the candidate's competence and behaviors in a way that can be measured and observed. The people responsible for recruitment and selection in Mexico explained: "Our starting point is the job's description. We develop an assessment based on the competencies." A highlight of the selection process is that a psychological test is performed online. The recruitment and selection coordinator sends the candidate the web link. The candidate can answer the questions anytime and anywhere. This is quite a different approach in the Mexican context, where the psychological test is traditionally conducted under the strict supervision of the recruitment and selection department. We were told that Novo Nordisk Mexico's approach is based on the basic values of trust and honesty. The firm claims to have an equal opportunity policy and absolute respect for the individuality of a human being. As the HR manager explained: "In Mexico, firms tend to apply the psychological test under supervision. However we depart from trust as a basic principle in the selection process." A manager at the Mexican division commented: "There is a complete lack of trust in some firms in Mexico, and of course when you arrive at an organization like Novo Nordisk Mexico, you say 'Can this really be true?' You have to pinch yourself to make sure you're not dreaming."

In terms of training and development, the challenge that Novo Nordisk in Mexico faces is to make employees accept other ways of thinking. The process that the firm follows starts with an induction process, then manager coaching, assessment based on competence, and feedback. The employees are responsible for their own development. The firm provides training programs that are aligned to the IDP (Individual Development Plans and Competencies) framework developed by the firm. In this context, the HR manager presented an unexpected point of view: "The biggest challenge in Mexico is to try to match the type of behavior to the NNWoM. We need to un-skill our 'old' Mexican skills to the 'new' way of management." In this sense, Novo Nordisk has three types of employees: (1) employees who have work experience in other firms that share the same types of values as Novo Nordisk to some extent, so that the way things are done in this firm are not completely "new" for this type of employee; (2) employees who need to forget the way they have been working in "old" management styles, and who the firm needs to coach to help them to understand and perform according to the NNWoM; (3) employees with no work experience, for whom it is relatively easy to learn the NNWoM. The HR manager commented: "Across Novo Nordisk we are working hard to implement a learning culture to help people build new competencies quickly." It seems that Novo Nordisk's challenge in Mexico is the assumption that the working values can be changed. Therefore, the challenge is Mexican culture: to make the employees believe in the firm's values and encourage the employees to put them into practice. Here, it is assumed that the focus is placed on employees who need to "forget the old management styles." The objective is to bring to the workplace the universal values that are practiced at home. A manager explained: "We cannot have a double standard, or a fake standard. We cannot work with certain values and live at home with others."

### *HR subsystem: appraisals and rewards*

The HR subsystem people flow shows that Novo Nordisk in Mexico trusts its employees from the first contact in the recruitment and selection process. Nonetheless, the HR manager stated: "Trust is good, but it is also necessary to implement some kind of control." Thus the performance appraisal process at Novo Nordisk is based on the Balanced Scorecard. According to one interviewee, employees know the firm's strategy and achievements throughout the different levels of the organization. The employees, together with their superior, set goals that will be measured at the end of the period. This is a process of open communication in which the goals are set in a fair way for both the employee and the firm.

In terms of rewards, the HR manager said: "Our compensation system is competitive in the local market. In addition to this, all employees have the right to gain the productivity bonus, from the office boy to the director of the Mexican subsidiary." In Mexico, a firm with a single type of productive bonus scheme is rare. In addition, the firm claims to offer a non-monetary form of compensation: the satisfaction of working in a job that makes a difference in the fight against diabetes. There is a sense of pride in working in a firm that aims to make a positive change in society. Finally, it seems that Novo Nordisk in Mexico is working to guarantee that employees can maintain a natural balance between work and leisure time that ensures that they have a full life packed with enjoyment and fulfillment both at work and at home.

### HR subsystem: employment relations

The employment relations subsystem encourages employee participation. The HR department works to encourage open communication. For example, one manager pointed out: "In our team, there is no way to avoid participation in the decision processes. This is a typical Danish culture characteristic." Another employee said: "Here everything takes time. Perhaps too much democracy is not right for all the processes. We have several rounds of discussions, trying to reach a consensus and consider all the opinions, in order to take a final decision." According to our observations in Denmark, this comes from their long tradition of a democratic political system, which has been embedded in the decision process. On the contrary, the boss is the boss in Mexico, and he (masculine society, e.g. House *et al.*, 2004) is the one who makes the decisions.

As with any process of culture change, it has been difficult to implement the NNWoM in Mexico: "In Mexico we are not used to having a framework to manage people." According to our findings, one of the challenges faced by Novo Nordisk in Mexico is how to manage the real openness and freedom given to Mexican employees – for example flexible working hours, working from home, setting of professional goals.

## Discussion and conclusions

The study can be summarized by two points: (1) national contextual factors seem to be important aspects for implementing HR systems, yet do not totally determine the assimilation of HR systems that were designed in developed countries and are implemented in emerging economies; and (2) trust, openness, participation, non-discrimination, and honesty, among other values, support HR performance subsystems, which help to create a strong corporate culture that employees endorse. Nevertheless, we suggest caution when interpreting these results because this study is exploratory and the results cannot be generalized. It would be interesting to study how other MNCs carry out HR practices in Mexico as we plan for a future research agenda of "best" HR practices in Latin America.

Highly selective recruitment, sharing of information, investment in training, and participation in decision making are HR practices integrated in the high-performance HR subsystems (Bamberger and Meshoulam, 2000) that Novo Nordisk has implemented in Mexico. The process for implementing these practices takes Mexican contextual factors (e.g. idiosyncrasies) into consideration. For example, employee personal networks (Elvira and Davila, 2005a; Worm and Michailova, 2003) are important sources for recruitment. Online psychological testing, job designs based on competence, and rewards based on the Balanced Scorecard are common practices that have to be supported by information technology, even though technological literacy in Mexico is relatively low and the infrastructure is poor (Olivas-Lujan, Ramirez, and Zapata-Cantú, 2007). These factors have been a challenge for this Danish firm because Novo Nordisk cannot rely on the way institutions work in Mexico to operate HRM practices as they do in Denmark.

It seems that the NNWoM system is derived from the Scandinavian management style (Schramm-Nielsen, 1991) in which institutions play a key role. Denmark has been described as a stable society in terms of its political and economical development with low power-distance, egalitarianism, and consultative decision making (Schramm-Nielsen, 2000, 2001; House *et al.*, 2004). The results of this case study seem to confirm these cultural and management values in Novo Nordisk in Mexico. However, Mexico presents a different profile in its economical development, as well as in its social factors and patterns of relationships within an organization. According to researchers, Mexico presents higher levels of power-distance and lower levels of egalitarianism: decisions are based on the hierarchical level (House *et al.*, 2004). Nevertheless, the tentative results from our analysis support the strong influence of Novo Nordisk's organizational culture in establishing a management style that appears to be the opposite of the contextual factors found in Mexico.

The process of operating HR subsystems of people flow, appraisal and rewards, and employment relations which are related to the five dimensions from the Great Place to Work Institute México is affected by both contextual factors surrounding the firm and the organizational culture. It is interesting to find openness in Mexican employees who are willing to "assimilate" different management styles according to NNWoM. Apparently employees feel comfortable with this style, as Novo Nordisk has been ranked as one of the best places to work in Mexico.

The basic premise of this study is that Novo Nordisk in Mexico acknowledges the contextual factors when implementing a high-performance HR practice model (Bamberger and Meshoulam, 2000), in particular in professional development investment. The firm's acknowledgment does not mean that Novo Nordisk is changing its core values in order to operate HR subsystems in Mexico. On the contrary, Mexican employees need to adapt to the NNWoM. However, the NNWoM is not a completely new way of management found in Mexico, because this case can be related to other organizations that operate under the same types of universal values and ways of management (e.g. Elvira and Davila, 2005b). Thus the Abramo and Montero (2000) argument that Latin American countries present "precarious human capital policies" could be misleading. However, the case presented indicates that we need to rethink the configuration of the "best"

HR practices that are designed elsewhere and are then implemented in Latin American countries.

## Notes

1 We wish to express our gratitude to the staff at Novo Nordisk in Mexico and Denmark for their collaboration in this research. We also appreciate professors Anabella Davila and Marta Elvira for their helpful comments on earlier drafts. This project has been funded by the Endowed Research Chair for European Studies within the School of Government, Social Sciences and Humanities at the Tecnologico de Monterrey, Mexico.
2 Novo Nordisk holds the copyright on the NNWoM model, which is used in this case study with permission from Novo Nordisk. The description and discussion of NNWoM in this case study do not entitle Professors Ramirez and Zapata-Cantú the right to use this model for other purposes not presented in this case study. This case study is not intended to show effective or ineffective handling of decision or business processes of Novo Nordisk in Mexico.

## References

Abramo, L. and Montero, C. (2000) "Origen y evolución de la sociologia del trabajo en América Latina," in E. de la Garza (ed.), *Tratado Latinoamericano de Sociología del Trabajo*, Mexico City: El Colegio de México, Facultad Latinoamericana de Ciencias Sociales, Universidad Autónoma Metropolitana and Fondo de Cultura Económica.

Alvesson, M. and Kärreman, D. (2007) "Unraveling HRM: Identity, ceremony, and control in a management consulting firm," *Organization Science*, 18: 711–723.

Bamberger, P. and Meshoulam, I. (2000) *Human Resource Strategy: Formulation, Implementation, and Impact*, London: Sage.

Bartusch, C. and Lindgren, K. (1999) "A grounded theory of national cultures' impact on Swedish–German business relationships," *Studies in Business Administrative and Informatics*: 2, 1–22.

Cavalcanti, H. B. (2002) "Sociology of work in Latin America: Notes from a dynamic discipline," *Work and Occupations*, 29(1): 5–31.

Co-Industri (2007) "Industrial relations in Danish industry," Copenhagen, Denmark. Online. Available HTTP: http://www.co-industri.dk/sw209.asp (accessed September 6, 2007).

Davila, A. and Elvira, M. M. (2007) "Psychological contracts and performance management in Mexico," *International Journal of Manpower*, 28: 384–402.

Dingwall, R. (1997) "Accounts, interviews and observations," in G. Miller and R. Dingwall (eds.), *Context & Method in Qualitative Research*, London: Sage.

EIU (Economist Intelligence Unit) (2005) "EU economy: The Nordic Model – a third way?," New York: EIU ViewsWire.

Elvira, M. M. and Davila, A. (2005a) "Special research issue on human resource management in Latin America," *International Journal of Human Resource Management*, 16: 2,164–2,172.

Elvira, M. M. and Davila, A. (2005b) *Managing Human Resources in Latin America: An Agenda for International Leaders*, Oxford: Routledge.

Federacion Mexicana de Diabetes, Mexico (2007) Online. Available HTTP: http://www.fmdiabetes.com/v2/paginas/d_numeros.php (accessed September 25, 2007).

Gomez, C. and Sanchez, J. I. (2005) "HR's strategic role within MNCs: Helping build social capital in Latin America," *International Journal of Human Resource Management*, 16: 2,189–2,200.

Great Place to Work Institute México (2007) Online. Available HTTP: http://www.greatplacetowork.com.mx/best/lists.php?year=current&idListName=mx&detail=1&order=rank (accessed September 25, 2007).

Haug, R. (2004) "Industrial Revolution to 1980: The history of industrial democracy in Denmark and Norway," *International Journal of Management*, 21: 135–143.

Hoskisson, R. E., Eden, L., Lau, C. M., and Wright, M. (2000) "Strategy in emerging economies," *Academy of Management Journal*, 43: 249–267.

House, R. J., Hanges, P. J., Javidan, M., Dorfman, P. W., and Gupta, V. (2004) *Culture, Leadership, and Organizations: The GLOBE Study of 62 Societies*, London: Sage.

Huselid, M. A. (1995) "The impact of human resources management practices on turnover, productivity, and corporate financial performance," *Academy of Management Journal*, 38: 635–672.

Instituto Nacional de Salud Pública, Mexico. Online. Available HTTP: http://www.insp.mx/ (accessed September 25, 2007).

International Diabetes Federation. Online. Available HTTP: http://www.idf.org/ (accessed September 25, 2007).

Legge, K. (1995) *Human Resource Management: Rhetorics and Realities*, Chippenham: Macmillan Business.

Lenartowicz, T. and Johnson, J. P. (2002) "Comparative managerial values in twelve Latin American countries: an exploratory study," *Management International Review*, 42: 277–279.

Lorenz, E. and Wilkinson, F. (2003) "FORUM organisational change, human resource management and innovative performance: Comparative perspectives," *Cambridge Journal of Economics*, 27: 239–241.

Macduffie, J. P. (1995) "Human resource bundles and manufacturing performance: Organizational logic and flexible production systems in the world auto industry," *Industrial and Labor Relations Review*, 48: 197–221.

Martin, J. (1992) *Culture in Organizations: Three Perspectives*, New York: Oxford University Press.

Mexican Ministry of Economy (2005) Online. Available HTTP: http://www.shcp.gob.mx/ (accessed December 10, 2006).

Michailova, S. and Worm, V. (2003) "Personal networking in Russia and China: Blat and Guanxi," *European Management Journal*, 21: 509–519.

Novo Nordisk (2006) *Novo Nordisk Annual Review: Financial, Social and Environmental Performance 2006*, Bagsværd, Denmark: Novo Nordisk A/S.

Olivas-Lujan, M. R., Ramirez, J., and Zapata Cantú, L. (2007) "e-HRM in Mexico: Adapting innovations for global competitiveness," *International Journal of Manpower*, 28: 418–434.

Pfeffer, J. and Veiga, J. (1999) "Putting people first for organizational success," *Academy of Management Executive*, 13: 37–38.

Ramirez, J. (2005) "Technology, culture and HRM: A 'neo-contingency' Anglo-French comparison," unpublished thesis, University of Newcastle upon Tyne, England.

Ramirez, J. and Fornerino, M. (2007) "Introducing the impact of technology: A 'neo-contingency' HRM Anglo-French comparison," *International Journal of Human Resource Management*, 18: 924–949.

Ryan, A. M., Wiechmann, D., and Hemingway, M. (2003) 'Designing and implementing global staffing systems: Part II best practices', *Human Resource Management*, 42: 85–94.

Schramm-Nielsen, J. (1991) "Danish managerial style – What is Scandinavian about it?", in J. Schramm-Nielsen, (ed.), *Management in Scandinavia: Differences and Similarities*, Copenhagen, Denmark: CBS.

Schramm-Nielsen, J. (2000) "How to interpret uncertainty avoidance scores: A comparative study of Danish and French firms," *Cross Cultural Management – An International Journal*, 7: 3–11.

Schramm-Nielsen, J. (2001) "Cultural dimensions of decision making: Denmark and France compared," *Journal of Managerial Psychology*, 16: 404–423.

Scott, W. R. (1995) *Institutions and Organizations*, Thousand Oaks, CA: Sage.

Sun, L. Y., Aryee, S., and Law, K. S. (2007) "High-performance human resource practices, citizenship behavior, and organizational performance: A relational perspective," *Academy of Management Journal*, 50: 558–577.

Terpstra, D. E. and Rozell, E. J. (1993) "The relationship of staffing practices to organizational level measures of performance," *Personal Psychology*, 46: 27–48.

UNCTAD (2005) Online. Available HTTP: http://www.unctad.org/Templates/Startpage.asp?intItemID=2068&lang=1 (accessed March 20, 2005).

Vargas-Hernández, I. (2007) "Las 100 Mejores Empresas para Trabajar en México' [The 100 Best Places to Work in Mexico], *Mundo Ejecutivo*. Online. Available HTTP: http://ejecutivo.mundoejecutivo.com.mx/articulos.php?id_sec=11&id_art=677&idejemplar=25 (accessed October 2, 2007).

Wood, S. and Albanese, M. (1995) "Can we speak of a high commitment management on the shop floor?," *Journal of Management Studies*, 32: 215–247.

World Bank (2005) "Infrastructure Public Expenditure Review (IPER) – Mexico." Online. Available HTTP: http://www-wds.worldbank.org/external/default/WDSContentServer/WDSP/IB/2005/11/23/000160016_20051123095117/Rendered/INDEX/3348310MX.txt (accessed October 1, 2007).

Xiao, Z. and Tsui, A. S. (2007) "When brokers may not work: The cultural contingency of social capital in Chinese high-tech firms," *Administrative Science Quarterly*, 52: 1–31.

Yin, R. K. (1989) *Case Study Research: Design and Methods*, Beverly Hills, CA: Sage Publications.

# 9 Performance management in knowledge-intensive firms

## The case of CompuSoluciones in Mexico

*Anabella Davila and Marta M. Elvira[1]*

> If one day I needed to leave the company, I would use not only my resume to seek
> a new job but also my performance evaluation from CompuSoluciones.
>
> (CompuSoluciones President's assistant, 30)

Research on performance management (PM) has increasingly focused on how knowledge plays into improving business competitiveness and the corresponding challenges for effective performance appraisal (PA). In particular, studies have aimed to understand better how human resources (HR) practices increase knowledge (Despres and Hiltrop, 1995; Thite, 2004) and how appraisals influence the performance of knowledge workers (Smith and Rupp, 2004; Wilson *et al.*, 1994). This effort is critical for knowledge-intensive firms (KIFs), that is, organizations that compete with sophisticated knowledge or knowledge-based products using the intellectual skills of highly trained employees, who comprise a very large proportion of their workforce (Alvesson, 1995, 2004; Blacker, 1995). Thus, the context of KIFs presents an important challenge to traditional HRM practices, especially in terms of appraising knowledge workers' effort and output.

In general, research into PM systems highlights the problematic nature of evaluating performance in practice (Hall *et al.*, 1989; Shen, 2004; Thite, 2004). The main challenge is twofold. First, defining the content of what is perceived and apprised as performance is difficult (Aycan, 2005), perhaps even harder in KIFs (Alvesson, 1995, 2004; Blacker, 1995). Second, managing the personal aspect of appraisals by superior and subordinate, as well as providing and receiving feedback about performance, involves subjective judgments (Jawahar, 2006; Lee and Akhtar, 1996). Research has thus focused on these issues to improve PM. An underlying assumption is that improving employee performance will redound in improved organizational performance (den Hartog *et al.*, 2004), investing performance management with strategic importance. This argument also applies to KIFs, where individual employee competencies are key for organizational performance (Alvesson, 2004). Therefore, we aim to understand how HRM policies and practices can be optimally integrated to link individual and organizational performance in KIFs.

This chapter draws on an empirical study of CompuSoluciones, a medium-size Mexican IT consulting firm chosen by the Great Place to Work Institute of Mexico as an outstanding company in 2007. CompuSoluciones ranked 33rd among the top 100 companies and 5th among the top 20 for women in the country. A key theme emerging in the study is that combining different PM practices is necessary to align individual and organizational performance.

We start with a brief description of PM systems to build an analytical framework for understanding the appraisal process in KIFs; then, we explore organizational characteristics and HRM approaches within KIFs and use the framework to present findings derived from interviews. We conclude with a discussion of key PM strategies learned from this case study.

## Performance management

Employee performance appraisal is a component of organizational performance management systems (den Hartog *et al.*, 2004; Guest, 1997). Typically, the definition of performance involves considerable complexity and subjectivity. PM theory recognizes the many factors involved in performance, and therefore requires HR involvement in proportion to the level of performance complexity (Guest, 1997). From an HR perspective, performance appraisal refers to activities used to assess employees, develop their competencies, improve performance, and allocate rewards (Fletcher, 2001). Specifically, HR is responsible for building the bureaucratic apparatus that line managers use for appraising performance.

Decomposing PA into a series of activities helps identify three main areas: (1) the content of performance; (2) the appraisal process itself; and (3) the outcomes of the appraisal. Research on appraisal content continues focusing on measurement tools and their application, stressing individual contributions that are hard to identify and to measure objectively (den Hartog *et al.*, 2004; Fletcher, 2001; Guest, 1997). Therefore, organizations use group, organizational unit, and organization-wide performance measures (Rynes *et al.*, 2005).

Research on the appraisal process is extensive, particularly concerning the feedback interview. We know that feedback interviews are most effective when focusing on the task performed and least effective when focusing on employee personal traits. In any case, employees need to learn when they are underperforming or not meeting expectations in order to improve their performance (Kluger and DeNisi, 1996).

Regarding appraisal outcomes, research has focused on rewards and recognition as they are closely tied to individual satisfaction and perceptions of justice. Yet individual or group rewards and recognition also have downsides such as perceived inequality. Therefore, organizations increasingly rely on multiple tools to minimize these limitations. Balancing individual and group rewards depends on the levels of task interdependence and required collaboration (Rynes *et al.*, 2005), as well as on the organization's desire to promote individual accountability vs. collective coherence (OECD, 2004).

An overarching question is how to develop flexible PM systems to improve responsiveness to organizational change while maintaining a sense of unity and providing a sense of satisfaction and fairness. Combining different PA practices may contribute to HR's role in linking individual and organizational performance. This approach guides our exploration of PA in a Mexican KIF.

## Knowledge-intensive firms and HRM

KIFs generate products or services using the knowledge of their workers as their main asset. This sector typically includes law, accounting, management, and engineering or computer consultancy firms, advertising agencies, research and development units or high-technology companies. While the concept usually overlaps with that of professional organizations, KIFs belong to a much broader organizational category because they are not limited to specific professional norms or regulated by the professional market through credentialing mechanisms. Instead, KIFs are concerned with their own set of organizational norms and with applying science to satisfy client needs, not developing basic science (Alvesson, 1995, 2004). Alvesson (2004) identified a set of structural characteristics specific to KIFs, mainly derived from how work is managed and organized. In KIFs:

1   work is performed by highly qualified individuals who use intellectual skills;
2   tensions exist between autonomy and organizational hierarchy;
3   ad hoc organizational forms emerge continuously;
4   needs arise for alternative communication and coordination mechanisms oriented to problem solving vs. decision making;
5   work is client-centered and, consequently, the assessment of the quality of work and its output is subjective and uncertain.

Research suggests that a tension exists between structural characteristics of work in KIFs and HR practices as we know them (Despres and Hiltrop, 1995). For starters, work features in a KIF emerge from the worker, not from the transformation of raw materials into a tangible product, as is the case in manufacturing. Given this context, how can HRM adapt effectively to these organizational and employment characteristics (Alvesson, 2004; Smith and Rupp, 2004; Thite, 2004)?

Two main challenges for employment management in KIFs include the retention of knowledge workers and their motivation in order to develop loyalty and commitment to the organization (Alvesson, 2004, 2000; Thite, 2004). Although common in any organization, these challenges are severe in KIFs because workers are often the pivotal resource for developing competitive advantage: workers could leave the company in groups to form their own company, taking with them key employees or clients (Alvesson, 2004). Therefore, HRM systems and practices in KIFs are highly oriented to the quality and motivation of individuals (Smith and Rupp, 2004; Thite, 2004).

Alvesson (2004) argues that HRM can contribute to a KIF's competitive advantage by focusing on either the human capital or the human process advantage. Human capital advantage builds on hiring the best individuals and, importantly, on retaining them. Thus HR practices such as staffing and rewarding are critical to recruit and retain qualified personnel. Performance is seen as the output of key individuals and this makes commitment and loyalty vital for the organization (Alvesson, 1995). The human process advantage focuses on creating an organizational climate conducive to human interaction and collaborative work. From an HR perspective, according to Alvesson, performance in this view is an organizational outcome more than an individual contribution, requiring management to develop a corporate culture with the "right orientation" (2004: 140).

The extent to which human capital and/or human process advantage paths complement each other depends on labor market conditions, a KIF's internal wage scale, and the attractiveness of the job. Because of resource scarcity, both paths represent trade-offs for the firm and are thus prioritized differently (Alvesson, 2004). For example, upwards labor market dynamics could challenge the strategy of hiring the best qualified individuals, so the firm might choose to stress working conditions. The firm's reputation and compensation budget, together with high complexity and uniqueness of the work involved, could require following the human capital path over the human process advantage. The issue is how best to allocate resources to either HR path in order to determine performance management.

PM methods also belong to the reward and motivation system in KIFs. From this perspective, it is critical for KIFs to understand knowledge workers' needs beyond financial incentives, considering optimal approaches to assess the ambiguity of knowledge work and its output. Symbolic aspects of knowledge work require human process conditions that facilitate positive evaluations and an organizational atmosphere conducive to learning and development. Research findings suggest that knowledge workers appreciate participating in novel and challenging tasks and downplay the relative significance of pay and other benefits. Thus retaining and motivating qualified personnel requires a combination of means: pay, other financial benefits, challenging tasks, opportunities for learning and development, a proper organizational climate, and congenial social relations (Alvesson, 2004; Smith and Rupp, 2004).

Moreover, knowledge workers need to perceive rewards as directly connected to the intended performance metrics defined by top management. However, existing empirical research in KIFs shows that performance ratings and pay are de-coupled. That is, knowledge workers find that merit increases are unrelated to performance ratings (Smith and Rupp, 2004). If other organizational factors might affect rewards and recognition of knowledge workers, what purpose do PM systems serve in KIFs? How can PM systems be managed to link effectively individual and organizational performance? Alvesson (2004) suggests that HRM strategies need to be broadly defined because of their influence on other organizational practices within KIFs. We explore these questions in the specific setting of CompuSoluciones, after describing the profile of KIFs in Mexico.

### Knowledge-intensive firms in Mexico

As is the case in most emerging economies, Mexico is experiencing a knowledge management era. Management understands the implications of the shift from labor- to knowledge-intensive firms, and is eager to adjust its practices to this new organizational paradigm. Because we explore PM systems in a Mexican IT consulting firm, we start by describing briefly the nature of IT firms in the country following a recent study that classified them in four groups according to their workers' profile (UAM, 2004):[2] selective, integrative, software-factory, and software-strategy firms.

Selective firms (12 percent of Mexico's KIFs) seek individuals with a college degree plus additional studies such as higher levels of technical training or certifications. They employ a great proportion of IT experts, while clerical functions are generally outsourced. These firms focus on areas of interest to top and middle management such as business consulting, distributed systems, mathematics, industrial processes, strategic and operations management (UAM, 2004).

Integrative firms (23 percent) seek individuals with just a college degree. The main responsibility of these IT workers is to test the components of a software program or its functionality. They install software development programs and packages already acquired.

Software factories (21.1 percent) do not typically employ individuals with college degrees, but rather those having technical training with certifications. These firms employ the largest percentage of software developers and programmers, whose high skill levels serve systems programming, test integration modules, and analyze and design systems. These firms' organizational structures are less sophisticated than those of selective firms.

Firms with a weak software strategy (44.6 percent) employ individuals with neither university diplomas nor technical training due to a focus on software testing. Using few outsourced services, these firms have the lowest ratio of IT personnel to clerical staff. These firms offer limited development and show little interest in consulting or strategic management knowledge. They focus mainly on operational skills (UAM, 2004).

The above classification of IT firms helps us assess the extent to which key assumptions for retaining and motivating knowledge workers and for managing HR in KIFs apply in Mexico. Labor market dynamics and average educational levels of IT workers, together with shortages of trained personnel, can lend priority to recruiting over retaining personnel. In addition, knowledge workers themselves might be more concerned about job security than about motivational aspects of work.

Mexico is currently experiencing favorable macroeconomic conditions for improving industry performance and the IT industry plays an important role in growing economic performance and increasing competitiveness. However, the size of the industry remains quite small for an emerging economy relative to that of the BRIC[3] countries. Federal programs exist promoting skill development and support for local IT firms such as Programa para el Desarrollo de la Industria del Software[4] (OECD, 2006). Moreover, analysts suggest that to professionalize the

IT industry, firms' internal management should adopt best practices and invest in strategic core competencies to ensure a differentiating strategy (UAM, 2004). One OECD (2006) recommendation is that regional/local best practices exchange should be encouraged, so that IT enterprises learn from local experience to build global competitiveness.

Most recommendations to help professionalize IT firms in Mexico target either macro aspects of the industry (e.g. investment) or micro themes (e.g. strategic intent) (OECD, 2006; UAM, 2004). Few recommendations involve HRM issues unless they are included under the general 'best practices' umbrella. While there is a keen concern about the quality of IT specialists and their employment, little attention is given to the HRM systems that support knowledge workers. In this chapter we aim to fill this gap by examining PM systems in a Mexican IT consulting firm. PM is a major component of HRM because of its impact on staffing strategies, training and development programs, rewards and recognition, and career planning.

## Method

### Research site

CompuSoluciones is a medium-size Mexican IT consulting company that has become a leading national wholesale supplier of hardware and software for important multinationals such as HP, IBM, Lenovo, Microsoft, Oracle and SAP. In 1989, it appeared in the Expansion 500 companies list for the first time.[5] In 2006 sales reached the company's record for the previous four years (US$131,339,000). Started in 1985 as a wholesale hardware supplier, today CompuSoluciones offers IT solutions through its four core businesses in sales and services of hardware, software, IT support, and associates' training certifications.

The company is headquartered in Guadalajara, Mexico and employs 277 individuals in three regional offices. Among employees, 37 percent are men and 63 percent are women.

### Interviews

We conducted this study in the firm's Guadalajara headquarters, after obtaining access through the company's HR director. In May 2007 we held a grand tour interview (Spradley, 1979) with the HR Director regarding the firm's performance appraisal practices. Interview analysis indicated that PA has a key strategic role in this company, so we requested open access to interview a sample of managers and subordinates. Having obtained approval, we interviewed seven managers and seven subordinates during a week in September 2007. Our specific requirement was to interview individuals directly involved with the PA process. CompuSoluciones' HR director was committed to our research objectives and offered her support by allowing us to report the findings without restrictions on the identity or information about the company.

We conducted semi-structured interviews, each one lasting an average of 60 minutes. Questions focused on the content, process, and outcomes of appraisal practices and on HR's role within the PM system. All interviews were tape-recorded and transcribed via word-processor for prompt retrieval during the analysis phase. Field notes were also taken and company documents used to gain familiarity with the organizational context. These documents included the Company History and the Cultural Audit Report. Most interviews were conducted in different meeting rooms; only two happened in the informant's private offices. Summary demographic data for our subjects is as follows: the average age of managers is 40 and that of subordinates 28; the average tenure of managers is 13 years and that of subordinates is 4 years; the President of the company holds a doctorate, two managers have a master's degree, four managers and six subordinates have a university diploma and only one person completed vocational studies.

### *Coding analysis*

The success of PM processes depends to a great extent on the alignment of individual appraisal practices to organizational strategic objectives. A coding analysis was pertinent to this study because it allowed us to start by describing appraisal practices such as the use of the 360° survey and other practices. As we learned about PA dynamics in the firm, we moved to more interpretive coding. For example, we developed categories for strategies, conditions, and consequences that actors gave to the PM system. Then we used a pattern coding strategy searching for more inferential and explanatory themes. At this stage we identified interrelations among salient categories and started to conceptualize our findings (Miles and Huberman, 1994). In doing this we were able to link data at the three levels of coding and identify how individual PA practices are aligned to organizational performance strategies at CompuSoluciones. We stopped the interview and analysis process when we reached theoretical saturation (Glaser and Strauss, 1967), that is, when a new interview or coding did not add a new category to the analysis process.

## Findings

### *CompuSoluciones' strategic intent*

The company presents itself as a 21-year-old Mexican firm oriented to the integration of IT solutions for medium-size and large organizations through alliances with complementary firms.[6] Its business model integrates IT solutions for hardware, software, and services. The company's vision includes four main strategic intent themes: to offer excellent client service, to develop employees personally and professionally, to live up to commitments, and to be profitable. All these themes are to be achieved based on solid principles and values.

However, company growth challenged the alignment of strategic themes to the company's principles and values so that in 2004 a "Values Committee" was established. The purpose of this committee was to work with employees to rescue the company's roots on principles and values, creating the *Picselin* acronym in Spanish. Picselin stands for: participation (*participación*), integrity (*integridad*), trust (*confianza*), service (*service*), dedication (*entrega*), loyalty (*lealtad*), and innovation (*innovación*). To strengthen company values among all organizational members the company had the first employee Picselin Convention in 2005. That same year, CompuSoluciones' performance was ranked 365 in the Expansion 500 list.

## Performance management at CompuSoluciones

Organizational PM starts with staffing practices. Personnel recruitment and selection filters individuals who meet the value profile required by the company. The premise here is that only individuals who can espouse company values will create a harmonious work environment. HR then revises monthly personnel indicators such as turnover, vacancies, safety, and work climate. For example, turnover rates decreased from 20 percent in 2004 to 16 percent in 2006.

Organizational performance is monitored via financial, operational, and personnel indicators with reachable yet challenging objectives. These objectives cascade to each business unit, and from there to each employee. The company provides business units with organizational resources including operational budgets, adequate personnel and a competency-development plan, strategic market information, IT management systems, financial resources for unit initiatives, and a performance measurement tool consisting of both area-based and individual-based work objectives. This performance measurement system for individuals consists of monthly objectives focused on horizontal work processes and oriented to specific results. That is, objectives are designed to include the goals of all departments involved in the workflow: for example, the credit department needs to consider purchasing department objectives for improvement. Objectives are proposed by an employee, approved by the supervisor, and reviewed monthly. Objectives should also be auditable. However, it is the individual who determines whether he/she fulfilled the expected work objectives during the first days of the month. The outcome of this system directly affects an employee's monthly salary, 15 percent of which is tied to the achievement of work objectives. Individual performance measurement also serves as input for the 360° annual evaluation.

## Performance appraisal at CompuSoluciones

Several appraisal practices are used for evaluating performance, including a Third Level Program, a Peer Recognition Program, a 360° survey, and a contest recognizing the Employee Who Best Represents Company Values.

The Third Level program encourages employees to hold a personal interview every six months with the manager of their immediate supervisor. The purpose is for managers of the third level to hear directly from employees input about different issues that might influence company performance or their specific job. This is an open interview held in company time. At the end of the interview the third-level supervisor fills out a form listing key topics discussed with the employee for follow-up.

There is also a Peer Recognition program based on employees' own criteria to recognize a peer who has done outstanding work. This year-round program is called Aros (rings) emulating the company's corporate logo (see www. compusoluciones.com). Employees receive electronic rings for different reasons such as staying in the company for one year or longer, becoming a supervisor, or participating in interdepartmental committees. However, the rings an employee receives are to recognize others' good work, not to be kept personally. In other words, employees give their rings to other employees when they consider that a peer's job needs recognition. An employee has three months to decide who deserves a ring or else the ring loses its value, benefiting no one. Eventually the awarded rings represent points that can be exchanged for tangible benefits such as time off, training courses outside of the firm, free movie or theater tickets, among a long list of choices. Still rules exist for awarding rings; for instance, the recipient of a ring cannot give it back to the person from whom he/she received it (a month has to elapse for this to be licit). Employees cannot give a ring to their supervisors and can only recognize the same peer three times per year. The ring program is based on the assumption that employees value rewarding peers, consequently creating a harmonious work climate and contributing to team spirit. The company displays the top employees receiving rings from their peers, with the goal of developing a sense of pride and belonging.

The 360° survey is paramount to individual performance evaluation in this firm. Questions in this survey are based on the Picselin set of values and designed according to the competencies that each individual needs in his/her organizational position. The survey implementation process has evolved and been refined. Usually, each employee's work is appraised by 12 individuals: five are required to be among people with whom the employee interacts daily; then come the immediate supervisor and the third-level supervisor; the remaining raters are selected by the employee him/herself with supervisor approval. The supervisor and HR manager check that employees avoid naming close friends or acquaintances with emotional ties and who could therefore provide biased evaluations.

The 360° survey is managed through the company's intranet and secured via passwords. Once an individual selects the employee to appraise, the webpage displays relevant information about him/her. For example, the person's picture stays visible the entire time a survey is open. Interviewees mentioned this feature as reminding them that they are appraising a human being, and although the survey is answered anonymously they take the assignment seriously. Appraisers also have access to the individual's monthly performance measurement trajectory. Interviewees stated that this information is important to help them relate the employee's work accomplishment with job attitudes, facilitating a more objective appraisal. Finally, the number of electronic rings received by the individual is also displayed, which interviewees also suggested helped balance the subjectivity involved in appraisal.

Because the survey requires providing explanations for low ratings, since 2006 the company has required attendance at feedback-giving training sessions. Interviewees expressed that before participating in this training they did not know how to use or handle feedback, so HR screened all comments to eliminate those considered inappropriate. Today employees learn how to offer and receive feedback, and feel more comfortable focusing on making suggestions for improving others' jobs.

The outcome of this 360° survey has several consequences for employee records. It is a major component of the yearly salary raise, as are the company's overall performance, monthly individual performance measurements, and labor market dynamics. Promotions are also based on the 360° survey appraisal, besides an individual's performance measurements, and competency development. Other outcomes from this survey include professional development opportunities, such as candidacy for scholarship awards for post-graduate education. Opportunities to apply for a home-office program (telecommuting) are also open to outstanding achievers.

Note that the company places special emphasis on the feedback process after appraisal. Supervisors and subordinates are required to discuss personally the appraisal results. This feedback interview focuses on three main themes: areas the employee accepts and is willing to change; areas the employee disagrees with but he/she is willing to change; and areas the employee disagrees with and is not ready to change. After agreeing with the supervisor, both individuals need to elaborate a development plan targeting those competencies that the individual needs to improve. Plans typically include taking specific in-company training or external training courses. Most interviewees mentioned having received recommendations for specific readings and books from the company's library. Interviewees described this feedback process as an effort on the company's part to help employee improvement; as far as they know, employees do not leave due to low performance appraisals.

The feedback mechanism includes improvements in the PA practice itself. HR managers and interviewees mentioned that at the end of the 360° process supervisors and subordinates are asked for their input on both the appraisal instrument and process. According to interviewees the PA practice changes yearly as HR incorporates employee improvement suggestions.

Other PM practices at CompuSoluciones exist. Interviewees described several instances that occur during events, such as an award for the Employee Who Represents the Company Values. Employees vote for the person that they consider represents company values best and the recipient receives a symbolic award.

Although generally interviewees denoted a good collective understanding of the PM system at CompuSoluciones and described it as positive for improving organizational performance and personal development, interviewees also mentioned some system drawbacks. A major concern was the number of questions in each evaluation. Some interviewees indicated they end up writing the same things about every person. Others mentioned that some questions were redundant, making it difficult to distinguish their real meaning. This perceived constraint and the consequent time investment make them feel uncomfortable with the formality of the process.

Regarding objectivity in evaluations, some interviewees recognized the 'recency effect', i.e. the challenge to remember an employee's yearly overall performance relative to recent incidents. This effect could reduce the effectiveness of appraisal practices.

Additionally, the relationship between appraisal outcomes and yearly salary increment was unclear for a few interviewees. To them, salary increments appear unrelated to appraisals because eventually there is an annual meeting where the top management team (president, directors, and managers) reviews salaries and makes decisions on pay raises. Therefore, individual performance appraisal does not guarantee automatic salary increases. Interviewees recommended having more open meetings with supervisors and HR staff where all inquiries can be answered and clarified.

Although all interviewees agreed on the use of the 360° survey for personal improvement, they also mentioned inconsistent follow-up on the personal development plan. Interviewees favored instituting a periodic follow-up instead of the yearly assessment of improvement.

Despite these comments, interviewees stated clearly that good performance appraisals are obtained by living the values of the company, following its policies, and, most importantly, demonstrating collaboration.

The description of the PM system just presented has helped us identify CompuSoluciones' strategies to align individual and organizational performance. Now we turn to the conceptualization of these strategies.

## Emergent strategies for performance management in KIFs

PM systems are complex because of the multiple factors involved, including subjective performance perceptions and challenging feedback situations (Aycan, 2005; Jawahar, 2006; Lee and Akhtar, 1996). PM complexity escalates in KIFs settings because of its relationship to measuring competencies for knowledge workers. Thus, research on HRM practices in KIFs has evolved around two key strategies: human capital or human process advantage (Alvesson, 2004). In addition, KIFs' job structures demand additional coordinating and problem-solving efforts with a heightened need for extensive communication (Alvesson, 2000). Because of the difficulty for HR to follow either strategy in isolation, it appears wise to integrate both strategic approaches, as seems to be the case in CompuSoluciones. Ultimately, KIFs face the challenge of retaining and motivating knowledge workers (Alvesson, 2004), a challenge which should involve HR practices. CompuSoluciones seems to do so quite successfully, at least in managing PM systems, or so the findings from this case study suggest.

CompuSoluciones experiences similar human resources problems to those portrayed in the KIFs literature. Based on Mexico's classification of KIFs, the company fits an integrative profile requiring employees with college degrees but no additional technical training, and focusing on testing hardware and software systems or their functionality (UAM, 2004). With integrative firms comprising 23 percent of the industry, the need to retain and motivate key personnel is paramount. HR issues are so important for this firm that HR indicators (such as the turnover index) serve as key metrics of organizational performance.

The PM system plays a strategic role at CompuSoluciones. An analysis of its content, process and outcomes indicates that it is used as an incentive to align employee behavior with strategic intent themes and with the firm's principles and values. CompuSoluciones' PM system is, however, quite complex. It has evolved and improved over time using input from employee feedback.

Moreover, the PM system encompasses multiple appraisal practices, some more or less bureaucratic and others rather informal. Some practices balance the vertical and horizontal structure of the organization; others target its levels of centralization and delegation. Some practices favor a human capital advantage strategy, yet all of them target the human process advantage.

Analyzing these organizational patterns suggests that performance in this company has at least a triple meaning: first, it relates to an employee's individual results; second, to the overall company performance; and, third, to employee attitudes towards collaborative work and a harmonious work environment – thus the need to use multiple appraisal tools targeting each specific aspect of performance. Managing multiple appraisal tools is challenging and requires significant resources. CompuSoluciones formalizes those appraisal practices directly linked to top management's definition of performance, namely, economic value based on the principles and values of the company. These practices are: the performance measurement system, the 360° survey, and the Aros (rings) program. The main underlying assumption is that a work environment based on the Picselin set of values will result in high financial performance. Other appraisal practices such as the Third Level program, the feedback interview, and the contest seem less formal in interviewees' opinion.

The PM system at CompuSoluciones also plays a strategic role as an integrative organizational mechanism linking individual to organizational performance. The variety of practices serves to integrate vertically supervisors' understanding of performance with employee performance measurements, the Third Level program, and the feedback interview process. By contrast, other bureaucratically managed practices serve to integrate horizontal workflow. For example, employee performance measurement follows from established objectives that include horizontal coordination of work, the 360° survey, the rings program, and the contest, all requiring peer evaluation based on daily interactions. From this analysis we surmise that linking individual to organizational performance depends on how well a company balances the outcome of performance appraisal practices both vertically and horizontally (see Table 9.1).

Similarly, PA practices that facilitate vertical integration are centralized at the supervisor level, and practices that favor horizontal integration are decentralized at the subordinate level. The appropriate balance could also depend on the firm's HR strategy (see Table 9.2). That is, in the more centralized PA practices CompuSoluciones seems to follow a human capital advantage; by contrast, in the

*Table 9.1* Performance appraisal practices as organizational integration mechanisms

|  | Vertical integration mechanisms | Horizontal integration mechanisms |
|---|---|---|
| Performance Measurement System (objectives) | X | X |
| Third Level Program | X | |
| Peer Recognition Program (ring) | | X |
| 360° survey | | X |
| Feedback interview | X | |
| Employee Who Represents the Company Values | | X |

more decentralized PA practices CompuSoluciones targets the human process advantage. In sum, CompuSoluciones relies to a greater extent on managers to develop human capital and to a greater extent on employees to build a harmonious and collaborative work climate.

## Conclusions

CompuSoluciones, a medium-size consulting company in information technology ranked 33th among the Great Places to Work in Mexico and 5th for working women in 2007. CompuSoluciones performance management strategies link individual with organizational performance, shedding light on the fundamental research question of how to appraise knowledge workers and the output they produce.

The underlying strategies for managing PM systems found in this case study appear as follows: (1) because of the complexity and variety of performance definitions, CompuSoluciones uses multiple appraisal practices; (2) because of the need for high task coordination, problem- solving efforts, and intensive communication within KIFs, CompuSoluciones uses appraisal practices that function as organizational integration mechanisms – vertically and horizontally; (3) because of the need to develop a human capital and a human process advantage, CompuSoluciones uses appraisal practices that are centralized at the supervisor level and decentralized at the subordinate level.

*Table 9.2* Performance appraisal practices supporting HR strategy

|  | Human capital advantage | Human process advantage |
|---|---|---|
| Performance Measurement System (objectives) | X | X |
| Third Level Program | X | X |
| Peer Recognition Program (ring) | | X |
| 360° survey | | X |
| Feedback interview | X | |
| Employee Who Represents the Company Values | | X |

These strategies encompass various theoretical perspectives on PM systems, suggesting the need to connect strategic HRM to organizational research via the study of PM: PM systems appear to serve as an integrative mechanism to centralize or decentralize decisions beyond the systems' incentive effects. This comprehensive role of PM systems in CompuSoluciones is supported by a clear strategic intent based on consistent principles and values promoted by top management and based also on managers and high levels of staff commitment to the appraisal process.

## Notes

1 The authors would like to thank Tecnologico de Monterrey, Campus Ciudad de Mexico, for the grant received for this research.
2 Firms in the sample included: IBM, Neoris, Hildebrando, Softtek, Qualita, ITS, EDS, Bearing Point, SyC, Unisys, Accenture, Adam Technologies, Netropology, Oracle, Kaizen Software, Kernel, Gedas, Migesa, PISSA, Cap Gemini, DSS, Siga, Assa, CTI, DynaWare, Qarta Sistemas, KeD, Cima, Nauter, STI, and others (UAM, 2004).
3 Brazil, Russia, India, and China.
4 Software Industry Development Program.
5 A major business press magazine.
6 From company history documents: *CompuSoluciones: El Mayorista de Valor que Integra Soluciones y Servicios* [CompuSoluciones: The value supplier firm for integrating solutions and services].

## References

Alvesson, M. (1995) *Management of Knowledge-Intensive Companies*, New York: de Gruyter.

Alvesson, M. (2000) "Social identity and the problem of loyalty in knowledge-intensive companies," *Journal of Management Studies,* 37(8): 1,101–1,123.

Alvesson, M. (2004) *Knowledge-Work and Knowledge Intensive Firms*, Oxford, UK: Oxford University Press.

Aycan, Z. (2005) "The interplay between cultural and institutional/structural contingencies in human resource management practices," *International Journal of Human Resource Management*, 16(7): 1,083–1,119.

Blacker, F. (1995) "Knowledge, knowledge work and organizations: An overview and interpretation," *Organization Studies*, 16(6): 1,021–1,046.

den Hartog, D. N., Boselie, P., and Paauwe, J. (2004) "Performance management: A model and research agenda," *Applied Psychology: An International Review*, 53(4): 556–569.

Despres, C. and Hiltrop, J. M. (1995) "Human resource management in the knowledge age: Current practices and perspectives on the future," *Employee Relations*, 17(1): 9–23.

Fletcher, C. (2001) "Performance appraisal and management: The developing research agenda," *Journal of Occupational and Organizational Psychology*, 74: 473–487.

Glaser, B. G. and Strauss, A. L. (1967) *The Discovery of Grounded Theory: Strategies for Qualitative Research*, Chicago: Aldine.

Great Place to Work Mexico (2007) *Las mejores empresas para trabajar en Mexico* [Best companies to work for in Mexico], Mexico: Great Place to Work Institute. Retrieved 09/10/07 from: http://www.greatplacetowork.com/best/list-mx.htm.

Guest, D. E. (1997) "Human resource management and performance: A review and research agenda," *International Journal of Human Resource Management*, 8(3): 263–276.

Hall, J. L., Posner, B. Z., and Harder, J. W. (1989) "Performance appraisal systems: Matching practice with theory," *Group & Organization Studies*, 14(1): 51–59.

Jawahar, I. M. (2006) "Correlates of satisfaction with performance appraisal feedback," *Journal of Labor Research*, 27(2): 213–236.

Kluger, A. N. and DeNisi, A. (1996) "The effects of feedback interventions on performance: A historical review, a meta-analysis, and a preliminary feedback intervention theory," *Psychological Bulletin*, 119(2): 254–284.

Lee, J. S. Y. and Akhtar, S. (1996) "Determinants of employee willingness to use feedback for performance improvement: Cultural and organizational interpretations," *International Journal of Human Resources Management*, 7(4): 878–890.

Miles, M. B. and Huberman, A. M. (1994) *Qualitative Data Analysis: An Expanded Sourcebook*, 2nd edn., Thousand Oaks, CA: Sage.

OECD (2004) *Trends in Human Resources Management Policies in OECD Countries. An Analysis of the Results of the OECD Survey on Strategic Human Resources Management*, Paris: OECD.

OECD (2006) *ICT Diffusion to Business in Mexico: Peer Review*, Country Report Mexico, Paris: OECD.

Rynes, S. L., Gerhart, B., and Parks, L. (2005) "Personnel psychology: Performance evaluation and pay for performance," *Annual Review of Psychology*, 56: 571–600.

Shen, J. (2004) "International performance appraisals: Policies, practices and determinants in the case of Chinese multinational companies," *International Journal of Manpower*, 25(6): 547–563.

Smith, A. D. and Rupp, W. T. (2004) "Knowledge workers' perceptions of performance ratings," *Journal of Workplace Learning*, 16(3): 146–166.

Spradley, J. P. (1979) *The Ethnographic Interview*, New York: Holt, Rinehart and Winston.

Thite, M. (2004) "Strategic positioning of HRM in knowledge-based organizations," *The Learning Organization*, 11(1): 28–44.

Universidad Autonoma Metropolitana [UAM] (2004) *Estudio para Determinar la Cantidad y Calidad de Recursos Humanos Necesarios para el Desarrollo de la Industria de Software en Mexico* [Study to Determine the Quantity and Quality of Human Resources Needed for the Development of the Software Industry in Mexico], Mexico: UAM.

Wilson, D., Mueser, R., and Raelin, J. (1994) "New look at performance appraisal for scientists and engineers," *Research–Technology Management*, 37(4): 51–55.

# 10 Walking the talk of safety in South America

*Jorge A. Gonzalez and Lorena R. Perez-Floriano*

Multinational enterprises that operate in Latin America must recognize several contextual factors that influence organizational practices and behaviors. There is a need for both centralization and local responsiveness (Bartlett and Goshal, 2002); therefore, organizations must compromise the cost savings associated with generalizing a practice in a region with the greater degree of local responsiveness. Although this is true for many business practices, the management of human capital is subject to localized needs in greater detail than other business functions. In particular, a major concern for both organizations and their employees is the physical and psychological well-being of this human capital. Universally, unsafe work conditions affect the well-being of employees, but dealing with national context reveals the importance of localizing the implementation of risk management and prevention systems.

In this chapter we present a synthesis of two studies and subsequent management action that constitutes both a novel research intervention and best managerial practice dealing with workplace risk in Latin America. We believe that the research we carried out in this organization draws important lessons for companies operating in Latin America, and perhaps other regions. The managerial implications and recommendations we derived from the studies and the follow-up of management suggest that individual-level factors (i.e. knowledge), environmental and historical conditions (i.e. institutional and management trust), and group beliefs about appropriate behavior (e.g. cultural values) affect cognitions about hazard effects on workers' health, and ultimately influence safe behavior.

We also describe a framework for the development of safety practices based on personal trust between management and employee. It is based on current theory and our analysis of empirical data, which has been presented elsewhere (Perez-Floriano et al., 2007; Perez-Floriano and Gonzalez, 2007). We then use this framework to describe the human resource practices that support safety and describe novel and award-winning safety training and interventions that have been carried out at a multinational enterprise, TransInc (real name omitted). We argue that the best human resource management practices in industries with pervasive risk, such as the industry in which TransInc operates, imply the "safest" practices.

Although TransInc operates in several countries in Latin America, the experiences of the Argentinean and Brazilian subsidiaries of this corporation are used to highlight three important factors that influence safety systems' effectiveness.

First, the development, implementation, or transformation of safety systems must emphasize the development of trust. Second, such trust can only flourish through the acknowledgment of local culture and the cultivation of relationships among leaders and employees. Third, allowing the development of personal, albeit hierarchical, relationships between management and employees fosters interpersonal trust and a strong personal tie.

This multinational enterprise has successfully transferred a risk management and risk communication system from its North American headquarters to various operations abroad. Despite a satisfactory degree of success, the South America subsidiaries questioned whether formulation and implementation success would still warrant additional localization efforts beyond existing practice. Given that they were dealing with people's lives and safety, they considered this to be a top priority. The research study resulted in several suggestions to be considered in the localization of the safety system. These results, reported in Perez-Floriano and Gonzalez (2007), show that the cultural values exhibited by employees in three different Latin American cities (Sao Paolo, Rio de Janeiro, and Buenos Aires) differed. These differences influence how people perceived risk and construed the meaning of work hazard danger. In addition, the results indicated that the extent to and manner in which employees trusted the communication of risk by power institutions, such as management, government, and unions, was related to their acceptance of workplace risk and risk management programs (Perez-Floriano *et al.*, 2007).

Because the interpretation of these results focuses on the need for trust, we argue that the development, implementation, and transformation of safety systems must also emphasize the development of trust. For instance, for a safety system to be successful in reducing risk, employees must trust its rules and recommendations. However, national culture and other contextual factors influence whether people are more likely to trust the procedures. Details such as the mode of communication (oral or written), its source (leaders or colleagues), and its formality (rules or practices) can influence whether employees accept and follow such procedures. In our research we surmised that it would be fruitful to emphasize the development of interpersonal, rather than institutional, trust. Differences in cultural values, noise in the transfer of a safety system from headquarters to a foreign subsidiary, and the impersonal nature of a system of rules and procedures can harm trust in the system and be detrimental to its implementation. The managerial implications of the results of the two studies (Perez-Floriano *et al.*, 2007; Perez-Floriano and Gonzalez, 2007) suggested that while the transfer of a system can be successful, its "localization" to Latin America can increase trust in the system, and hence employee adherence to it. We describe how a managerial focus on three important and interrelated factors – cultural values, trust, and personal relationships – can increase safety.

## The urgency of workplace safety and its relationship with national, cultural, and industry factors

Research into and management of best practices in workplace safety are critical in Latin America. The International Labor Organization (ILO) reports that the toll of occupation-related death, injury and sickness has leveled off in developed countries, but that it is increasing in developing economies, including Latin American countries. Globally, every year 1.7 million people die because of work-related injuries and diseases and 268 million people have on-the-job accidents. Part of the problem is that differences in the presence and implementation of laws about safe processes, differences in training and skills to work with new technology, different attitudes about the quality and condition of equipment and other insti-tutionalized practices can lead to faulty assessment and poor risk management practices. In essence, the off-shoring of dangerous processes, which goes along with opportunities for employment and increased national production, also introduces opportunities for accidents.

Second, industry factors must be considered. Multinational organizations that operate in industries where danger is commonplace recognize the importance of managing job hazards. They often develop risk management systems that are implemented in their home countries and then are often transferred to other locations where they also operate or are copied by companies abroad. The success of a centralized design and subsequent international transfer of risk and safety management systems can be measured by its success in reducing the rate of on-the-job injuries and deaths. However, the international transfer of risk management and safety systems may still leave some room for failure if local factors are not considered. This is of the utmost importance for organizations operating in industries with a high risk of injury or death which, at the same time, value corporate social responsibility.

Therefore, the cultural context in which the subsidiaries of multinational enterprises are embedded is also important. Even when data indicate that inter-national operations are becoming safer, multinational enterprises around the world cannot disregard how differences in cultural values and the manner in which these differences influence communication, trust, and organizational behaviors affect the manner in which people perceive risk, construe danger, and act accordingly.

## Safety at TransInc

TransInc is an American-based multinational operating in more than 40 countries and it is considered a leader in terms of technological innovation, service, quality, and safety. It emphasizes both global and local components in its international strategy, given that it serves the needs of a wide array of companies around the world, including local and multinational corporations in Latin America. It is an industry leader in a product that implies dangerous installation and maintenance because accidents and fatalities are likely to happen. As described by corporate management, its high-risk operation includes accidents such as crushes, electro-cution, falls from 1.8 meters or higher, failures of electricity control, and motor vehicle crashes. Therefore, managers have implemented a wide range of human resource initiatives for improving safety in the workplace. The decade of the 1990s was characterized by increasingly open global competition in the industry. Nonetheless, quality and industrial security were some of the most common themes of interest for the company, along with the introduction of new products and technologies. Today, regularly administered safety audits focus on prevention by detecting near-miss accidents.

The headquarters-based safety management program at TransInc is focused on prevention. This approach can only succeed if accidents do not happen through a constant improvement of conditions that might lead to an accident. At TransInc, managers seek to create a culture of trust where people are involved and informed of preventive measures and their rationale. They have developed a communication system for the identification, notification, and analysis of near-miss accidents (those that did not result in injuries but had the potential to do so). They have changed from a culture of correction to one of prevention and prediction; by rewarding the report of near misses and penalizing accident occurrence they increased near-miss report by more than 400 percent in a two-year period (personal communication with senior manager at TransInc).

The implementation of an American-made risk communication and management system in its foreign operation has resulted in the reduction of the number of fatalities and accidents worldwide. This includes South America, where the company has a history of improving its safety processes and systems such that the incidents and near misses had reached an asymptote effect. However, the leaders recognized that cultural factors influence how employees assess risk and follow the safety procedures. The international transfer of American safety procedures has been successful, but managers believed that safety levels could still be improved. Therefore, the organization agreed to participate in a study carried out by Jose Flores under the direction of the second author. The data were collected from November to December 2002. The purpose of the study was to identify cultural, psychological, and organizational factors that could help the organization to understand, shape, and ultimately improve future safety management programs at TransInc.

At TransInc, we studied the extent to which exposure to danger of workers who install and maintain elevators would pose a health risk in this organization. The company's management described the principal injuries and health risks that could occur through accidents with objective data provided by the firm. It is interesting to note that the incidence rate in Argentina was the highest, and workers in Buenos Aires perceived a much higher likelihood for accidents on the job. The incidence rates[1] in terms of accidents per year at the time of data collection were Buenos Aires 4.15, Rio de Janeiro 1.39, and Sao Paolo 1.36. This rank order is the same for perception of risk from hazard exposure given by the study participants at the three sites.

## A focus on culture and cultural values

Culture is related to risk perception and resulting behavior. This indicates that it is imperative for multinational organizations in high-risk industries to understand how culture influences the manner in which people construe risk and danger. Insofar as a group has one cultural orientation that is predominant over another (e.g. people from the United States score high on the individualism dimension), the dominant cultural orientation will determine the behavior of the group members (Douglas, 1978; Wildavsky and Dake, 1990). However, it is important to understand that even within a world region where cultures are considered similar, or within a national culture, one can expect to have some cultural differences related to risk perception.

Organizations that want to develop a high reliability operation with a strong culture of safety must understand workers' perceptions of risk and construal of danger. These could be a result of the complex interplay of culture, cognitions, and social factors.

In an international context, societal culture is an important variable to consider because the literature is beginning to relate culture to organizational safety (Janssens *et al.*, 1995; Kouabenan, 1998; Perez-Floriano *et al.*, 2007).

Values are a reflection of a person's desired state for an object or thing (Schwartz *et al.*, 2000). Differences in cultural values, such as individualism and collectivism, are related to safety. In a study of Argentina, United States, and France, the results showed that organizations in collectivist societies (e.g. Argentina) placed more value on safety versus productivity. On the other hand, the more individualistic Americans and French rated productivity as a higher priority (Janssens *et al.*, 1995). We believe that legal issues such as the presence of nationwide structures and safety procedures (e.g. OSHA – Occupational Health and Safety Administration) are likely to divert managerial concerns from personal issues to task issues. However, organizations may not be able to do this in national contexts where a more personal approach to safety is expected.

The seminal work by Hofstede (1980) identified cultural dimensions that are related to the perception of risk and danger in an organization. Values such as power distance and uncertainty avoidance are related to the manner in which people construe risk and danger and interpret safety rules and procedures. Uncertainty avoidance refers to the extent to which people dislike risk and ambiguous situations. People from high uncertainty avoidance groups have higher perceptions of danger and risk. In addition, power distance refers to whether people in a society believe that differences in power that exist in their society are legitimate. This dimension is likely to be related to a lower perception of risk when the communication of risk comes from those in managerial positions. People in high power-distance societies are likely to follow orders and believe what those in positions of authority say because they know what is best for them, and therefore they will feel safe. Lastly, people in countries that are high on both dimensions are more likely to believe that people in power can and should break the safety rules if needed given that they are the ones who created the rules in the first place.

Schwartz (1992) presents another large-scale survey of national cultural values, some of which have implications for risk perception, such as the values of security, conformity, self-direction, universalism, self-transcendence, and self-enhancement. The value of security relates to the importance placed on physical security, harmony, and stability and is directly related to perceptions of risk and danger.

The manner in which people follow safety rules may be related to the value of conformity, which represents obedience, self-discipline, and tradition, and the value of self-direction, which refers to independence of thought and action through creativity, imagination, intellect, and logic. Universalism, which relates to the importance of beauty, wisdom, tolerance, and protection of the environment, matters because it is related to the belief that everyone should have equal access to safety. People who hold values related to self-transcendence may worry about hazard exposure in general, while people who hold values related to self-enhancement (achievement and power) may express more concern about issues that affect them personally.

When Schwartz, Sagiv, and Boehnke (2000) assessed the relationship between values and worries, they looked at worries as perceptions that the state of a situation or object would change from its desired state and divided them in two types: micro worries that have to do directly with the person and those close to the person, and macro worries that have as their object external entities like wider society and the universe. They found that values accounted for more variance in macro than micro worries; self-transcendence values (universalism and benevolence) are associated with high macro and low micro worries and values associated with the self and its extensions. In addition, people holding values related to conformity may endorse safety regulations because they believe in authority and want to follow a caring leader, while people who hold universalism and benevolence values may care about justice, equality, their environment, and the well-being of their group as a whole.

We used Schwartz's (1992) theory of values to explore how cultural values relate to risk perception and found that different values explain perceptions of risk in each of the three cities where workers' attitudes to workplace risk were studied. Two types of risk were assessed: (1) health risks, an index assessing worry about injury and disease from exposure to dangers in the workplace; and (2) risk from job hazards, an index assessing the perceived degree of danger from exposure to selected job tasks and technologies. Among Porteños (people from Buenos Aires), those who supported the value of self-direction were less likely to express concern about hazard exposure, while the value of benevolence had the opposite effect. For Cariocas (those from Rio de Janeiro), the values of universalism and benevolence predicted perception of health risk. In contrast, self-enhancement (i.e. stimulation and self-direction) and conservation values (i.e. tradition and conformity) were negatively related to perceptions of health risk. Lastly, the model explained 45 percent of the variance for Paulistanos (people from Sao Paolo) and, consistent with the two other groups, self-enhancement values were negatively related to health risk.

The results for job hazards indicate that those who endorse the value of security reported feeling less risk from risk exposure. Those who held values related to self-enhancement and conservation were more likely to worry about hazard exposure in the workplace. For Porteños, the values of conformity, security, tradition, and stimulation predicted worry about exposure to job hazards. For Paulistanos, the results indicate that people endorsing the values of conformity, universalism, self-direction, and achievement are more likely to perceive danger from job hazard exposure. The cultural values measured did not predict perception of risk from job hazards for Cariocas.

In sum, the results indicate that different types of objects trigger risk perceptions and different values are linked to different types of concerns. On the one hand, health risks are more likely to trigger self-transcendence values. Conservation and self-enhancement related values are negatively related to health risks, while they are positively related to risk from job hazards. This could be an indication that people endorsing conservation and self-enhancement values will be focused on doing their jobs and achieving their goals through self-assertion. On the other hand, perception of risk from job hazard exposure is linked to self-enhancement and conservation values.

## A focus on trust

TransInc considers that its employees must trust and believe that they are in the business of safe delivery of people, and that safety is their top priority. TransInc has managed to integrate safety into all of its operations by devoting corporation efforts to eliminate employee injuries and disease. Error prevention is not only the basis for process improvement but also for health and safety initiatives in the workplace. Therefore, the corporation developed and integrated safety performance metrics that touch both clients and employees, promoting the adage that "The safe way is the only way." Many successful companies in North America use rewards to maintain safety practices among their employees, and TransInc is no exception. Nonetheless, this practice had been questioned by Latin American executives because they believe that the reward system had led to undesired behaviors, including hiding near-miss errors and employee communications that everything was working well when potential safety threats were present. One practice that was being considered to overcome such deficiencies was the Trust Index, developed at TransInc South America. This index is calculated by correlating the incidence rate with near-miss reports. A negative relationship indicates that workers are regularly reporting events or hazards that can potentially lead to accidents and fatalities; thus they trust the company to take action on hazard removal efforts, instead of expecting the "deaf ear syndrome." This promotes the development of trust between managers and employees, but prevents any backlash effects. Workers can contact the company's ombudsman through a toll-free number and report any management or peer misconduct. Also, they made available envelopes with paid postage that went from the branches to the corporate office in order to report safety concerns. TransInc suggested that these procedures were working effectively.

Our studies' results showed that employees at TransInc believed that the safety management at TransInc was trustworthy. However, it is likely that people from high power-distance countries, such as Brazil and Argentina, are less likely to voice their concerns in the workplace (Brockner *et al.*, 2001), while those in low power-distance cultures are more likely to express lower commitment and engagement if they do not participate in the decision process. TransInc believed that it was necessary to overcome this "trust" backlash.

General trust in leadership was another behavior we wanted to explore because of its relationship to safety in past research. For instance, Roberts (1993) found that people who perceived their work conditions as unsafe reported less trust in their organizations. In another study, Roberts and Baugher (1995) found that low perceptions of safe conditions and low trust lead to higher levels of work-related strain. This can result in a dangerous, vicious cycle because stress can eventually lead to lack of focus and work exhaustion, which could become a catalyst for accidents in situations of actual risk.

Given that safety rules are ascribed by leadership, we wanted to explore whether trust in government and the organization would influence risk perceptions. It is likely that people who trust in leadership are more likely to follow the rules that are given to them. On the other hand, more cynical and distrustful employees are more likely to see safety rules not as a sign of care and organizational support, but as a constraint on their work.

Perez-Floriano, Flores-Mora, and MacLean (2007) found that workers at TransInc trust the risk communication initiatives coming from the organization, but in contrast are likely to distrust risk communication information coming from management and unions. Trusting implies putting oneself in a vulnerable position, that is, at risk. Thus, to elicit people's support of safety prescriptions, risk communicators have to be perceived as trustworthy and address specific risks to the individual.

Part of the business context for TransInc is the government and thus the perception of the trustworthiness of government is relevant as well. Low levels of trust in government could be considered endemic to Latin American. Therefore, business operates in a zone of low trust where corruption is a way of doing business. The corruption index published by Transparency International (2007) consistently indicates that most Latin American countries score high on corruption. This does not favor the development of trust.

## A focus on personal relationships

The conclusion reached by our analysis of the role of culture and trust led us to believe that, as commented by Davila and Elvira (2005), personal relationships were of primary importance in Latin America. The development of personal relationships among employees has been cited as a very important resource in dangerous situations and moments of crisis (Weick and Roberts, 1993). It is natural to expect that this would be more important in collectivist societies that breed people-oriented corporate cultures (House *et al.*, 2004). We therefore surmised and suggested that personal communication of danger, risk, rules, and safety procedures among coworkers, and between leader and subordinate, would be a path to follow. This would be the best practice, to which workers would react appropriately (following rules and behaving in a secure manner) to a risk management communication program.

The high values of collectivism in Latin America do affect the development of personal relationships at work. Davila and Elvira (2005) suggest that group management is the best way to manage organizations in Latin America because of these values, instead of the presence of an individual focus. This suggests that the mutual reinforcement of safety rules and procedures is likely to be propagated and communicated in a personal and collective manner, where older and more tenured employees are likely to communicate safety procedures to others. It is likely that this takes less of a formal and task-oriented focus to make room for a personal and people-oriented one. With this focus, interpersonal care, emotions, and organizational citizenship behaviors become a very important aspect of success for a safety program.

As Janssens *et al.* (1995) stated, aside from values, managerial style and the company's decision-making style (paternalistic versus participative) predicted differences in the relationships between management's concern for employees and consideration of safety as a priority. The study conducted in France, Argentina, and the United States revealed that the collectivist Argentineans preferred a paternalistic management style, which implies care and concern from those in power. This paternalistic expectation implies that the task of the leader is to acknowledge the cultural orientations of employees and communicate the potential for danger in a manner that is appropriate for the local culture. The degree of trust that the employee places in his or her leader is a powerful determinant for the success of communication and acceptance of the safety initiatives (Zohar and Luria, 2004). Also, the leadership style and behavior of the manager are likely to influence the perception of danger and the manner in which the employee reacts to it. We suggest that developing a personal relationship between a leader and a subordinate is the best way to communicate risk and implement a safety program that has a successful influence on behavior.

This highlights the importance of management and leadership in the success of a safety system. Weyman and Clarke (2003) argue that managers' perception of risk in a given situation heavily influences employees' perceptions. They argue, therefore, that the decision maker's perception of risk heavily influences employee behavior and often becomes more important than objective measures of risk. It is very likely that this consideration becomes more important in Latin American nations. The people-orientation present in these cultures means that the relationship between leaders and members is much more important than in task-oriented cultures and organizations. Therefore, a closer relationship between managers and workers is likely to influence the communication of risk perceptions. In other words, rules and procedures may mean nothing to an employee unless the employee is aware of the leader's feelings about and belief in the present system. This does not imply loss of respect or hierarchical differences that may be expected in high power-distance cultures. Instead, it shows how personal and genuine concern from someone in a position of power can actually be more powerful than an impersonal rule or procedure that is communicated in writing or through other impersonal modes of communication.

Thus, two possible antecedents to safety stand out. First, the employee is more likely to follow the system (and hence behave in a safer manner) if he or she trusts the manager, including the manager's perceptions and ideas of what is safe or dangerous. Second, the likelihood that the employee is aware of the manager's perceptions is a function of the extent to which both manager and employee interact and discuss safety. This does not mean that formal or written procedures would not work, but that they need to be ratified through personal communication.

## Toward an integrative approach to human resource and safety practices

TransInc recognizes that they are dealing with people's lives, and any problems, even the smallest, must be fully accounted for. The results suggested that personalized approaches to communication that addressed the local culture differently for each city were needed. While North American-based procedures have proved successful in Latin America, it was recommended that additional localized interventions would still prove fruitful. The effective delivery of services requires an integration of best practice in organizational systems: human resources, safety, production, and commercialization focused on timely product delivery and customer satisfaction. In a corporation that deals daily with risk, the organization's strategy must be aligned with its safety program. In the English words of a Latin American executive at TransInc, they must "walk the talk." The corporation is successful in both safety and the financial bottom line because it follows this premise.

The research has suggested that trust in risk communication is related to health risk, but not to risk perception from job hazards. To increase workers' physical and psychological well-being in Latin America we suggested that a person-based participatory system that recognizes power differences and varying collectivism would be useful. This stems from the data: Paulistanos are more likely to support managerial procedures and regulations, trust the information provided by management, and endorse safety prescriptions that come from a source of authority because they are more likely to endorse conservation values than Porteños and Cariocas. However, this might limit the effective delivery of safety management programs. People endorsing self-transcendence values are more likely to voice hazards' presence than those who value conformity and tradition, who may unquestionably accept management orders.

As a result TransInc, striving to develop practices that are culturally sensitive and appropriate for workers in Latin American branches, implemented a contest. Workers were asked to have their children draw workers at TransInc performing their tasks in a safe manner. The parent then had to explain to their child what they did and how they did it. Through this contest, TransInc promoted the value of collectivism because employees would interact with their families and had to learn safety practices because they had to describe them to their kids, perhaps even help them draw them. The employees had an extra incentive to learn the details of safety practices, and they provided their families some peace of mind because the families realized that they could trust that the company was promoting the workers' safety. The idea worked wonderfully because the best drawings were sent to headquarters in the United States. Twelve drawings, chosen as the best, were printed in an annual calendar that was distributed to all employees in the Latin American branches.

In a recent interview, our contact acknowledged that the data generated from our studies have helped TransInc to reinforce and provide justification for its ongoing safety programs. Right after our research intervention he developed another initiative that showed person-orientation and collectivist values, the *show o milhão* (the Show of the Million). This consisted of a safety management quiz show that was intended to promote the learning of safety practices. Surprisingly, the implementation of this program led to both unexpected and successful outcomes. Usually, when the safety management technicians visit each city, they go over the task procedures, indicate the safety procedures, and give each technician a manual of procedures to keep and study. However, management felt that workers just paid lip-service to the formal training and task-centered communication process, and never looked at the manual again. Thus, part of the new training program was to have workers divide in teams and compete against each other to test their safety knowledge. The contest helped management uncover best practices and was instrumental in using and promoting group cohesiveness. The managers reported that workers were competing and enthusiastically debating about the best way to do the job tasks, and, as a result, the safety managers found that many technicians were more knowledgeable than they were about how to do the job properly.

Our contact also explained that the contest helped in the integration of employees from acquired companies, which in effect allowed personal communication and trust to positively influence the implementation of the safety system. Our contact states that TransInc acquires smaller companies that provide elevator maintenance and usually will keep most of the workers. The workers from the acquired companies tend to be older than the typical TransInc employee, and are not easily integrated into the company. On one occasion, our contact interviewee went to train an Argentinean branch that consisted of members of a recently acquired outlet and younger employees that were hired by TransInc. He said that the older workers were a little shy and separate from the rest of the group, while the younger workers were much more enthusiastic, self-confident, and socially integrated. However, as the contest evolved, it turned out that the older workers were much more knowledgeable about the systems and procedures of elevator installation and won the contest. This situation did not cause conflict between both subgroups; management found that the younger workers began to trust and respect the older workers, and the contest became a tool for social integration after an acquisition. Thus, TransInc inadvertently discovered a mechanism for social integration as well as safety training. The contest has now been established throughout the region.

We believe that the implementation of the new human resource and safety practices described here are best practices in alignment with the findings of our two studies.

Workers at TransInc trust their management to keep them safe in the workplace and are satisfied with their jobs. TransInc has found new ways to gain the trust of its employees that will keep them safe in their workplace, and this has been accomplished by focusing on their cultural values to gain their trust, and by developing programs that emphasize personal communication and integration instead of formal, task-centered communication.

## Note

1 Incidence rate is an index that indicates the number of illnesses and accidents times the base for 100 full-time equivalent workers and divided by the base of number of working hours divided by the total hours worked by all employees during the calendar year.

## References

Bartlett, C. A. and Goshal, S. (2002) *Managing across Borders: The Transnational Solution*, 2nd edn., Boston: Harvard Business School Press.

Brockner, J., Ackerman, G., Greenberg, J., Gelfand, M. J., Francesco, A., Zhen, X. C., Kwok, L., Bierbrauer, G., Gomez, C., Kirkman, B. L., and Shapiro, D. (2001) "Culture and procedural justice: The influence of power distance on reactions to voice," *Journal of Experimental Social Psychology*, 37(4): 300–315.

Davila, A. and Elvira, M. (2005) "Culture and human resource management in Latin America," in M. M. Elvira and A. Davila (eds.), *Managing Human Resources in Latin America*, Oxford, UK: Routledge.

Douglas, M. (1978) *Cultural Bias*, London: Royal Anthropological Institute of Great Britain and Ireland.

Hofstede, G. (1980) *Culture's Consequences: International Differences in Work Related Values*, Beverly Hills, CA: Sage.

House, R. J., Hanges, P. J., Savinar, M., Dorfman, P. W. and Gupta, V. (2004) *Culture, Leadership, and Organizations: The Globe Study of 62 Societies*, Thousand Oaks, CA: Sage.

Janssens, M., Brett, J. M., and Smith, F. J. (1995) "Confirmatory cross-cultural research: Testing the viability of a corporation-wide safety policy," *Academy of Management Journal*, 38: 364–382.

Kouabenan, D. R. (1998) "Beliefs and the perception of risks and accidents," *Risk Analysis*, 18(3): 243–252.

Perez-Floriano, L. and Gonzalez, J. A. (2007) "Risk, safety and culture in Brazil and Argentina: The case of TransInc Corporation," *International Journal of Manpower*, 28(5): 403–417.

Perez-Floriano, L. R., Flores-Mora, J., and MacLean, J. (2007) "Trust in risk communication in organizations in five countries of North and South America," *International Journal Risk Assessment and Management*, 7(2): 205–223.

Roberts, J. T. (1993) "Psychosocial effects of workplace hazardous exposures: Theoretical synthesis and preliminary findings," *Social Problems*, 40: 74–89.

Roberts, J. T. and Baugher, J. E. (1995) "Hazardous workplaces and job strain: Evidence from an eleven-nation study," *International Journal of Contemporary Sociology*, 32: 236–249.

Schwartz, S. H. (1992) "Universals in the content and structure of values: Theoretical advances and empirical tests in 20 countries," in M. P. Zanna (ed.), *Advances in Experimental Social Psychology*, 25, New York: Academic Press, pp. 1–65.

Schwartz, S. H., Sagiv, L., and Boehnke, K. (2000) "Worries and values," *Journal of Personality*, 68(2): 309–346.

Takala, J. (2005) *Press Release, ILO/05/21*, International Labour Organization. Available at: http://www.ilo.org/public/english/bureau/inf/pr/2005/21.htm (accessed November 20, 2006).

Transparency International (2007) "Corruptions perceptions index 2007." Available at: http://transparency.org/policy_research/surveys_indices/cpi/2007

Weick, K. E. and Roberts, K. H. (1993) "Collective mind in organizations: Heedful interrelating on flight decks," *Administrative Science Quarterly*, 38(3): 357–405.

Weyman, A. K. and Clarke, D. D. (2003) "Investigating the influence of organizational role on perceptions of risk in deep coal mines," *Journal of Applied Psychology*, 88: 404–412.

Wildavsky, A. and Dake, K. M. (1990) "Theories of risk perception: Who fears what and why?," *Daedalus*, 119(4): 41–60.

Zohar, D. and Luria, G. (2004) "Climate as a social-cognitive construction of supervisory safety practices: Scripts as proxy of behavior patterns," *Journal of Applied Psychology*, 89(2): 322–333.

# 11 Executive staffing practices in US-Mexican joint ventures

## A staffing model for IJV executives

*Pramila Rao*

In World War Two, the most strategic decision was not General Montgomery's combat decisions, but rather Prime Minister Churchill's selection of General Montgomery in his team as a leader. All other advantages in the war flowed from this fundamentally important staffing decision.

(Peter Boxall)

As globalization in the form of mergers, alliances, and joint ventures continues to increase, it is critical to understand the staffing practices of global executives. Global executives lead, direct, and inspire employees in different cultures to achieve strategic goals for organizations (Schuler, 2001). The focus of this chapter is to provide a detailed understanding of the staffing practices of the CEO, Vice-President, and all directors below the Vice-President (or the equivalent to these titles) in US-Mexican joint ventures located in Mexico and the US. This chapter also provides a description of executive staffing practices in US-Mexican joint ventures, identified for the first time in the US literature.

International joint ventures (IJVs) exist when two parent firms pool assets and resources to achieve strategic goals in a new independent organization (Shenkar and Zeira, 1987). IJVs are formed for several reasons, such as leveraging the local partner's knowledge (Makino and Beamish, 1998), creating economies of scale (Mondragon, 1997), increasing bargaining power with foreign governments (Neupert and Montoya, 2000), enhancing competitive positioning (Geringer and Frayne, 1990), and sharing inevitable business risks and costs (Lemak *et al.*, 1994).

Specifically in the Mexican context, Mexican joint ventures indicated they form such alliances due to access to superior technology, collaboration with established brand names, and product expertise of the partner. Further, an interesting point to note was that Mexican firms who formed such alliances did so mainly to block domestic competition from local firms. Mexicans in this study perceived that the US firms formed strategic alliances with Mexican firms predominantly to access new geographic markets, capture the partner's market knowledge, and access new customers (Gillespie and Teegen, 1995).

The North American Free Trade Agreement (NAFTA) has dramatically increased commercial interaction between the USA and Mexico (Celaya and Swift, 2006). Understanding executive staffing practices in US-Mexican joint ventures is very significant as the number of US-Mexican IJVs formed continues to increase (Gillespie and Teegen, 1995) due to Mexico's geographic proximity to the United States (Neupert and Montayo, 2000) and also Mexico's proximity to Latin America allowing US-Mexican joint ventures to expand into the Latin American market more easily (Neupert and Montayo, 2000).

Though IJVs are so widely prevalent, IJV failures (Schaan, 1988) occur at a high rate of 50 percent to 70 percent (Schuler, 2001). An IJV is considered a failure when it ceases its business operation as a joined independent entity due to radical cultural or strategic differences between parent firms (Kogut, 1989). Some of the typical problems leading to joint venture failures include conflict over control of the IJV (Schaan, 1988), improper partner selection (Lane and Beamish, 1990), parent firms having differing goals (Miller *et al.*, 1997), and incompatible human resource management practices (Lorange, 1996; Schuler, 2001).

In the human resources domain, executive staffing practices have been identified as being among the critical reasons for the failures of international joint ventures (Lorange, 1996). Executive staffing, considered a control mechanism, is an ongoing process of influence and hence a very big source of contention between parent firms (Geringer and Frayne, 1990; Schaan, 1988). Though executive staffing is so critical, surprisingly little is known of how US-Mexican IJVs recruit and select their employees.

Few studies have examined staffing practices in US-Mexican joint ventures (Martinez and Ricks, 1989; Stephens and Greer, 1995). None of these studies addresses how executives of IJVs are recruited and selected. This empirical study addresses that paucity in research by the primary driving research question: What are the predominant executive staffing practices (recruitment and selection) currently being followed in US-Mexican joint ventures located in Mexico? The study reveals that current executive staffing practices are influenced both by national culture and staffing practices from other multinationals.

The next section discusses the theory for this research.

## Resource-based view and executive capital

Traditionally, organizations competed on the basis of technology, financial capital, access to cheap labor, access to different markets, and innovative products. Most of these traditional frameworks of competition provided organizations with competitive advantages, such as high-quality products, excellent service, speed, innovation, and customization (Delery and Doty, 1996). However, most of these traditional ways of competing could be imitated and transferred from one firm to another and hence did *not* provide sustainable competitive advantages for organizations. Organizations have begun to look inward toward their employees and the management of those employees for unique sources of competitive advantage. An increased awareness that human resource management practices (e.g. recruitment, selection, and training) could provide organizations with successful approaches for sustainable competitive advantage has more recently emerged (Barney, 2001).

Further, many organizations realized that it was difficult to duplicate human capital or specific management practices. Following the resource-based view of the firm, employee skills are considered unique, complex, and difficult to imitate, and hence as providing an unparalleled sustainable competitive advantage (Barney, 2001).

Executive human capital has been identified as a critical source of sustainable competitive advantage for organizations. Boxall (1994) argues that executives drive the strategic orientation of a firm and also translate an organization's goals into business realities. Further, they strategically lead their organizations in a business environment that is unpredictable (Kesler, 2002; Yeung and Reddy, 1995). Therefore, the recruitment and selection process of executive capital is a significant strategic decision for organizations today. Understanding how organizations recruit and select their executive capital is paramount.

Schuler (2001) underscores the importance of executive human capital in international joint ventures. He argues that in a global context such as IJVs executives have to successfully lead and integrate *both* the domestic and overseas operations, which requires a certain exceptional skill set. Therefore, the staffing process for such executive capital is an important one. While successful domestic executives define strategic business goals, enhance business opportunities, and provide inspiring leadership, global executives have similar responsibilities, but operate in a broader business context and different cultural context. These global leaders define both global and country-specific strategic goals, integrate global profits, and provide leadership that inspires in different cultural contexts (Yeung and Reddy, 1995).

Further, several scholars (Hannon *et al.*, 1995; Lorange, 1996) have articulated that executive leadership in IJVs is even more complex, making successful staffing a well-thought-out and systematic process. The organizational structure is characterized by shared ownership, decision-making, and control, all of which increase corporate complexity. Executives in IJVs simultaneously report to two parent firms from diverse cultures (Hannon *et al.*, 1995).

The next section provides details of the Mexican cultural framework and its implications for executive staffing.

## Mexican culture: implications for executive staffing

Traditionally, human resources in Mexico was considered "a family matter." Frequently friends and family were hired solely based on the fact that they needed a job or they knew somebody in an organization. However, an increased presence of multinationals in Mexico has led to a heightened emphasis on the human resources function (Bensinger, 2003; Urteaga-Trani, 2003).

Constant exposure of Mexican businesses to multinationals has brought attention to the fact that attracting, selecting, training, and retaining employees of the highest quality could provide organizations with sustainable competitive advantage. Human resource leaders in Mexico acknowledge that human capital can provide organizations with a definite competitive advantage (Emmond, 2005).

Researchers (Hofstede *et al.*, 1990) suggest that multinationals have a strong influence on local human resource practices. Local organizations look up to multinationals and adopt their management practices gradually. Kras (1995) and Trompenaars (1994) suggest that the increased presence of US and other multinationals has been a driving force in changing some of the traditional values of the Mexican work culture, such as hiring predominantly from among family members. A case in point, United Parcel Service (UPS) in Mexico emphasizes using interviews and resumes in its hiring process and not hiring employees' family members (Dorroh, 2003).

The cultural framework of any country provides a backdrop in understanding the prevalence of current management practices. Mexico has been identified as having high power distance, high uncertainty avoidance, and high collectivism (Hofstede, 1991), which have demonstrated implications in staffing practices (Ryan *et al.*, 1999).

The literature on selection practices in Mexico (Kras, 1995; Martinez and Ricks, 1989) consistently suggests that Mexicans prefer to recruit and hire employees that they personally know or have established a relationship with socially. Such social referrals are common for high-level executive positions, where loyalty and trust are very important executive selection criteria. Researchers (Martinez and Dorfman, 1998) contend that such networking becomes a problem only when social friendships supersede work competence.

The collectivist culture of Mexico also places a strong emphasis on "grooming internal candidates." This cultural trait is evidenced in their national politics and is extended to their corporate boardrooms also. Scholars attribute this "grooming tendency" to the collectivist trait of being supportive, trusting, and nurturing of their in-group members (Elahee *et al.*, 2002).

Organizations from high uncertainty-avoidance cultures, such as Mexico, prefer to have elaborate information about applicants. A reflection of this cultural trait in staffing practices is an emphasis on checking employer references and also using different methods of employment testing (Fritsch, 2000; Ryan *et al.*, 1999). Organizations from such cultures tend to obtain employer references of applicants by contacting previous employers to verify employment information (Fritsch, 2000; Ryan *et al.*, 1999), something that is becoming very difficult to implement in the US (Gatewood and Field, 1998). Such extensive information about the applicants brings predictability into the recruiting and hiring process, which is highly valued in such cultures (Triandis, 2004). An example of employment testing in executive selection is the use of personality tests such as Kolbe tests, which are frequently used in Mexico to assess employees' traits, behaviors, and their potential success in organizations.

The increased presence of multinationals (Urteaga-Trani, 2003) has put a premium on getting quality executive talent. However, there seems to be a lack of supply to meet this growing demand that requires unique leadership skills (Emmond, 2001). Therefore multinationals are turning towards external sources, such as professional search agencies, to locate executive talent worldwide. For instance, Korn/Ferry in Mexico has a sophisticated database of more than 60,000 executive profiles. These agencies are able use their professional networking expertise to locate worldwide talent, which is very important for multinationals (McCoy, 2004).

The method on seeking elaborate information on executive applicants, such as current age, family background, work background, marital status, photos, and number of children, is very prevalent in Mexico. Staffing practices that demonstrate this cultural trait are reflected in both interviews and biodata (O'Connell *et al.*, 2002). Such detailed personal information is very important in the Mexican and Latin culture. Such extensive personal informa-tion helps the organization understand the applicant's family, which includes the extended family, and thereby aids in decisions, such as executive relocation. Employees in Mexico prefer to live close to their extended family as well (O'Connell *et al.*, 2002).

Physical appearances are very important in Mexico because applicants are portrayed as symbols of the company. Messenger (2004) states that in Mexico executives would dress in brand-name shirts, ties, and wear expensive watches in an open display of their power and social status. Such personal display of brand names contributes to the company's image, signals personal efficiency, and also provides a sense of uniformity in organizations.

The economic culture of Mexico has seen a dramatic trend in recent years towards being with global competitors. The Mexican government is investing heavily in the information technology (IT) industry as it realizes that it lags behind several Asian economies in the IT field. The government has announced an incentive program called Prosoft to achieve $5 billion worth of Mexican soft-ware by 2013 and also make Mexico a software leader in the Latin American region (Emmond, 2005; Navarrete and Pick, 2002). Organizations in Mexico are embracing this new digital culture and its impact on human resource practices. Several organizations are adopting e-training and online services for staffing and compensation practices (Emmond, 2005).

## The complexity of staffing in IJVs

The collaboration of two independent organizations from different geographical, cultural, and economic backgrounds adds tremendous complexity to the executive staffing management process (Schuler, 2001). Primarily, the perceptions of human skills and talent differ between parent firms from different cultural backgrounds

(Lorange, 1996). For instance, American organizations prefer technical expertise as the driving criterion in selecting executive personnel, while Mexican organizations consider interpersonal skills to be a very important criterion (Triandis, 2004).

Second, parent firms place differing priorities on staffing executive personnel for the IJV. Some parent firms assign exceptional executives, while others assign mediocre executives to the venture. Mediocre personnel are generally assigned when IJV organizations are not very important to the parent firms' business portfolio (Lorange, 1996; Schuler, 2001).

Third, the method of executive selection among parent partners from different national backgrounds is challenging. While domestic organizations vary widely in their executive selection practices, such a distinction is magnified in the IJV context as cultural norms dictate different practices (Ryan *et al.*, 1999). For instance, in the European context, organizations in the UK predominantly use board interviews to select executives, while, in contrast, organizations in France generally use multiple individual interviews (Shackleton and Newell, 1991). In the North American context, US organizations predominantly use interviews, resumes, and employer references for executive selection (Sessa and Taylor, 2000), while generally Mexican corporations rely on personal relationships and networking for executive selection (Kras, 1995).

Fourth, there is an imposition of the dominant partner's human resource policies on the IJV. A parent firm is dominant by being a leader in capital, resources, or technology. Studies have shown that US parent firms, whether majority or minority partners, tend to impose the parent human resource policies on IJV management (Stephens and Greer, 1995). A case in point, Stephens and Greer (1995) demonstrated that US parent firms imposed their staffing policies (selection criteria) in US-Mexican IJVs regardless of whether such practices were appropriate in the Mexican context.

Fifth, parent multinational firms struggle to identify local international executive talent as such employees require exceptional competencies. Executives usually have to lead, perform, direct, and integrate their operations across geographically, culturally, and economically diverse groups (Mejia-Gomez and Palich, 1997). Therefore several multinationals adopt an ethnocentric approach to staffing (Lin and Germain, 1999), causing negative feeling among IJV host nationals.

The intricacies of the IJV staffing process call for a thorough understanding of how executives are recruited and selected so that multinationals can formulate the most appropriate staffing practices. The primary goal of this study was to describe the current executive staffing practices and also understand the influence of firm characteristics on staffing practices.

## Methodology

The primary goal for this empirical research was to identify the predominant executive staffing practices (recruitment and selection) currently being followed in US-Mexican joint ventures located in Mexico. The information on the population of joint ventures (104) was obtained from a variety of sources such as published directories, internet search engines, relevant business leaders, US-Mexican Chamber of Commerce, popular press (such as *Wall Street Journal, Fortune*), college professors, and publishers.

The main organizational informant was the IJV's Human Resource Director (*Director Recursos Humanos*) or the General Manager of Industrial Relations (*Gerente General de Relaciones Industriales*), who provided his/her response either through efax or email attachments. The survey was translated and back translated from English to Spanish using the four-step recommended process (Brislin *et al.*, 1973).

Fifty-four responses were received, for a response rate of 49 percent, which researchers consider very high for international research (Harzing, 2001). The survey was developed based on a review of the literature, review of previous surveys, input from Mexican business leaders, and expert business professors (see Table 11.1).

## Results

### *Executive staffing practices (recruitment and selection)*

Professional search agencies (67 percent), succession planning (65 percent), internet recruiting (35 percent), and internal advertisements (35 percent) were considered as the most important *recruitment methods* in attracting executive candidates. One-on-one interviews (88 percent), employer references (82 percent), and biodata instruments (77 percent) were the most frequently used *selection practices* to obtain information about executive candidates. Personality tests (63 percent), assessment centers (49 percent), cognitive ability tests (43 percent), and foreign language testing (43 percent) were the most frequently used methods of executive testing.

This empirical study also analyzed the influence of firm characteristics on executive staffing practices using regressions and ANOVA. Regression analyses revealed that firm size (measured as the number of full-time employees) significantly predicts succession planning ($\beta = .305$; $p < .05$), biodata ($\beta = .418$; $p < .05$), referral from current employees ($\beta = -.481$; $p< .05$), and group panel interviews ($\beta = .412$; $p < .05$). Equity structure was found to be significant for employer references ($\beta = .489$; $p < .01$), and group panel interviews ($\beta = .380$; $p < .05$). Firm age (years of operation) was found to be significant for trade journal advertisements/professional associations ($\beta = -.317$; $p < .05$), employer references ($\beta = .360$; $p < .01$), and foreign language tests, ($\beta = -.555$; $p < .01$). Corporate location (Mexico) was found to be significant for personal references ($\beta = .478$; $p < .01$), family connections ($\beta = .460$; $p < .01$), succession planning ($\beta = .400$; $p < .01$), and foreign language tests ($\beta = -.370$; $p < .05$). Resource dependence on the Mexican partner was significant for internet recruiting ($\beta = .348$; $p < .05$), succession planning ($\beta = .364$; $p < .01$), and assessment centers ($\beta = .355$; $p < .05$). ANOVA tests revealed that industry type was significant for foreign language tests (F values = 2.869; sig.011), professional search agencies (F values = 2.346; sig.03), and succession planning (F value = 2.199; sig.043).

*Table 11.1* Demographic details of US-Mexican IJVs

| Demographic Data | % |
|---|---|
| *Industry sectors* | |
| Manufacturing | 53 |
| Service | 43 |
| *Primary industry* | |
| Automotive | 21.6 |
| Chemicals | 15.7 |
| Consumer products | 13.7 |
| Construction engineering | 9.8 |
| Transportation | 7.8 |
| Real estate | 7.8 |
| Communication | 5.9 |
| Retail sales | 3.9 |
| Textiles | 3.9 |
| Legal | 2.0 |
| Other | 5.9 |
| *Firm age* | |
| Less than 3 years | 17.6 |
| More than 3 years, less than 5 years | 9.8 |
| More than 5 years, less than 7 years | 11.8 |
| More than 7 years, less than 9 years | 15.7 |
| More than 9 years, less than 11 years | 15.7 |
| More than 11 years | 29.4 |
| *Corporate location* | |
| Mexico | 71 |
| US | 26 |
| *Equity structure* | |
| 50–50 | 43 |
| 51(US)–49(Mexico) | 14 |
| 40(US)–60(Mexico) | 10 |
| 49(US)–51(Mexico) | 8 |
| *Firm size* | |
| Less than 250 | 39 |
| Between 250 and 1,000 | 29 |
| More than 1,000 employees | 29 |

N = 51

## Discussion

### *Executive staffing practices*

Professional search agencies were identified as the most important recruiting practice in US-Mexican joint ventures. These executive search agencies have become quite prevalent in Mexico as several multinational companies relocating to Mexico are looking for upper executive talent, which is scarce and in high demand. Professional search agencies provide an unbiased and objective opinion about executive clients, which is very important for parent partners of the joint ventures. They help identify the best client (Emmond, 2001; McCoy, 2004).

McCoy (2004), President of Korn/Ferry Internacional, S.A. de C.V., Mexico, in a personal telephone interview with the researcher articulated the prominent reasons that professional search agencies are an important recruiting tool for US-Mexican joint ventures. McCoy (2004) emphasized that professional search agencies provide an "objective view of talent" and "no bias" which is very critical for joint ventures, working with two different cultural partners. Joint venture partners are concerned that partners might promote their own employees, in an attempt to have more control. Professional search agencies could mitigate this concern. Second, these executive firms have an extensive database that can locate quality executive talent worldwide, thereby bringing the most qualified applicants to these joint ventures. The key in such high-profile recruiting is not limiting the executive search to the national boundaries of Mexico but networking worldwide for the best talent. On average, Korn/Ferry takes three months to locate the most qualified executive applicants. Moreover, professional search agencies pay special attention to the culture of the organization, and identify executive applicants who have a good fit with the organizational culture.

Goldberg and Cerullo (2006) emphasize that hiring the most qualified applicants gives a definite sustainable competitive advantage. In today's dynamic business environment, hiring the most qualified person is the best brand name a company can have. This is even more critical for global executives, whose competencies and skills are developed over years to become unique and inimitable (Spreitzer *et al.*, 1997).

Succession planning was rated the second most important recruitment method in attracting executive candidates. In Mexico, there is a preference for "grooming candidates" to upper-level positions right from entry-level junior positions. In collectivist cultures, such as Mexico, qualities such as trustworthiness, loyalty, dependability are extended only to in-group members, such as current employees of the organization (Martinez and Dorfman, 1998). A propensity for succession planning is an extension of such a cultural preference; employees who have developed a personal and business relationship with other employees will be considered an important source in the executive recruitment pool.

Everton (2004) argues that leadership capabilities in multinationals require an unusual set of competencies, which take time to learn. Therefore developing and identifying executive individuals, such as in succession planning, within the context of the multinational organizations can be used as an "inimitable" source of competitive advantage by organizations. Ibarra (2007) indicates that succession planning can help develop employees within the organizational and industry context, making them a rich source of talent.

Internet recruiting was ranked as the third most important method for recruiting executive candidates. Internet recruiting is a recent phenomenon in Mexico, as employees fear loss of confidentiality in submitting their resumes on the internet (Mejias, 2000). Internet penetration in Mexico is increasing rapidly and the country has seen great growth in its use since 2000. In this global race to hire the best talent, Mexico does not want to lag behind and has implemented this current method of proactive executive recruiting (Emmond, 2005; Navarrete and Pick, 2002).

Smith and Rupp (2006) state that the paramount advantage of e-recruiting is not its speed or cost, but its ability to tap the most qualified executive person across the globe. Global executives take time to learn and develop mastery of their job since it requires complex competencies, such as business knowledge, leadership skills, language skills, and cross-cultural sensitivity (Spreitzer *et al.*, 1997).

Internal advertisements were also ranked as an important method of executive recruitment. In multinational jobs, such as joint ventures, executives take time to attain mastery over their complex competencies. Therefore it is quite common to identify and seek high-performing talent internally as current employees have already established a sense of familiarity with the culture and values of the organization (London and Sessa, 1999). Further, at such a high level, selection is considered developmental because global executives are selected for development in different new learning environments (Weeks, 1992).

An interesting revelation of this study was that the *least used recruiting method* for attracting executive candidates was referral from family members (2 percent). While researchers (Davila and Elvira, 2005; Martinez and Dorfman, 1998) indicate that Mexicans are strongly influenced to recruit family members, this study points *to the contrary for executive staffing*. This could be because organizations in this study were multinationals and these organizations usually transcend local human resource practices (Hofstede *et al.*, 1990).

Among executive selection practices, one-on-one interviews were identified as the most frequently used. The universal appeal of interviews is not surprising, as employers in any country would undoubtedly want to meet candidates in person before making any hiring decisions (Huo *et al.*, 2002). While in the US interviewers look for qualities such as individualism, optimism, curiosity, problem solving, embodying the American tradition, counterparts in Mexico look for different qualities such as interpersonal skills, loyalty, and team working skills of candidates (De Forest, 1998).

The culture's emphasis on interpersonal relationships makes interviews an ideal place to explore applicants' interpersonal relationship skills. Teamwork and cooperation are compelling qualities for executive candidates in the Mexican corporate environment, which can be assessed in an interview process (De Forest, 1998; Triandis, 2004; Luthans *et al.*, 1997). Further, researchers indicate that using staffing practices (Schuler, 2001) that reflect local practices can bring the best talent and therefore be a definite source of competitive advantage.

Employer references have been identified as the second most frequently used selection practice. Employers in Mexico seek elaborate employment opinions from prior employers who have worked with applicants, so as to establish the credibility of their past work accomplishments. Employers from such cultures need to have as much information as possible on applicants before making a hiring decision (De Forest, 1998).

Biodata was ranked as the third most frequently used selection practice in US-Mexican joint ventures. In contrast to the US, in Mexico biodata tend to provide comprehensive information on applicants' educational, employment, and personal history. Having more information about applicants adds predictability to the hiring process, especially in a culture high on uncertainty avoidance. It also ensures getting as much information as possible before hiring (O'Connell *et al.*, 2002).

The least used selection practice was family connections (6 percent). Family connections are a selection method for hiring applicants predominantly because they are personal friends or relatives (Davila and Elvira, 2005; De Forest, 1998). The integration of two different national cultures in a multinational setting could possibly diminish the use of traditional local human resource practices (Hofstede *et al.*, 1990).

Personality tests were the most frequently used method of executive testing. In collectivist cultures like Mexico, the intention of such comprehensive testing (Ryan *et al.*, 1999) is to make sure that there is harmony in the workplace, which is highly valued in collectivist cultures (Davila and Elvira, 2005). Further, psychometric tests such as Kolbe and Cleaver help employers identify important employee characteristics, such as being detail-oriented and entrepreneurial (Ryan, 1992).

### Executive staffing practices and firm characteristics

This study provides evidence for the role of firm characteristics (age, size, equity structure, resource dependence on parent partners, corporate location, and industry sector) on executive staffing practices.

"Younger" joint ventures relied more on trade journal advertisements/professional associations in their recruiting efforts as such sources have a good database of information to begin identifying potential applicants working in similar business environments (Harzing, 2001). "Younger" joint venture operations used foreign language tests more frequently in their selection efforts because emerging multinationals that seek extensive operations in Mexico have recognized the critical importance of bilingual skills. On the other hand, "older" joint ventures relied on recommendations from their current employees, especially for upper executive positions. This could be because current employees are in a good position to observe and identify high-performing fellow peers working in similar work environments (Harzing, 2001).

Larger joint ventures used more succession planning, biodata, and group panel interviews and used less referral from current employees. This is consistent with the staffing literature's argument that larger organizations (with their large internal pool of employees) tend to use staffing policies that develop internal employees, such as succession planning (Harzing, 2001). Larger organizations used more biodata as they have resources to validate and develop biodata instruments (Harzing, 2001). Large joint ventures used more group panel interviews as generally in large multinationals several upper executives from different functional divisions are involved in group panel interviews for selecting applicants (Harzing, 2001). Large joint ventures relied less often on referral from current employees. Usually large multinationals target high-performing internal employees within the company or from their other subsidiaries and affiliates. Leveraging executive talent among affiliates and subsidiaries is quite a common staffing practice for large multinationals as familiarity within the industry and company helps such executives perform better (Harzing, 2001).

Equity ownership structure influenced staffing practices, as indicated by earlier studies (Shenkar and Zeira, 1987). The more US equity was held by the joint venture, the less frequent use of employer references. As the IJVs for this study were all located in Mexico, using employer references would mean completely relying on the host country nationals' recommendations. In Mexico's collectivist culture, employer recommendations might not actually reflect the job potential of the applicant. Therefore IJVs that have more US equity would rely less on local employer references, which could have a subjective bias (Schuler *et al.*, 1996). The more US equity structure held by the IJV, the greater the use of group panel interviews. Staffing studies in the US have demonstrated that group-panel interviews were the predominant method of hiring upper-level executives, and therefore the more equity the US has in the IJV, the more likely they are to use predominant staffing practices from their national origins (Sessa and Taylor, 2000).

Personal references, family connections, foreign language testing, and succession planning were used more frequently as executive staffing methods when the corporate location of the IJV was in Mexico. The use of personal references and family connections as predominant selection methods in Mexico has been emphasized repeatedly by several researchers (Kras, 1995; Schuler *et al.*, 1996) and is confirmed in this empirical study. Succession planning is important in the Mexican culture as group members (employees in the organization) are preferred to external members having developed a strong personal and professional relationship with their peers and superiors (Triandis, 2004).

The use of foreign language testing is more frequent when the corporate location of the IJV is in the US. This contributes to an earlier observation that there is an increased emphasis on Mexican employees demonstrating English competence when multinationals in Mexico have their corporate headquarters in the US. Such a bilingual workforce helps better communication between corporate offices with their foreign affiliates (Sargent and Matthews, 1997).

This study contributes to and advances the finding of an earlier study (Martinez and Ricks, 1989) that dependence of the IJV on parent partners for critical resources (such as capital and markets) does influence human resource practices. The IJV that is dependent on the Mexican parent partner is more likely to adopt and use staffing practices that are locally established in the national origins of its parent partners. The more dependent the IJV was on the Mexican partner, the more important was internet recruiting and succession planning in its recruitment efforts, and the more frequent was the use of assessment centers in its selection efforts. The method of testing in assessment centers (multiple tests and interviews) is appealing to Mexicans, who prefer to have elaborate and additional information on applicants before making any hiring decisions (Ryan *et al.*, 1999).

This study also contributes to the finding of Harzing's (2001) earlier study on multinationals that specific industry types influence executive staffing practices. Construction and engineering industries used more foreign language testing than textiles, as more construction and engineering companies in this study had their corporate offices in the US. Therefore IJVs that had their corporate location in the US preferred to use foreign language testing of Mexican employees.

Communication industries used more professional search agencies than chemical industries. In the sample for this study, communication industries were usually larger and also established (for a longer time) than chemical industries, and hence more likely to have the financial resources to use such recruiting efforts. Succession planning was more important in consumer industries than real estate. In the sample for this study, consumer industries were larger (more full-time employees) and hence more likely to use staffing methods where internal employees are groomed and developed (Harzing, 2001).

## Conclusion

This study describes current executive staffing practices in US-Mexican joint ventures, identified for the first time in the US joint venture and staffing literature. Based on these results, future research can investigate testable hypotheses on whether certain staffing practices are associated with higher organizational effectiveness. The results provide practitioners with a better understanding of the current state of executive staffing practices and can help them formulate better executive staffing practices. Further, the results have shown the influence of firm characteristics on executive staffing practices.

Scholars (Huo *et al.*, 2002; Laroche, 2002; Ryan *et al.*, 1999; Schuler, 2001) assert that multinational organizations should consider local staffing practices to be "best practices" as they are bound to attract the most qualified local talent. Ryan *et al.* (1999) argue that not considering local practices could create dysfunctional effects in the staffing system as qualified applicants will not like being recruited or selected on criteria they are not familiar with. Adopting local practices also guarantees that the applicant's skills, knowledge, and abilities are evaluated in the local context.

## References

Barney, J. (2001) "Is the resource-based 'view' a useful perspective for strategic management research? Yes," *Academy of Management Executive*, 26(1): 41–56.

Bensinger, K. (2003) "The top business schools (a special report); Heading south; far south: Mexico boasts the top two foreign business schools in the latest WSJ survey," *Wall Street Journal (Eastern Edition)*, New York, September 17: R12.

Boxall, P. (1994) "Placing HR strategy at the heart of business success," *Personnel Management*, 26(7): 32–35.

Brislin, R., Lonner, W., and Thorndike, R. (1973) *Questionnaire Wording and Translation. Cross-cultural Research Methods*, New York: John Wiley.

Celaya, L. and Swift, J. (2006) "Pre-departure cultural training: US Managers in Mexico," *Cross Cultural Management*, 13(3): 230–236.

Davila, A. and Elvira, M. (2005) "Culture and human resources management," in M. M. Elvira and A. Davila (eds.), *Managing Human Resources in Latin America*, London and New York: Routledge.

De Forest, M. (1998) "Hecho en Mexico: Tips for success," *Apparel Industry Magazine*, 59(9): 98–106.

Delery, J. and Doty, H. (1996) "Modes of theorizing in strategic human resource management: Tests of universalistic, contingency, and configurational performance predictions," *Academy of Management Journal*, 39(4): 802–835.

Dorroh, J. (2003) "Respect in office," *Business Mexico*, 13(11): 1–3.

Elahee, M., Kirby, S., and Ercan, N. (2002) "National culture, trust and perceptions about ethical behavior in intra- and cross-cultural negotiations: An analysis of NAFTA countries," *Thunderbird International Business Review*, 44(6): 799–815.

Emmond, K. (2001) "Matchmakers," *Business Mexico*, 10(12): 28–30.

Emmond, K. (2005) "Investing in IT," *Business Mexico*, 15(5): 22–28.

Everton, W. (2004) "Growing your company leaders: How great organizations use succession management to sustain competitive advantage," *Academy of Management Executive*, 18(1): 137–138.

Fritsch, P. (2000) "For Mexico's Fox: No cronies needed? Headhunter team is hired to select cabinet prospects," *Wall Street Journal (Eastern Edition)*, New York, July, 14: A12.

Gatewood, R. and Field, H. (1998) *Human Resource Selection*, 4th edn., Orlando, FL: Harcourt Brace.

Geringer, M. and Frayne, C. (1990) "Human resource management and international joint venture control: A parent company perspective," *Management International Review*, 30: 103–117.

Gillespie, K. and Teegen, H. (1995) "Market liberalization and international alliance formation: The Mexican paradigm," *Columbia Journal of World Business*, 30(4): 58–69.

Goldberg, J. and Cerullo, M. (2006) "Research staffing – the right staff," *Brand Strategy*, June: 56–58.

Hannon, J., Huang, I., and Jaw, B. (1995) "International human resource strategy and its determinants: The case of subsidiaries in Taiwan," *Journal of International Business Studies*, 26(3): 531–555.

Harzing, A. (2001) "Who's in charge? An empirical study of executive staffing practices in foreign subsidiaries," *Human Resource Management*, 40(2): 139–158.

Hofstede, G. (1991) *Cultures and Organizations. Software of the Mind*, London: McGraw-Hill.

Hofstede, G., Neuijen, B., Ohayv, D., and Sanders, G. (1990) "Measuring organizational cultures: A qualitative and quantitative study across twenty cases," *Administrative Science Quarterly*, 35(2): 286–316.

Huo, P., Huang, H., and Napier, N. (2002) "Divergence of convergence: A cross national comparison of personnel selection practices," *Human Resource Management*, 41(1): 31–44.

Ibarra, P. (2007) "The myths and realities of succession planning," *Public Management*, 89(1): 24–28.

Kesler, G. (2002) "Why the leadership bench never gets deeper: Ten insights about executive development," *Human Resource Planning*, 25(1): 32–44.

Kogut, B. (1989) "Expatriate reduction in American multinationals: Have we gone too far," *ILR Report*, 27: 22–30.

Kras, E. (1995) *Management in Two Cultures. Bridging the Gap between US and Mexican Managers*, Yarmouth: Intercultural Press.

Lane, H. and Beamish, P. (1990) "Cross-cultural cooperative behavior in joint ventures in LDCs," *Management International Review*, 30: 87–102.

Lemak, D., Arunthanes, W., and Moore, N. (1994) "A guide to joint ventures in Mexico," *Multinational Business Review*, 2(1): 19–27.

Lin, X. and Germain, R. (1999) "Predicting international joint venture interaction frequency in US–Chinese ventures," *Journal of International Marketing*, 7(2): 5–23.

London, M. and Sessa, V. (1999) *Selecting International Executives: A Suggested Framework and Annotated Bibliography*, Greensboro, NC: Center for Creative Leadership.

Lorange, A. (1996) "A strategic human resource perspective applied to multinational cooperative ventures," *International Studies of Management and Organization*, 26(1): 87–103.

Luthans, F., Marsnik, P., and Luthans, K. (1997) "A contingency matrix approach to IHRM," *Human Resource Management*, 36(2): 83–89.

McCoy, H. (2004) Personal telephone interview with President, Korn/Ferry Internacional, S.A. de C.V., Mexico.

Makino, S. and Beamish, P. (1998) "Performance and survival of joint ventures with non-conventional ownership structures," *Journal of International Business Studies*, 29(4): 797–818.

Martinez, S. and Dorfman, P. (1998) "The Mexican entrepreneur: An ethnographic study of the Mexican empresario," *International Studies of Management and Organization*, 28(2): 97–123.

Martinez, Z. and Ricks, D. (1989) "Multinational parent companies' influence over human resource decisions of affiliates: US firms in Mexico," *Journal of International Business Studies*, 20(3): 465–487.

Mejia-Gomez, L. and Palich, L. (1997) "Cultural diversity and the performance of multinational firms," *Journal of International Business Studies*, 73(3): 309–335.

Mejias, C. (2000) *Latin American Trends in Human Resources*, Alexandria, VA: Society for Human Resource Management.

Messenger, R. (2004) "Style matters," *Business Mexico*, 14(7): 30–32.

Miller, R., Glen, J., Jaspersen, F., and Karmokolias, Y. (1997) "International joint ventures in developing countries," *Finance and Development*, 34(1): 26–30.

Miller, P. (2007) *The Mexican TSP Initiative: Positioning the Mexican Software Industry through TSP/PSP*, Software Engineering Institute. Retrieved from: www.sei.cmu.edu/news-at-sei/features/2007/01/01-feature-2007-01.html

Mondragon, C. (1997) *Strategic Alliances in Mexico: The Case of Wal-Mart-Cifra*, University of Texas.

Navarrete, C. and Pick, J. (2002) "Information technology expenditure and industry performance: The case of the Mexican banking industry," *Journal of Global Information Technology Management,* 5(2): 7–29.

Neupert, K. and Montoya, R. (2000) "Characteristics and performance of Japanese foreign direct investment in Latin America," *International Journal of Public Administration*, 23(5): 1,269–1,283.

O'Connell, M., Hattrup, K., Doverspike, D., and Cober, A. (2002) "The validity of 'mini' simulations for Mexican retail salespeople," *Journal of Business and Psychology*, 16(4): 593–599.

Rianhard, C. (2002) "E-Learning," *Business Mexico*, 12(9): 57–58.

Ryan, J. (1992) "Striving for the best," *Business Mexico*, 2(5): 49–50.

Ryan, A., McFarland, L., Baron, H., and Page, R. (1999) "An international look at selection practices: Nation and culture as explanations for variability in practice," *Personnel Psychology*, 52(2): 359–391.

Sargent, J. and Matthews, L. (1997) "NAFTA, the financial crisis, and the multinational management in Mexico," *International Executive*, 39(3): 375–392.

Schaan, J. (1988) "How to control a joint venture even as a minority partner," *Journal of General Management*, 14(1): 4–16.

Schuler, R. (2001) "Human resource issues and activities in international joint ventures," *International Journal of Human Resource Management*, 12(1): 1–52.

Schuler, R., Jackson, S., Jackofsky, E., and Slocum, J. (1996) "Managing human resources in Mexico: A cultural understanding," *Business Horizons*, 39(3): 55–61.

Sessa, V. and Taylor, J. (2000) *Executive Selection: Strategies for Success*, San Francisco: Jossey-Bass and the Center for Creative Leadership.

Shackleton, V. and Newell, S. (1991) "Management selection: A comparative survey of methods used in top British and French companies," *Journal of Occupational Psychology*, 64(1): 23–36.

Shenkar, O. and Zeira, Y. (1987) "Human resources management in international joint ventures: Directions for research," *Academy of Management Review*, 12(3): 546–557.

Smith, A. and Rupp, W. (2006) "Managerial challenges of e-recruiting: Extending the life cycle of new economy employees," *Online Information Review*, 28(1): 61–63.

Spreitzer, G., McCall, M., and Mahoney, J. (1997) "Early identification of executive potential," *Journal of Applied Psychology*, 82(1): 6–29.

Stephens, G. and Greer, C. (1995) "Doing business in Mexico: Understanding cultural differences," *Organizational Dynamics*, 24(1): 39–55.

Triandis, H. (2004) "The many dimensions of culture," *Academy of Management Executive*, 18(1): 88–93.

Trompenaars, F. (1994) *Riding the Waves of Culture: Understanding Diversity in Global Business*, Burr Ridge, IL: Irwin Publishing.

Urteaga-Trani, R. (2003) "Mexico: A competitive location," *Area Development Site and Facility Planning*, 38(7): 42–46.

Weeks, D. (1992) *Recruiting and Selecting International Managers*, New York: Conference Board.

Yeung, A. and Ready, D. (1995) "Developing leadership capabilities: A comparative study in eight nations," *Human Resource Management*, 34(4): 529–547.

# 12 Western ethical theories and their relevance to HRM in Latin America

*Jorge M. Herrera and Carolyn Erdener*

The study of ethics in human resource management (HRM) in Latin America is becoming increasingly important as organizations competing internationally often face a different set of ethical beliefs than those within their own societies. Globalization has increased the significance and influence that organizations have worldwide, therefore it is important to explore ethical practices and their influences on areas such as decision-making on individuals, societies, and organizations in different parts of the world. Human resource (HR) practices are intricately tied to the ethical beliefs of cultures as HR seeks to bridge the needs of working individuals and organizations within the framework of the values, beliefs, morals, and attitudes of the society in which the organization operates. The study presented here was designed to contribute to the development of best ethical practices in HRM in Latin America by assessing data on how business ethics is currently taught and practiced. It is based on the most relevant literature available, using well-known Western ethical theories as a starting point.

Complex ethical pluralism increases the potential for intrapersonal and interpersonal ethical conflict and is difficult to manage as it contributes to moral ambiguity and confusion about the parameters of ethical dilemmas (Erdener and Márquez, 2005; Erdener *et al.*, 2007). For example, in addition to well-known Western ethics concepts such as *deontology*, *teleology*, *justice*, and *individual rights*, Latin American understandings of ethics are rooted in a particularist tradition regarding personal relationships (Márquez and Erdener, 2007). "Latin Americans tend to place the goals of the in-group over and above the goals of society at large. Thus, the law is seen somewhat flexibly in view of these personalistic relationships" (Husted, 2002: 417). In Latin America, HRM is focused on the person, with the HR professional serving as an advocate for employees rather than merely representing the organization (Elvira and Davila, 2005: 2,265). There is an inherent dignity placed on social relationships in Latin America that creates a unique code of ethics that may be incongruent with the general code of conduct organizations require.

Regional and national differences among Latin American countries must be considered when analyzing ethical beliefs and practices. "[D]espite their superficial linguistic and historical similarities, 'each country has a unique history and geography and other elements that contribute to the culture of its people'"

(Albert, 1996: 329; cited in Lenartowicz and Johnson, 2003). These differences influence HRM practices. For example, "employees in Mexico are entitled by law to continue receiving any benefit, service, or bonus that has been paid for two consecutive years, and profit sharing is mandated by law at the rate of 10 percent of pretax profits" (Cascio, 2006: 486).

Very little published research has addressed the linkages between HRM and business ethics, especially in Latin America. "The practice of HRM varies widely in the region due to organizational ownership and types, top management belief in the value of HRM and the degree of professionalism in HR personnel" (Osland and Osland, 2005: 2,221). Nonetheless, the literature on human resource management, cross-cultural management, and business ethics research focused on Latin American countries does provide a frame of reference, analysis, and observation.

## Definition of terms

### *Business ethics vs. international business ethics*

The concept of business ethics has been popularized in the West and therefore encompasses Western philosophies, religions, cultures, value systems, languages, and meanings. We use the term "Western" to mean European and US values and beliefs. In practical terms, business ethics is how moral principles are applied to everyday business decisions. However, "business communities cannot claim that their set of ethical values is necessarily universal" (Donaldson and Dunfee, 1999: 47). Therefore, it is important to ask to what degree Western ethics concepts are applicable to a region of the world with significantly different histories and cultures. In other words, how universal are the widely used business ethics concepts taught and practiced in the US and Europe?

Cullen and Parboteeah define international business ethics (IBE) as "[pertaining] to those unique ethical problems faced by managers conducting business operations across national boundaries" (2005: 628). If it is true that "background shapes the foreground" (Cooper, 2004: 2), then given the varying histories of Latin American countries, they might perceive a particular event differently from each other and from countries with different "backgrounds." This does not take into consideration the "background" of individuals making ethical decisions in HR departments. "Different cultural values and institutional systems necessarily mean that people may not always agree on what one 'ought' to do" (Cullen and Parbotteah, 2005: 628). Critical questions arise when looking at international business ethics from this perspective. For example, how are ethical problems addressed while conducting business across national boundaries? Whose background is used as the basis for ethical decision-making? It may be useful to broaden the definition of IBE as follows: International business ethics is impartial, inclusive and representative of the philosophies, religions, cultures, value systems, languages, and meanings of the regions of the world where the ethical dilemma occurs (Herrera, 2005).

The ethics concepts and theories used in this study are those that appear most frequently in the literature and in business ethics texts. The list is not meant to be exhaustive but representative of the Western conceptualization of ethics. The concepts and theories are *absolutism*, *autonomy*, *deontology*, *egoism*, *justice*, *natural rights*, *relativism*, *social contract theory*, *teleology*, *universal morality*, and *utilitarianism* (see Table 12.1).

## Relevant research on Latin America

### HRM research on Latin America

HRM researchers interested in Latin America have investigated themes that are relevant to business ethics. Several studies examine HR issues in the US and

*Table 12.1* Western conceptualization of ethics

| | |
|---|---|
| Absolutism | The doctrine or practice of unlimited authority and control; despotism; predestination (Preble, 1963). |
| Autonomy | Independent control of one's own life or not being controlled from the outside (Cooper, 2004). |
| Deontology | The science of moral obligation (Preble, 1963). Nonconsequential ethics. Some property besides good consequences determines what is right and wrong (Cooper, 2004). |
| Egoism | The doctrine that the supreme end of human conduct is the perfection of happiness of the ego, or self, and that all virtue consists in the pursuit of self-interest (Preble, 1963). |
| Justice | Concerns the area of morality that deals with justifying and protecting rights or giving people their due (Cooper, 2004). |
| Natural rights | A theory based on the fundamental belief that individuals naturally have special moral standing as holders of rights (Cooper, 2004). |
| Relativism | The theory that truths are relative and may vary according to the individual, the group, the place or the time (Preble, 1963). A metatheory about morality that claims there are no universal values, so that the meaning of all values is constrained by the context that gave rise to them (Cooper, 2004). |
| Social contract theory | Based on the foundations of hypothetical ideal conditions for moral consent: everyone ought to act in accordance with principles of justice that would be chosen by free and equal rational people who come together to form a contract to establish a model community (Cooper, 2004). |
| Teleology | Focus on consequences or the results of the actions they produce (Carroll and Buchholtz, 2006). |
| Universal morality | Prescribes rights and duties for everyone, no matter what their station or what community they inhabit (Cooper, 2004). |
| Utilitarianism | The idea that we are obligated to maximize non-moral good in the world: always choose the option that promotes the greatest amount of happiness to everyone (Preble, 1963). |

Europe such as *performance appraisal, recruitment and selection, compensation, retention*, and *diversity*, and apply them in a Latin American context. While such studies typically do not explicitly discuss ethics, they provide insight into what may be important ethical considerations in Latin America.

International comparisons of compensation practices can provide useful information regarding perceptions of equity in different societies. Data from six Latin American countries were analyzed in an international comparison of compensation practices (Lowe *et al*., 2002). The findings illustrate a large gap between employees' scores for the current status versus the ideal. Large gaps between the current status of compensation practices and the ideal may indicate a strong perception of inequity or injustice. The ethics concept of *justice* deals with justifying and protecting rights, or giving people their due (Cooper, 2004).

Country comparisons of performance appraisal systems can be beneficial in understanding possible ethical HRM practices. A study of the use of performance appraisal in Mexico, Australia, Canada, Japan, South Korea, China, Taiwan, the US, and a group of four unspecified Latin American countries found that the greatest gaps between employees' expectations and reality were in Mexico (Milliman *et al*., 2002). Although the pattern regarding promotion decisions was similar, the average responses to questions about determining promotability indicate a relatively low emphasis on this in Mexico, though Mexico (and the four-country Latin group) showed the highest means for the use of performance appraisals in determining promotability (Milliman *et al*., 2002). *Justice* and *social contract theory* could also be related conceptually to this gap between reality and the ideal.

International studies on diversity are also useful in understanding the ethics behind HRM decisions. In the US HRM literature, diversity management is broadly understood to include many kinds of diversity such as gender, ethnicity, disability, or national origin. In the Latin American context, however, diversity management research focuses mainly on women in the workplace (Maxfield, 2005; Muller and Rowell, 1997; Osland and Osland, 2005; Zabludovsky, 2001). Women managers are significantly under-represented in Latin America, forming 25 percent of the workforce as compared to a global average of 40 percent, according to data gathered by the International Labor Organization (Maxfield, 2005: 249). However, the concentration of women managers is higher in services and commerce as well as in the functional areas of marketing, accounting, and HRM. Diversity, in general, can be conceptually linked to *universal morality* as it prescribes rights and duties for everyone, regardless of their station in life (Cooper, 2004).

### Business ethics research on Latin America

Business ethics literature focuses on topics such as *bribery, corruption*, or *corporate policy*. This research identifies differences in ethics that can affect interactions across countries. Major differences indicate likely sources of friction (Erdener and Torbiörn, 1999) that can impede organizational function.

Considerable empirical research on ethical aspects of corruption exists in the academic and practitioner literature, including an ongoing focus on Latin America.

Numerous empirical studies have demonstrated a significant negative relationship between corruption and economic growth (Wilhelm, 2002). According to Donaldson and Dunfee, corruption violates the *efficiency hypernorm*. "Hypernorms are principles so fundamental that, by definition, they serve to evaluate lower-order norms ... They represent norms by which all others are to be judged" (Donaldson and Dunfee, 1999: 46). The ethics concept of the *efficiency hypernorm* may relate to *social contract theory*, *universal morality*, and *natural rights* (see Table 12.1). Efficiency is a hypernorm because it is in the best interest of all societies to promote economic welfare and social justice (Donaldson and Dunfee, 1999: 57). Corruption may also violate the ethics concepts of *utilitarianism* and *justice* because it is not in the best interest of the majority, nor is it fair for contracts to be awarded to the few corrupt individuals with deep pockets. Another ethics concept that corruption violates is *autonomy*, because entrepreneurs who produce the best product or service do not have control of their own fate in a corrupt environment where free enterprise is compromised.

A series of papers exploring the effects of personal relationships in Mexico address a new theoretical construct identified as relational ethics. These studies use content analysis of short essay responses to a vignette in which ethical decision-making involves relationship considerations. Three competing ethical orientations were identified, each emphasized by approximately one-third of the subjects: *personal friendship*, *professional standards*, and *business interest* (Márquez and Erdener, 2005). These studies find that interpersonal relationships may be subject to widely shared norms for ethical conduct that, to varying degrees, contrast sharply with professional and business interests. Relational ethics may be conceptually linked to *social contract theory*. In Latin America, rather than being merely a way to make a living, work is central to the social life of the person, creating an "intricate and implicit contract between workers and their employers" (Elvira and Davila, 2005: 2,265).

### Cross-cultural management research on Latin America

"Kluckhorn, Hofstede, Turner, and Trompenaars, and many other management theorists have shown the importance of cultural differences to business – but the further issue of ethical implications of many of these differences remains unexplored" (Donaldson and Dunfee, 1999: 47). The most widely used conceptual framework for cross-cultural comparison is the national culture model proposed by Geert Hofstede (1980, 2000). Hofstede's model has the advantage of having been far more widely used in empirical research than any other model. Each of the dimensions in the model – *individualism–collectivism*, *masculinity–femininity*, *power distance*, and *uncertainty avoidance* – may have implications for Business Ethics. For example:

> In collectivist cultures, morality is defined in terms of the benefits for the in-group (family, friends, work companies, etc.), implying the maintenance of solidarity (Triandis and Bhawuk, 1997) ... in a highly individualistic country,

individualism is viewed as a strength and the major reason for the country's accomplishments.

(Beekun *et al.*, 2003: 269)

The collectivistic end of the *individualism–collectivism* dimension of national culture could be linked conceptually to the ethics concept of *relativism*. One of the hallmarks of collectivistic cultures is the distinction between in-groups and out-groups. Such distinctions produce a dualistic ethics system or double standard according to which it is ethically correct to maintain different standards of accountability for in-group versus out-group members (Erdener and Márquez, 2005; Erdener *et al.*, 2007a). The individualistic end of this dimension could be linked to the ethics concept of *egoism* if one looks at individualism from the viewpoint of Adam Smith's self-interest concept.

## *Methodology, policies, practices, and ethics in HRM in Latin America*

In order to help fill the gap that exists in the study of HRM and ethics, two new survey instruments were distributed in Mexico: the first is a survey for HR professionals and the second is directed at college or university professors teaching HR or organizational behavior (OB). HR professionals were chosen because they are most knowledgeable about the ethical environment of their HR departments and can provide valuable information about the relationship between ethical policies and practices. HR and OB professors were chosen because they can identify the ethics concepts they teach and have an informed opinion as to the application of these concepts in HR departments. This will help determine to what degree Western ethical theories are applicable in Latin America and to better understand the Latin American conceptualization of ethics. The purpose of this is to contribute to the development of a framework for best ethical practices in HR departments in Latin America.

The HR professional survey seeks to determine the extent to which HR policy and practice in Latin America are guided by the eleven Western ethics concepts previously mentioned (Table 12.1). In addition, this study also explores how these concepts are related to one another in policy and practice and to determine if there are broader considerations that explain the degree to which each of the ethics concepts is reflected in HR policy and practice.

The professors' survey seeks to determine the extent to which they teach ethics concepts and their opinion as to how frequently HR practices in companies are influenced by these concepts. This study also seeks to explore whether a relationship exists between the ethics concepts being taught and what is being practiced and if there are broader considerations that explain the degree to which each of the ethics concepts being taught is reflected in what is being practiced in HR departments.

Each survey has a double-scale series of questions based on well-known Western ethics concepts (Table 12.1). The HR professionals use this scale to answer questions that compare HR *policies* with *practices*. In contrast, the HR and OB professors use this scale to answer questions that compare the ethics concepts they *teach* with what they believe is the frequency with which these concepts are *practiced* in HR departments. It is important to study the relationship between what is being taught and what is being practiced in order to improve the preparation and ethical performance of future managers and HR professionals.

The name of the concept is not provided as the respondent may not be familiar with the terminology, but a clear definition of each ethics concept is given. As an example, the left-hand side reads, "How frequently do the *policies* of the HR department reflect that one should always choose the option that promotes the greatest amount of happiness to the greatest amount of people?" (utilitarianism); while the right-hand side reads, "How frequently do the *practices* of the HR department reflect that one should always choose the option that promotes the greatest amount of happiness to the greatest amount of people?"

The same method is followed for the double-scale section of the survey for HR and OB professors. As an example, the left-hand side reads, "Do you *teach* the concept in your class that states that duty, not necessarily good consequences determines what is right and wrong?" (deontology); while the right-hand side reads, "In your opinion, how frequently do the *practices* of HR departments in Latin American companies, specifically in your country, demonstrate the concept that duty, not necessarily good consequences, determines what is right and wrong?"

The survey for HR professionals also includes a variety of exploratory statements about the organizational environment, feelings and attitudes, and concerns and conflicts. Similarly, the survey for HR and OB professors also asks a variety of exploratory questions about variables that may affect their ethics teaching in their classes.

An online survey was administered to HR professionals and HR and OB professors in Mexico during the spring of 2007. As no useful established lists were found for the target population and taking into consideration that personal relationships are extremely important in Latin America, it was decided that the best method to reach the target population was snowball sampling. A total of 60 subjects were contacted altogether regarding the survey, and 20 surveys were completed, for a response rate of 33 percent.

The HR professionals' estimations of the degree to which policy and practice reflect each of the ethical concepts were examined for evidence of linear relationships between the concepts as measured by Pearson's correlation coefficient; the HR and OB professors' estimations of the degree to which what is being taught and practiced reflects each of the ethical concepts were examined in a similar way. Frequency tables were developed to analyze the results of the exploratory questions which sought information about a variety of influences on ethical policies, practices, and teaching.

### *HR professionals' evaluation of HR policies regarding ethics*

First, strong positive correlations were found in the degree to which each company's HR policies reflected *utilitarianism*, *deontology*, *natural rights*, *social contract theory*, and *autonomy*. As each of these concepts generally addresses the relationship between the individual and society, this finding suggests that the HR policies of the respondents' companies are influenced to some extent by the idea that people have a duty to preserve everyone's rights, including allowing people to have independent control of their lives for the common good of all.

Second, the degree to which each company's HR policies reflect the concepts of *universal morality* and *justice* exhibited a strong positive correlation, indicating that HR policies are influenced by each company's commitment to the general idea that everyone, regardless of social status, has rights and duties that need to be protected (justice).

Finally, moderate to strong positive correlations were noted in the degree to which each company's HR policies reflect *egoism, absolutism, relativism,* and *teleology.* From this finding, one can conclude that HR policies are shaped by each company's commitment to the idea that the actions of individuals are for their own best interest, and that they will use their authority to achieve their desired results (control). One may conclude that differences in the degree to which each company's HR policies reflect the eleven concepts in Table 12.1 are a function of three broad ethical considerations – the individual vs. society, justice, and control.

### *HR professionals' evaluation of HR practices regarding ethics*

Strong positive correlations were found in the degree to which HR practices reflected *utilitarianism, deontology, natural rights, social contract theory, universal morality, justice,* and *autonomy.* This finding indicates that the HR practices of the respondents' companies are influenced, to a greater or lesser extent, by the idea that individuals believe that organizations are seen as members of the community and, as such, have a duty to protect employees. Individuals believe that everyone has rights as well as duties, but that individuals may act in a way that is different from corporate policy if they believe that they are acting in the best interests of the community (individual vs. society).

Also, the degree to which HR practices reflect the concepts of *egoism, absolutism, relativism,* and *teleology* exhibited a moderate to strong positive correlation, indicating that HR practices are influenced by each company's belief in the general idea that individual actions are in an individual's best interest and he or she will use his or her authority to achieve the desired results (control). One may conclude that differences in the degree to which HR practices reflect the eleven concepts in Table 12.1 are a function of two broad ethical considerations – the individual vs. society and control. In the Latin American context, individual vs. society may be interpreted as personal relationships vs. organizational rules. This is the same pattern that was observed for the third factor for the HR *policies* section. However, the table of correlations for *policies* showed a pattern that has to do with the general idea of justice, while the table of correlations for *practices* did not identify this trend. It may be that a difference exists in the perception of what exists in writing as policy and what is being practiced regarding the concept of justice in general.

### HR ethics in policy and practice

*Justice* was the ethics concept most often reflected in HR policy. *Social contract theory*, *universal morality*, *natural rights*, and *autonomy* are also widely prevalent. *Egoism*, *teleology*, and *absolutism* were the concepts least often reflected in policy. Results of the survey of HR professionals indicate that, of the eleven concepts measured, *natural rights* is most often reflected in HR practices. *Social contract theory*, *justice*, *universal morality*, and *absolutism* were also widely reflected in practice. Among the concepts least often reflected in HR practices are *egoism*, *autonomy*, and *teleology*. Comparing the rankings of policy and practice, two important findings are noted. First, although *autonomy* is often reflected in policy, it is not often practiced. Second, according to HR professionals, while *absolutism* is not often reflected in the HR policies, it is frequently seen in practice. Perhaps the presence of absolutism in practices, but not in policy, is evidence of a high power distance (or paternalism) at the middle management level, while the presence of autonomy in policy, but not in practice, may be evidence of the existence of an organizational global HR management strategy. This is an example of the conflict that emerges in Latin America, where personal relationships heavily influence HR practice in an increasingly global environment where HR policies are meant to be universal (38 percent of the corporations surveyed were foreign owned). This person-centred view of HR management is increasingly at odds with the performance-centred view predominant in global companies and creates a hybrid cultural environment (Elvira and Davila, 2005: 2,265).

These findings indicate that a discrepancy exists between the organization's HR strategy and its implementation at the departmental level, and the findings lend support to the idea that in Latin America a hybrid management model has evolved to resolve the chasm between global processes and local management practices (Davila and Elvira, 2005: 3).

### The ethics concepts that HR and OB professors teach

First, strong positive correlations were found in the degree to which *utilitarianism*, *natural rights*, *social contract theory*, and *universal morality* are taught. This finding indicates that the ethics concepts professors teach are influenced to some degree by the idea that everyone has rights and duties regardless of his or her position in life, and organizations should act for the greater good of all while preserving individual rights (egalitarianism).

Second, the degree to which the curriculum reflects the concepts of *egoism*, *deontology*, *relativism*, and *teleology* exhibited a strong positive correlation, indicating that the degree to which the professors teach the ethics concepts is influenced by the idea that what is good for the individual and what is right and wrong depends on the situation, regardless of the consequences (relativism).

Finally, the degree to which the curriculum reflects the concepts of *absolutism* and *autonomy* exhibited a strong positive correlation, indicating that the ethics concepts the professors teach are also influenced by the idea that while people may want or seek control over their own lives, the reality is that they are largely controlled by hierarchical systems (control).

One may conclude that differences in the degree to which the ethics concepts professors teach reflect the eleven concepts above are a function of three broad ethical considerations: egalitarianism, relativism, and control. In the Latin American context, relativism may be interpreted as ethical pluralism. Donaldson and Dunfee include the concept of "moral free space" to account for strongly held cultural beliefs that may be in conflict with more universal norms (Donaldson and Dunfee, 1999: 53).

### HR and OB professors' evaluation of HR practices regarding ethics

First, strong positive correlations were found in the degree to which the professors surveyed believed HR practices reflected *absolutism*, *autonomy*, and *teleology*. This finding indicates that, according to the professors, HR practices are influenced to a greater or lesser degree by the idea that while people may want control of their own lives, they are limited by hierarchical systems. This could lead to the avoidance of negative consequences by following company rules on the surface, but acting in other ways to fulfill their wishes for autonomy (control).

Second, the degree to which HR practices reflect the concepts of *deontology*, *relativism*, and *universal morality* exhibited a strong positive correlation, indicating that the professors believe that HR practices are influenced by each company's commitment to the general idea that while people have equal rights regardless of who they are, they may not be applied equally because many of the rights people have depend on individual circumstances (fairness).

Finally, strong positive correlations were found in the degree to which HR practices reflect *egoism*, *social contract theory*, and *justice*, indicating that the professors believe that HR practices are influenced by each company's commitment to the general idea that individuals are concerned with the pursuit of their individual goals and that the HR role is to protect and care for their employees in pursuit of those goals within the rules/framework of the organization (justice).

One may thus conclude that the professors believe that differences in the degree to which HR practices reflect the eleven ethics concepts discussed are a function of three broad ethical considerations – control, fairness, and justice.

### Exploratory questions

HR professionals' responses to a series of exploratory questions to examine the reasons ethics concepts are applied in the HR departments indicate that ethical issues are handled in an informal manner. While 88 percent said that their organization was concerned with the well-being of the employees in general, only 38 percent are satisfied with the general attitude of the organization regarding ethics. HR professionals indicated that outside influences such as legal requirements for the organization to behave ethically and pressure from the community or other organizations contribute to the ethical behavior.

Answers to exploratory questions for HR professionals related to internal and external influences on ethical practices revealed that the areas which had the most influence on ethics practices were: the organization's policies, the organization's general concern for the well-being of employees, the respondent's personal knowledge about ethics, and the respondent's personal interest in ethics. The areas indicated as having some influence on ethical practices in HR but less than those above were: concern for ethics among company leaders, concern for ethics among HR managers, pressure from outside organizations, and concern for public image.

Of the factors indicated as having the most influence on ethical practices, two are organizational in nature: policies and concern for employees; and two relate to the individual: personal knowledge and interest of the HR professional. This may be a sign of a gap between organizational strategy and individual goals regarding ethical practices, and creates an opportunity for assessing the organizational culture and creating or improving training and development programs. In a Latin American context, the literature supports the idea that this apparent dichotomy may be an indication of the strength of the person – the dignity of the individual – as central to his or her actions with respect to ethical practices and his or her relationship with others vs. the organization (Elvira and Davila, 2005; Erdener and Márquez, 2005).

The survey for HR and OB professors also asked exploratory questions. The professors reported very few constraints on ethics teaching in their courses. An interesting finding is that 80 percent indicated that their own experience regarding ethics affects their teaching of ethics, not necessarily their personal interest in ethics or the ethics content in the text.

## Concluding remarks

The study of ethics in HRM in Latin America is crucial to the economic development of the region. Global competition demands continuous improvements in efficiency and the deployment of increasingly innovative competitive advantages. It is essential for organizations to minimize costly ethical dilemmas by increasing their efforts to understand and improve ethical conduct in HRM.

The question of the universality of the Western ethics concepts naturally comes to mind as these concepts have been popularized in the US and Europe and have found their way into the literature and textbooks in other regions of the world. The responses from the professionals and professors surveyed indicate that Western ethics theories and concepts are broadly applicable in Mexico and, by extension, Latin America, especially those countries with similar national characteristics such as power distance and uncertainty avoidance. While further research is needed to better understand the differences that exist between Mexico and other Latin American countries, for the purpose of an initial approach Mexico can be used as a reliable representative of the region.

This study highlights the need for dialogue and cooperation between the academic community and organizations in order to improve the knowledge and performance of HR professionals. It also demonstrates the importance of working to merge organizational HR strategy with what is occurring on a daily basis in HR departments. These two general observations have implications for curriculum development and call for new and innovative training and development strategies that are congruent with the Latin American context. The findings of this work lend support to the idea that HR in Latin America cannot simply adopt generic HR strategies developed in other regions of the world without serious adaptation to the local culture and tradition. HR in Latin America can evolve into a distinctive competitive advantage with new and creative strategies that will meet the challenge of today's global environment.

# References

Albert, R. D. (1996) "A framework and model for understanding Latin American and Latin/Hispanic cultural patterns," in D. Landis and R. Bhagat (eds.), *Handbook of Intercultural Training*, 2nd edn., Thousand Oaks, CA: Sage.

Beekun, R. I., Stedham, Y., and Yamamura, J. H. (2003) "Business ethics in Brazil and the US: A comparative investigation," *Journal of Business Ethics*, 42(3): 269–279.

Carroll, A. B. and Buchholtz, A. K. (2006) *Business and Society: Ethics and Stakeholder Management*, 6th edn., Mason, OH: Thomson/South-Western.

Cascio, W. F. (2006) *Managing Human Resources: Productivity, Quality of Work Life, Profits*, 7th edn., Boston: McGraw-Hill.

Cooper, D. E. (2004) *Ethics for Professionals in a Multicultural World*, Upper Saddle River, NJ: Pearson/Prentice Hall.

Cullen, J. B. and Parboteeah, K. P. (2005) *Multinational Management: A Strategic Approach*, 3rd edn., Mason, OH: Thompson/South-Western.

Davila, A. and Elvira, M. (2005) "Culture and human resource management in Latin America," in M. Elvira and A. Davila (eds.), *Managing Human Resources in Latin America*, Abingdon, Oxon: Routledge.

Donaldson, T. and Dunfee, T. (1999) "When ethics travel: The promise and peril of global business ethics," *California Management Review*, 41(4): 45–63.

Elvira, M. and Davila, A. (2005) "Emergent directions for human resource management research in Latin America," *International Journal of Human Resource Management*, 16(12): 2,265–2,282.

Erdener, C. and Márquez, P. (2005) "A preliminary investigation of business ethical reasoning in Mexico, China, and the US: Implications for emerging theory," *Proceedings*, Southwest Academy of Management, Dallas, Texas, March 1–5.

Erdener, C. and Torbiörn, I. (1999) "A transaction costs perspective on international staffing patterns: Implications for firm performance," *Management International Review*, 39(3), Special issue on IHRM: 89–106.

Erdener, C., Márquez, P., and Mendez, J. (2007) "Cultural perspectives on managerial ethics and corruption: Lessons for HRM," paper presented at the International Association for Business and Society, Florence, Italy, May 31–June 3.

Gomez, C. and Sanchez, J. I. (2005) "HR's strategic role within MNCs: Helping build social capital in Latin America," *International Journal of Human Resource Management*, 16(12): 2,189–2,200.

Herrera, J. M. (2005) "What are we teaching in international business ethics?," paper presented at the Society for the Advancement of Management Conference, Las Vegas, Nevada, April 3–6, published in the Conference *Proceedings*, 43–54.

Hofstede, G. (1980, 2000) *Culture's Consequences*, Beverly Hills, CA: Sage.

Husted, B. (2002) "Culture and international anti-corruption agreements in Latin America," *Journal of Business Ethics*, 37(4): 413–422.

Lenartowicz, T. and Johnson, J. P. (2003) "A cross-national assessment of the values of Latin American managers: Contrasting hues or shades of gray?," *Journal of International Business Studies*, 34(3): 266.

Lowe, K. B., Milliman, J. B., De Cieri, H., and Dowling, P. J. (2002) "International compensation practices: A ten-country comparative analysis," *Human Resource Management*, 41(1): 45–66.

Márquez, P. and Erdener, C. (2007) "Relational ethics in Mexico," Working Paper, ITESM, Mexico City, Mexico.

Maxfield, S. (2005) "Modifying best practices in women's advancement for the Latin American context," *Women in Management Review*, 20(4): 249–261.

Milliman, J., Nason, S., Zhu, C., and De Cieri, H. (2002) "An exploratory assessment of the purposes of performance appraisals in North and Central America and the Pacific Rim," *Human Resource Management*, 41(1): 87–102.

Muller, H. J. and Rowell, M. (1997) "Mexican women managers: an emerging profile," *Human Resource Management*, 36(4): 423–435.

Osland, A. and Osland, J. (2005) "Contextualization and strategic international human resource management approaches: The case of Central America and Panama," *International Journal of Human Resource Management*, 16(12): 2,218–2,236.

Preble, R. C. (1963) *Standard Dictionary of the English Language*, international edn., Britannica World Language Dictionary, New York: Funk and Wagnalls Co.

Wilhelm, P. G. (2002) "International validation of the corruption perceptions index: Implications for business ethics and entrepreneurship education," *Journal of Business Ethics*, 35(3): 177–189.

Zabludovsky, G. (2001) "Women managers and diversity programs in Mexico," *Journal of Management Development*, 20(4): 354–370.

# 13  Business schools in Latin America

## Global players at last?

*Henry Gomez-Samper[1]*

Across Latin America, several MBA degree programs have in recent years become internationally accredited by AACSB International, AMBA, and EQUIS. Painstakingly prepared self-assessment reports of the region's leading schools have been reviewed by one or more of these bodies; in turn, dozens of teams made up of North American or European professors have made site visits to screen achievements and challenges faced by schools applying for accreditation. Can the region's business schools now be considered world class? How do the region's best schools compare with those they emulate? What challenges do these schools face as they vie for regional leadership and global positioning? How has Latin America's political left turn impacted schools such as IESA, in Venezuela?

International certification of Latin American schools is itself a recognition that management education in Latin America has come of age. Leading business schools in several of the region's countries have significantly influenced business practices by preparing students for a career in management, and offering executive education programs to local and multinational companies, public agencies, and varied organizations. Accreditation by international bodies is an outcome of long-standing efforts to promote worldwide standards for management development, largely dating from the 1980s. In 1989, the International Management Development Network (INTERMAN) paved the way for cross-region accreditation by linking AACSB, the leading certifying association of US schools, together with the European Foundation for Management Development (EFMD), the Council of Latin American Schools of Administration (CLADEA), and other regional associations.

Before examining the kinds of external and internal challenges currently faced by leading Latin American business schools, consider how they got started and evolved.

### Origins and decades of hardship

Business education is comparatively new to Latin America. Graduate schools of management are about to become half a century old – more than half a century again following the establishment of the first business schools in the United States, such as Wharton at the University of Pennsylvania (1881), Dartmouth

College (1900), and Harvard University (1908). In the 1960s, business schools sprouted across less-developed regions, charged with transferring twentieth-century know-how to backward economies. In Latin America, rigid or politicized academic structures hindered educational innovation, but civic and business leaders successfully attracted generous support from international agencies and foundations to establish graduate study in management at institutes outside universities. Independent schools emulating the North American business school model, to mention a few, range from ITAM in Mexico to INCAE in Costa Rica, IESA in Venezuela, ESAN in Peru, and EAESP in Brazil.[2] Early development of most of these schools was backstopped by a US institution, such as Harvard at INCAE, Stanford at ESAN, and, at IESA, an advisory board of five business schools chaired by the dean at Northwestern's Kellogg School of Business. In time, schools of economics and administration based at state and private universities emulated and built on programs introduced by the new, free-standing institutes.

Troubling barriers plagued the newly launched schools. In some countries not a single Ph.D. in a management-related field was to be found. Backstop support came with visiting faculty from the US, paid for by the Ford Foundation or USAID, and doctoral fellowships for future faculty to study abroad. But returning faculty were seldom offered a salary commensurate with their training, and financially strapped schools charged them with teaching loads that left little or no time for serious research. Not surprisingly, many high-powered faculty members spent most of their time on consultancies, or simply left the school. Also, international aid to support business education soon dwindled.

Latin America's stride to development following the Second World War was founded on the promise of local manufacturing. By coupling new industry with management training, the kind of social and economic progress heretofore restricted to the industrialized world was to be sparked. But the prospects for real progress soon became illusory; much of what the schools taught – largely a carbon copy approach to what North American business schools offered at that time – had little relevance to the needs, opportunities, and problems encountered by Latin American managers. Victims of a technology transfer trap, local schools took decades to mobilize research and curricular programs suited to Latin America's business and public agency management needs. Moreover, local companies seldom shared privileged management information with probing academics. Trade reforms in the 1990s lifted industry protection from foreign competition and, in time, companies and business schools found common ground. Nonetheless, progress in management research that draws deeply on the local context is barely under way (Gómez-Samper and Dávila, 2008).

Other troubles that for decades plagued Latin American business schools relate to the region's financial turbulence, impacting operating costs, faculty retention rates, and the opportunity to raise funds for academic and physical plant growth. For most countries, the 1970s and 1980s were years of double-digit inflation and failing investor confidence. The 1990s brought financial distress to both business and the population at large as speculative attacks were made on local currencies, followed by massive devaluations that wiped out savings and wealth.

These episodes, experienced by all countries in varying degrees, were highlighted by financial crises in Mexico and Argentina in 1995, Brazil in 1997, and, worst of all, Argentina again in 2001. By 2007, inflation in most of the region's countries except Venezuela had been contained; with Venezuela awash with unprecedented oil revenue, its free market exchange rate reached three times the official rate as a result of severe exchange controls and widespread concern that an essentially market-based economy might be replaced by state controls and property limits.

Interestingly enough, Latin America's financial and economic volatility has provided something of a competitive advantage to leading business schools, whose graduates – particularly those with business experience – are widely viewed as more resilient managers than those trained by schools based in more stable settings.

Nowadays, Latin American business schools face a daunting curricular issue. In a globalizing economy, students expect preparation for a career in management that may play out in their home country or just about anywhere. For both the schools and their faculty, this requires developing study programs adapted to the local business context, coupled with curricular inputs drawing on state-of-the-art management knowledge. Nonetheless, the leading schools are better positioned than ever before to address this challenge. Many have become prestigious academic institutions in their home countries as a result of their influence on management practice, buttressed by pioneering studies that examine a wide range of issues bearing on the region's economic and social development. Some schools have partnered with other leading schools in and outside of the region to undertake joint research or executive education programs. Moreover, growing integration of global management education has loosened the traditional US hold, acquainting Latin American schools with European models that are more akin to local management development needs.

## Challenges faced by Latin American business schools

Several factors, some external in origin and others internal to the schools themselves, have burdened business school development in Latin America. Internal factors limiting school development are perhaps greater for free-standing graduate business schools than for those attached to a university. The latter boast access to essential fields of knowledge drawn from other departments, and to undergraduates as a source of enrollment. Also, in universities research resources are more readily available. Although universities often plague faculty with bureaucratic formalities, free-standing business school faculty may be required to take on undue administrative and institutional service demands. In these schools, the faculty's role in promoting school growth is crucial; more than any other constituent, faculty determine the school's capacity to attract students to its different programs, and raise support for research and development. Yet for faculty members with superior research skills, the time allocated to committee work and promoting the institution makes for huge opportunity costs.

External factors common to the region also impact business school development. These vary from one country to another, with some countries making greater progress than others in promoting educational reform or joining a global economy. We will consider the following: (1) a small or nonexistent academic market; (2) a comparatively small pool of qualified university graduates; and (3) social and political threats to business.

### Small or nonexistent academic market

No business school in Latin America competes openly for qualified faculty in an academic market. North America's steady supply of freshly trained talent, spewed out by a resource-rich economy, enables business schools to vie with each other to attract qualified candidates to pursue an academic career. In contrast, leading Latin American business schools must either search out international faculty, or "grow their own" at huge cost. Many of the schools hire bright MBA graduates as full-time researchers or teaching assistants for two or more years, assess their performance and encourage the best – often on school salary plus fellowship support – to obtain a doctorate abroad. Hence, future professors are hired and their skills honed over a period spanning five or six years before they qualify for an assistant professorship. Such slow and expensive grooming carries the risk that upon completion of the doctorate fellowship awardees may choose not to return home, leave the school to set up their own management consultancy, or work for higher pay in industry. Even when such grooming is successful, few schools are able to build and retain a core faculty that focuses on the full range of specialties that comprise each management discipline, e.g. in the study of organizations, human capital, organization behavior, and leadership, to mention some.

One reason why Latin American schools are often short of faculty in certain areas of specialization is that comparatively few compete effectively in the global market of academics, given disparate salary levels, let alone cultural and language differences. Yet these limitations appear to be fading, as evidenced by international faculty recruiting experience at several Chilean schools and Colombia's University of Los Andes' business school, which recorded an impressive surge in the latest ranking of the region's schools by *AméricaEconomía* (2007). Salaries may be lower than in North America, but local purchasing power and lifestyles hold appeal.

Universities in Brazil, Mexico, and certain other countries boast doctoral programs in business and related disciplines that have expanded the supply of local academic talent. Doctoral students are acculturated in small groups by core faculty, much the same as elsewhere, and drilled to undertake research on topics that are locally relevant. Nonetheless, even in Brazil, with large numbers of local doctorate holders, few faculty members compete for positions in different schools – perhaps because of a preponderance of state-supported institutions with rigid hiring and compensation practices. Moreover, given the opportunity for study in Europe or North America, few doctoral aspirants in business would likely make the choice of pursuing the degree in their home country. Not only is a local doctorate perceived as lacking the quality associated with a recognized US or European school; an overriding reason is that Latin American universities lag in world competitiveness, produce little knowledge, and lack a diversity of students and sources of financial support (*Economist*, 2005).

Latin America's expanding doctoral programs in management and related fields help fill a pressing need to build an academic market, and grow desperately needed qualified faculty to staff the burgeoning number of public and private, graduate and undergraduate business schools that dot the region. Nonetheless, the embryonic nature of the academic market has made for imperfections that dissuade talented faculty members from full-time service. In the US, a full-time business faculty member on a nine-month contract can seek support from a wide network of organizations to support research and publication output; in Latin America, a similarly trained faculty member might be on a twelve-month contract, but support sources for research are few. Worse yet, higher teaching loads seldom allow faculty members to spend three months on research. Neither has the market for business faculty as yet evolved a fluid flow of talent to and from public and private schools. Financially strapped private business schools faced with increased competition for qualified students from academically strengthened public institutions, as in Mexico, are known to scale down their faculty size at a time of year when alternative academic options for those displaced are hard to come by.

Several schools have crossed borders to broaden their market and strive for regional leadership. INCAE, established to serve small Central American countries, mounted academic and executive education programs half a continent away. Monterrey Tech enlisted scores of Latin American business schools to deliver its courses electronically. Chile's Catholic University (PUCCH) offered executive education courses in Central America, Colombia's Los Andes in the Dominican Republic, and in 2007 Venezuela's IESA launched an academic and executive education beachhead in Panama.

### *Small pool of qualified university graduates*

Despite mushrooming population growth, countries in Latin America feature a comparatively small pool of university graduates from which business schools can select qualified candidates for admission. Latin America's population is predominantly young, uneducated, and poor. Again, figures vary from one country to another. The most authoritative region-wide study shows the percentage of the population 25–59 years old with 13 or more years of education varies from a high of 30.1 percent in Panama to 27.9 percent in Chile, 22.5 percent in Mexico, and as low as 13.4 percent in Brazil (CEPAL, 2006). A rough assessment valid for some countries suggests that even if 7 out of 10 secondary school graduates enter college, perhaps only 1 out of 3 children age 7–13 finishes primary school; and among secondary education youth a scant 1 out of 10 may actually complete their studies. Among university graduates, a significant share is represented by women, many of whom are not career-oriented or, for other reasons, are unlikely to seek a graduate degree in management.

A small pool of qualified applicants for graduate study in business invariably leads to a limited supply of talent to fill management needs, particularly as globalization increases competitive demands on companies. Supply vs. demand pressures in the market for managers are further exacerbated as Latin America's population becomes increasingly polarized – comparatively small pockets of more advantaged groups that make up the modern economy, *vis-à-vis* a fast growing market comprised of the underprivileged masses, who nourish an expanding informal economy that already provides employment to more than one-half the region's labour force.

A second external constraint to increased enrollment stems from the high opportunity cost to talented Latin Americans who pursue full-time graduate study, given the high local demand for trained manpower. Unemployment is rare among such candidates as would qualify for admission to a first-rate graduate business school such as Mexico's Monterrey Tech, Brazil's EAESP, or Chile's Adolfo Ibañez University. In North America, an MBA is generally perceived as an investment that leads to handsome future earnings through higher salaries and other benefits; but in many a Latin American country, full-time enrollment in an MBA program may be perceived as extremely expensive in terms of income and promotion opportunities foregone during the fifteen to eighteen months required to earn the degree. This explains the huge growth that most leading schools have experienced in demand for part-time programs and the Executive MBA, offered outside normal business hours. Leading schools have also learned to market the Executive MBA more effectively, targeting older or more experienced students than those who enroll in full-time programmes.

### Social and political threats to business

Countries in Latin America are among those where 10 percent of the population live on less than $1 a day, and 25 percent on less than $2. Income inequality in Latin America as a whole is greater than in any world region; 10 percent of the population captures 48 percent of the national income, while the poorest 10 percent make do with a scant 1.6 percent – a ratio of 30:1, *two to three times* more unequal than any world region. Yet limiting the pool of qualified applicants is the least significant way such reality impacts the region's business schools.

Appalling social and economic conditions have persisted in Latin America despite strong economic growth in recent years, an outcome of free-market and macroeconomic reforms enacted in previous decades. Not surprisingly, voters in Latin America have increasingly turned to leftist political parties that promise to undertake radical measures to address poverty. The most extreme case is that of Venezuela, where President Hugo Chávez leads a government that is openly opposed to free markets, deploying oil-rich resources to influence governments in Argentina, Bolivia, Uruguay, and the Caribbean – not to mention past efforts to swan election returns in Mexico, Nicaragua, Peru, and, at the local level, Colombia by funding radical candidates; but political forces elsewhere voice similar rhetoric: blaming business – especially large multinational and locally owned firms – for the region's abject poverty and persistent inequality; and capitalizing on global demands that business must assume responsibility for overcoming poverty and other world ills (Austin and Coatsworth, 2007: 54).

Management schools cannot overlook the threats that political forces may bring to local business as one of their key stakeholders. For IESA, the leading business school in Venezuela, the changing political climate hit hard in January 2007, when its two best business patrons (a power company owned by the US multinational AES and the largest telecom company, partly owned by Verizon) were abruptly nationalized, cutting short the training of hundreds of managers in scheduled executive education programs. It was not the first time in Latin America that a business school was directly impacted by political forces. In 1979, Daniel Ortega's Sandinista government assumed power in Nicaragua; hostility to private enterprise increased, and in 1982 INCAE moved its main campus to neighboring Costa Rica. How soon will such political threats to business – and business schools – occur elsewhere in Latin America or, for that matter, other developing countries?

MBA curricula at leading Latin American schools now expose students to the region's social, economic, and political realities, and seek to prepare socially responsible managers. Research under way at several schools aims to develop effective and sustainable corporate social responsibility programs. Companies are being coached in launching ventures with low-income sectors as consumers, suppliers, and partners (Rangan *et al.*, 2007), and an expanding number of teaching cases on these and related issues are now on hand or soon will be. But other means must be found to enable business, together with government and civil society organizations, to forge decisive measures that will improve Latin America's social and economic outlook. Hence a real need exists for innovative, region-wide research to shape new kinds of business models, linking management schools with each other and with emerging business experience. Notwithstanding significant efforts currently under way, few schools of management anywhere are well prepared to address such formidable business and societal needs. Moreover, issues that bear on management in a state-oriented economy (*vis-à-vis* one that is market-based) hold little appeal for management faculty generally – even as some have begun to give it a try (Francés, forthcoming).

Talented and productive faculty members faced with demands to focus their research agenda on management needs in a politically threatened society or a state-oriented economy may well consider the opportunity cost too high. In much of Latin America, social and political threats to individual freedom and personal safety persist. Understandably, scores of business school faculty members have faced the painful decision for themselves and their family to relocate abroad – joining the legions who contribute to making Latin America a net exporter of management talent.

## Relocating to a school abroad: what it means to business school faculty

In today's global village, it's easy to hold that qualified business school faculty who are concerned over the economic or political outlook in their country may relocate elsewhere. But there's a world of difference between choosing to relocate within Latin America and moving to a developed country; and, if the latter, between a leading university and a school where demands on research output are comparatively modest. Leading business schools in Latin America triumphantly report the number of articles published by their faculty in international scientific information (ISI) journals; but in a prestigious US school, six articles in six years may be required for a new faculty member to qualify for promotion – accepted for publication not just by any ISI journal, but one of the top five!

Comments made by a few of those faculty who chose to relocate – some within Latin America, others elsewhere – shed light on the costs and benefits for the individual concerned. For the individual faculty member, migrating abroad means increased opportunity and better pay, and, for many, greatly improved personal security for themselves and their family; and, if from Venezuela, to flee from a country where government ideology is openly hostile to free enterprise values, coloring the kind of education children obtain in school.

But for a Latin, to break away from family, life-long friends, and former class-mates is no easy choice. Business school faculty members who relocate must also learn the local nuances of doing business and how these shape organizational and academic life in a different culture – even when moving to a neighbor country in Latin America. And if the move is made to a country outside of the region, pride may be a factor to contend with: productive business school faculty members in a Latin American country are likely to be nationally known, prestigious academic authorities who exert influence over business practice; but upon moving to an average US school, their image reach may not extend much beyond the local chamber of commerce. Moving to a different country means leaving behind an extended support group that includes family and friends who are doctors, lawyers, and other professionals; the newly relocated faculty member who is suddenly faced with a child's serious illness or a community emergency – e.g. evacuation from their California home because of a spreading forest fire – has a sobering experience.

As closely as the region's leading business schools strive to emulate the American model, the rules by which the academic game is played in the two courts remain worlds apart. The aforementioned example of publishing demands made by a leading US school on a new faculty member – as it happens, a talented Venezuelan – make for a widely different lifestyle *vis-à-vis* relocating to a leading school within Latin America. To produce the six articles in six years in top ISI journals, the Venezuelan benefits from a minimal teaching load, yet has little time left to spend with family or friends. Had he chosen to relocate to a leading school in the region, in a similar span of time he could turn out two or three papers based on serious research, spend quality time with his family, teach graduate and executive education courses, do some consulting, write up one or two teaching cases, and spare some time to read an occasional novel.

Consider another rule that varies in the two regions. Faculty members in Latin American schools often "moonlight" to make ends meet, for pay scales are generally well below the US or European average; hence relocating abroad holds, for many, considerable appeal. Too much moonlighting may harm both the individual and the school; but kept under control it can serve as a useful bridge between academia and "real-world" business practitioners. Some Latin American faculty produce their best teaching cases by moonlighting, helping firms solve what may appear to be banal management problems. Expanding class hours in executive education to earn additional income may be an alternative, but doing so likely cuts into research output.

Latin American schools that prod their faculty to publish in ISI journals, either to improve the school's MBA ranking or to qualify for international accreditation, face a dilemma that goes beyond the number of articles published or the kind of ISI journal accepting them. Top ISI journals prefer hypothesis-driven, often highly quantitative, esoteric research, not the inductive kind required in countries where little is known about how successful local organizations are actually managed. As noted by the *Economist* (2007), "inductive research tends to draw sneers from the editors of academic journals."

Happily, some rankings now score schools on their contribution to both journals they consider purely "academic" and ones they consider "practitioner" – i.e. the kind real-world managers might read. Practitioner journals have a far better chance of influencing management practice than do largely unread, theory-driven articles. This news augurs favorably for Latin American business schools that publish management reviews expressly directed at practitioners, including *Debates IESA*. On the other hand, such journals are seldom read outside their home country. Worse yet, featured articles generally lack the critical peer review of those written for an academic audience. Only articles appearing in academic journals enhance a faculty member's reputation and opportunity for relocating to a top school.

## Conclusions

In short, for the past 50 years leading Latin American business schools have faced challenges that in some respects dwarf those encountered in recent years by their counterparts in North America and Europe. The magnitude of these challenges has necessarily impacted the ability of these schools to adequately compensate their highly trained faculty, and attend as well to developing administrative support systems to reach and maintain the level of academic excellence required for international accreditation and for becoming major players in global management education. Latin American schools of business have undeniably come a long way, but as yet are hardly in the same league as research universities in developed countries.

Growing research and publication output by certain leading Latin American business schools now provides them with international visibility. Many of these schools now influence the practice of management in their home country, learn from successful local experience, and prepare students for positions wherever companies in a globalizing economy may take them. Some schools are pioneering the kind of knowledge development required to address the social, economic, and political challenges that plague the entire region, and stand to produce fresh approaches to strengthen the future of Latin American society. The business community, the schools' chief external stakeholder and the world's most powerful change agent, can make good use of such insights. Even the most renowned universities anywhere lack the talent and resources to address so daunting a task.

## Notes

1 Grateful appreciation is expressed to colleagues Patricia Márquez, Maximiliano González, and Eduardo Pablo for valuable ideas and suggestions.
2 Instituto Tecnológico Autónomo de México (ITAM), Instituto Centroamericano de Administración de Empresas (INCAE), Instituto de Estudios Superiores de Administración (IESA), Escuela Superior de Administración de Negocios (ESAN), Escuela de Administraçao de Empresas-Fundaçao Getulio Vargas (EAESP).

## References

*AméricaEconomía* (2007) "Especial MBA: Ranking América Latina," *AméricaEconomía* August 20.

Austin, J. and Coatsworth, J. (2007) "Convertir la incertidumbre en oportunidad: Las empresas y el vuelco político de América Latina" [Turning uncertainty in opportunity: Enterprises and the political turnaround in Latin America], *Harvard Business Review*, R0702D-E.

CEPAL (2006) *Panorama Social de América Latina – 2006*, Santiago, Chile: CEPAL.

*Economist* (2005) "The brains business," *Economist*, September 8.

*Economist* (2007) "Business schools and research: Practically irrelevant?," *Economist*, August 28.

Francés, A. (ed.) (forthcoming) *Compromiso Social: Gerencia para el Siglo XXI*, Caracas: Ediciones IESA.

Gómez-Samper, H. and Dávila, C. (2008) "Management in a turbulent and socially excluding business context: Insights from Latin America," *Galeras de Administración*, Bogotá, 18, January.

Rangan, V., Kasturi, J., Quelch, J. A., Herrero, G., and Barton, B. (eds.) (2007) *Business Solutions for the Global Poor*, San Francisco: Jossey-Bass.

# 14 Theoretical approaches to best HRM practices in Latin America

*Anabella Davila and Marta M. Elvira[1]*

Reflecting on the diverse case study research presented in this book, we discern nascent concepts for theory building on human resource management (HRM) in Latin America. At first sight, our contributors analyze divergent HRM practices in different contexts; yet a deeper look reveals notable common themes across the in-depth case studies. In this chapter, we identify those themes as lessons learned from *best practices* in the complex context of Latin America. Then, we elaborate on how theoretical approaches such as stakeholder management and cultural hybridism help us draw important lessons for understanding HRM in Latin America. Finally, we bring in the *new humanism* and *pragmatism* perspectives to build on our proposal for effective HRM in Latin America. By new humanism we mean an approach that balances the individual and economic perspectives of organizations. By pragmatism we refer to Santiso's (2006) view of "what is possible" in Latin America given the environmental complexity in which organizations have to function. While classic economic theories provide "magic formulas and lyric exaltations" (Santiso, 2006: 4), neglecting social realities and the historical development of the region, this pragmatic humanism focuses on the reality of Latin America's political economy.

## Best HRM practices in Latin America's complex context

The best practice research approach usually follows a universalistic perspective, assuming that general management practices can be transferred effectively to any context (Delery and Doty, 1996). Still, HRM practices should form a coherent system for controlling and developing human competencies in order to achieve strategic goals. Therefore, transferring a single "best HRM practice" to a different context would have a limited impact on the organization's performance (Schuler and Jackson, 2005). Moreover, organizations would gain limited performance benefits from copying or imitating a specific "best HRM practice" from "best employers."

Rankings of "best performing" companies are a growing trend in Latin America, as in other parts of the world. The business press publishes different rankings, such as *AméricaEconomía's*[2] "Best Banks," "500 Latin American Companies," or "Best MBAs." The Great Place to Work Institute initiated operations in Brazil in 1995 and today ranks firms for almost every country in the region (Great Place to Work Institute, 2007).

When HR scholars use "best companies" rankings, they usually seek to understand how such companies align business strategies with HR practices. Research suggests that part of this effect results from enhanced firm reputation when participating in these rankings, for example in the improved ability to attract talented employees (Joo and McLean, 2006). Rankings are usually based on financial performance metrics, employees' voluntary participation in cultural audit surveys, and/or HR practices profiles. In general, companies are evaluated according to a best-practice model derived from a global database (Great Place to Work Institute, 2007). Therefore, the assumption of universal management application underlies the best-company construct.

Our approach in this book follows a different assumption. Researchers here seek to understand what works in Latin America within each case study, not what works all the time under any circumstances. This approach carries a different connotation for the "best practice" concept and its resulting theoretical implications. When speaking of HRM practices, we note that each practice consists of the tool or instrument, the content of the tool, the management of the process involved in using such tool, and the outcome produced. While international human resources management (IHRM) research acknowledges that companies benchmark their practices to those of the best employers' lists (Joo and McLean, 2006), they focus mainly on the tool or instruments, rarely considering an HR practice as a whole, its role within in the HRM system overall, or its alignment with a particular corporate strategy or organizational context (Schuler and Jackson, 2005).

The studies in this book aim to fill the gap in understanding the HRM practices of "best companies" in their real-world setting as well as contribute toward building helpful "best practice" theory. Three of the case studies examine companies that participate in the "best place to work" ranking; one study examines a "best employer to work for" firm. Of these cases, two are European and two Latin American companies. Using thick description methodology, the researchers illustrate how the companies implement HRM practices in ways that might only make sense in Latin America, which is an uncommon approach in classic IHRM books. Specifically, the managers of Aracruz in Brazil (see Chapter 2) and Grupo San Nicolás in El Salvador (see Chapter 7) face violent contexts yet protect their employees without neglecting their commitment to the company. CompuSoluciones (see Chapter 9) and Novo Nordisk (see Chapter 8) in Mexico use HRM practices based on and tightly aligned with corporate values that place the individual at the center of their work, over and above the organizations' financial performance.

We surmise that a "best practice" research approach might benefit from taking this pragmatic, locally constructed view besides using managerial theories derived from the universalistic perspective. Universalistic management theories could hinder HRM and its role in Latin America in representing a search for "magic realism." Witness business schools in Latin America. Gomez-Samper (in Chapter 13) describes how these schools were challenged to achieve accreditation based on criteria defined by international agencies. Seeking accreditation, Latin American business schools were pressured to emulate North American or European models, orienting their scarce resources to this purpose. But because business schools in Latin America operate in an inhospitable economic and political environment, they cannot rely on a mature academic market and are far from being like American or European programs. In sum, "best practice" in Latin America is practice that matches Latin America's dynamic social reality.

## Key lessons for HRM in Latin America from different theoretical views

When starting this book we expected HRM practices to diverge across the lines of the different organizations and industries. We have, nevertheless, found convergence in the need for an interdisciplinary theoretical approach to best explain each case. Traditional models of management and organization offer only partial explanations for HRM complexity in a region where multiple contextual elements challenge the use of a single theoretical view. To understand HRM in Latin America's distinct environment of economic, political, and social instability, the role of the enterprise as a social institution, the value of the individual within a society, and the pragmatic character of governmental public policies, interdisciplinary views are required. We address these views next.

### *Stakeholder management*

We have argued elsewhere that the unstable environments surrounding HRM practices in Latin America call for novel theoretical frameworks in management and organization studies (Elvira and Davila, 2005a). Based on the research cases presented in this book, a seemingly fruitful perspective is stakeholder theory, which considers the impact of HRM systems on the organization's multiple stakeholders. HRM systems should thus be designed to satisfy key stakeholders' demands (Schuler and Jackson, 2005). This approach is broad enough to include singular stakeholders who might not exist in all societies. Importantly, it also assumes that various stakeholders' degree of legitimacy, power, or urgency affects organizational objectives (Donaldson and Preston, 2005; Mitchell, Agle and Wood, 1997). However, this premise could limit our understanding of indigenous stakeholders' demands and our ability to maintain valid and long-term relationships with diverse silent groups that lack such legitimacy or power. Such is the case in land ownership disputes.

Land ownership disputes between multinational corporations and indigenous people are not new in colonized countries. In Australia, for example, acknowledging the legitimization of a stakeholder group and its land claims is more a function of the colonizer economic and political elite than a natural social process (Banerjee, 2000). In Latin America, organizations and diverse stakeholders coexist and desire social integration regardless of their legitimacy or power. Three chapters of this book highlight the importance of redefining not only who key stakeholders are, but also what really matters to both the organization and the stakeholders in Latin America (see Chapters 2, 3 and 4). The case studies illustrate that it is not enough to design a socially responsible corporate strategy to satisfy indigenous stakeholders' needs; it appears to be necessary to share control rights and ownership-related privileges with employees. In violent conflict-ridden Colombia, the emphasis seems to be on mutual dependence, shared control, and high levels of cooperation among diverse stakeholders and the organization (see Chapter 3).

### Cultural hybridism

IHRM theory is enriched by a cultural perspective, which usually takes two approaches to understanding local management: a comparative approach (e.g. Hofstede, 1982) and an in-depth case study approach (e.g. D'Iribarne, 2002). Yet the cultural perspective of organizations and management has been criticized by post-modern Latin American researchers (e.g. Ibarra-Colado, 2006) as limited in its ability to explain why modern management theories do not work in the region. In other words, when theories developed abroad fail in Latin America, the general explanation is that culture alters management application. In this perspective, the outcome is defined in binary terms, that is, the "other," representing managerial modernity, and "us," using local managerial practices (Frenkel and Shenhav, 2006; Zabludovsky, 1989). Latin America's management is seen as requiring acculturation and modernization.

Lacking in these culture-oriented perspectives is usually a conceptually coherent account of how "culture" causes variations in managerial application. Post-modern arguments are limited, first, because they discount the historical mix of managerial formulas' origins (Garcia Canclini, 1990) and, second, because culture is seen as stable and pure, missing the historical hybridization process that tends to alter cultures through historical development (Shimoni and Bergmann, 2006). In other words, it is hard to deny the migration of management ideas and theories that irrigate local Latin American meanings and uncover indigenous interpretations (Micheli, 1994). The cultural thesis seems valuable to understand management in Latin America if we see hybridization as a process, not an outcome. When hybridization is seen as an outcome, the research strategy tends to be descriptive, focused on the means by which ideas and theories travel across the globe. For example, management textbooks could be seen as the primary source for acquiring foreign ideas and theories of management (Mills and Hatfield, 1998). Thus, the notion of hybridization is reduced to a merger or an integration of cultures, overlooking contradictions and rejections (Garcia Canclini, 1990).

Two theories treat hybridization as a process: the socio-cultural perspective (Garcia Canclini, 1990) and post-colonial theory (Bhabha, 1994). The socio-cultural perspective argues that hybridization is a dynamic framework for discovering intercultural contact points that might produce conflictive but negotiable responses for mutual enrichment (Shimoni and Bergmann, 2006). Hybrid configurations emerge from discrete structures or practices that existed separately and that are combined to generate new structures, objects, or practices (Garcia Canclini, 1990). Hybridization, in this view, might be rejected because it could produce insecurity or threaten egocentric self-esteem cultures. Communication technologies facilitate the appropriation of many elements from diverse cultures, but this perspective assumes that such elements would not be accepted indiscriminately (Garcia Canclini, 1990).

In contrast, post-colonial researchers argue that hybridization results from an authoritarian imposition of identity from powerful colonizers over colonized individuals (whether the imposition is objective or perceived is outside the scope of our argument). Yet colonized cultures are not silenced by the imposition of a homogeneous identity: Rejection behaviors produce mimicry responses that resemble those of colonizers but are not identical (Bhabha, 1994). In either perspective, hybridization as a process unravels when individuals appropriate other worldviews that make them generate alternative responses to diverse situations.

This book's in-depth case studies could contribute to our understanding of the hybridization process in the context of HRM practices. A hybrid approach challenges the dichotomy typical of cultural HRM studies in Latin America by rejecting a binary categorization of contrasting views regarding simple cultural identities. Moreover, the socio-cultural perspective of hybridization assumes that individuals are free to accept or reject hybrid influences. For Latin America, this suggests that theory can be built departing from two elements: on the one hand, diversity and, on the other hand, knowledge of individuals' position regarding inter-cultural relationships. For example, Gonzalez and Perez-Floriano (in Chapter 10) studied a high-risk work environment within a multinational corporation operating in Brazil and Argentina. They found that best HRM safety practices are designed more around individuals' concept of trust than the institutional meaning of safety. The study shows that the cultural values exhibited by employees in three Latin American cities (Sao Paulo, Rio de Janeiro, and Buenos Aires) differed, and that these differences influenced how workers perceived risk and construed the meaning of work hazard. The authors concluded that differences in cultural values influence the transferability of safety procedures from headquarters to the Latin American subsidiaries. Moreover, the impersonal nature of a system of rules and procedures could harm trust in the system and be detrimental to its successful implementation.

The studies also provide insights for identifying the element of diversity in the hybridization process within Latin America. First, the companies studied are hybrid in nature. We observe diverse ownership arrangements: mergers, acquisitions, multinationals, international joint ventures, and local private firms. All of the companies exhibit diverse cultures and operate successfully in the region. We also observe diversity in the HRM practices studied. Companies use multiple HRM practices targeting the same purpose. For example, Rao (in Chapter 11) discovered the simultaneous use of several recruitment and selecting practices by international (US-Mexico) joint ventures (IJV) operating in Mexico. The use of each practice was equally categorized as influenced by the IJV headquarters and as a local cultural bounded practice. Yet IJVs seemed able to manage successfully all staffing practices identified in the research.

## Novel conceptualizations

What does it mean to view HRM theory as a framework, with individuals sustained by a collectivity? Humanism, in the modern intellectual classic movement, is based on the idea of individual self-sufficiency. Today this rational anthropocentric view of the individual is progressively pushing away the individual from him/herself, overlooking his/her social well-being. Therefore, we see the value of a "new humanism" in contrast with this classic view. We propose that in Latin America the individual is valued as part of the collectivity. With this in mind, to work well HRM practices need to place the individual at the center of the organization and society. At CompuSoluciones (see Chapter 9), performance management systems include diverse practices for simultaneously developing human and social capital. The company keeps goals in balance for both individual and organizational performance, integrating the relevance of these elements in its organizational practices, something unusual for the IT industry. Similarly, in the acquisitions of two Brazilian banks by ABN AMRO successful integration strategies seem to result from the priority assigned to human issues over business strategy. Ultimately, integration leverages HRM as a strategic function (see Chapter 6).

By contrast, HRM practices should avoid focusing on society and subordinating the individual to the mass supra-ideology, as has been the case in some political systems in the region. In Latin America's ethical system, the individual is a very important unit within the collective social structure.

At the economic-political level, Santiso (2006) has found in Latin America a generalized conception of pragmatism. He sees Latin American governments moving away from classic economic and political theories as much as from idealistic views and utopian development solutions. Santiso (2006) argues that instead of following a specific economic development model, Latin America is now guided by what he calls pragmatism. That is, Latin America governments are gradually applying what can work, given the culture of the region and of each particular country. This pragmatic approach has helped the region attain stability recently, moving away from the economic "magic realism" that promised wondrous but impossible solutions for development in Latin America.

The pragmatic view includes culture and doses of idealism. We think of the hybrid automobile as a metaphor to explain the Latin American perspective: A hybrid car uses energy efficiently depending on energy requirements, while at the same time it provides a green and socially responsible solution to transportation. Yet Latin America's pragmatism is not unlimited; it has natural social and institutional constraints (i.e. those of international institutions that pressure the region for economic stability). Additionally, it is unclear whether the industrial development model adequately described all Latin American countries. Some countries, led by Venezuela, appear to be returning power to the state, seeking different – if not new – modes of development, and ones that might not prove sustainable in the long term.

Overall, Santiso's pragmatism combines with the "hope" permeating Latin America. We share his renewed optimism in learning from the companies represented in this book. These "best performing" companies demonstrate considerable creativity and innovation in the use and implementation of HRM practices. The companies also project hope because they seem to understand not only what works "best" but also under what circumstances.

## Stakeholders, new humanism, hybridization, and pragmatism: cornerstones for a proposed theoretical approach to best HRM practices in Latin America

This book offers an international, grounded theoretical and empirical approach for understanding HRM in Latin America. Novel conceptual frameworks emerge from the diverse case studies and HRM practices studied. While we note the usefulness of existing general management theories in the region, these theories are enriched with concepts or terms that are unique to Latin America because of its singular historical and cultural development. A common theme underlying "best HRM practices" is the inclusion of multiple stakeholders. HRM practices perform best when they include both powerful and silent stakeholders. Acknowledging a horizontal relationship, organization–stakeholder, in contrast to a hierarchical relationship of subordination could set the basis for a more comprehensive stakeholder theory for HRM in Latin America.

We conclude with a recommendation to continue using the cultural perspective to understand HRM in Latin America. Yet culture should be seen as a hybrid dynamic process that enriches societies because of the constant intercultural individual and group contact points. Enrichment could occur through conflict, via negotiated responses to differing cultural influences.

Building on the chapters' evidence, we propose the new humanism as a foundation for a hybrid cultural approach to HRM in Latin America. This approach departs from the existence of diversity in practices and takes into account individuals' position within intercultural relationships. Consider the roles played by businesses in Latin America. Environmental factors demand business roles, such as becoming part of the social support system (Elvira and Davila, 2005b). In this vein, Aracruz in Brazil, Hacienda Gavilanes or Indupalma in Colombia, and Grupo San Nicolás in El Salvador show how effective HRM serves as a link between the company and governmental institutions, expanding its role from the firm to society. Latin America has thus transformed business organizations into social institutions that facilitate balancing the needs of the individual and the development of society.

Latin America, as other world economies, has long defied rational economic models that do not consider the region's social reality and that aim to produce utopian transformations. Today, Latin America is increasingly adopting pragmatic methods of development. This pragmatism also characterizes business organizations and, specifically, the HRM practices studied in this book. Moreover, Santiso (2006) observes open-mindedness not only in economics but also in politics toward using diverse methods to suit the social reality of Latin America. This translates into flexible approaches for solving problems, for abandoning ideas that do not work and rapidly trying other ideas. Santiso labels this the silent arrival of the "political economy of the possible," which offers hope to a region exhausted by economic reform programs that have produced recurrent and severe economic shocks. Thanks to this pragmatic orientation in the region, managers are learning what works best and leading with an optimistic attitude of hope.

## Notes

1  The authors would like to thank Bryan W. Husted, Nora H. Martinez, and Jorge Rocha for their insightful comments on early versions of this chapter.
2  Regional business magazine.

## References

Banerjee, S. B. (2000) "Whose land is it anyway? National interest, indigenous stakeholders, and colonial discourses," *Organization & Environment*, 13(1): 3–28.

Bhabha, K. H. (1994) *The Location of Culture*, London: Routledge.

D'Iribarne, P. (2002) "Motivating workers in emerging countries: Universal tools and local adaptations," *Journal of Organizational Behavior*, 23: 1–14.

Delery, J. E. and Doty, H. D. (1996) "Modes of theorizing in strategic human resource management: Tests of universalistic, contingency, and configurational performance," *Academy of Management Journal*, 39(4): 802–835.

Donaldson, T. and Preston, L. E. (1995) "The stakeholder theory of the corporation: Concepts, evidence, and implications," *Academy of Management Review*, 20(1): 85–91.

Elvira, M. M. and Davila, A. (2005a) "Emergent directions for human resource management research in Latin America," *International Journal of Human Resources Management*, 16(12): 2,265–2,282.

Elvira, M. M. and Davila, A. (2005b) "Emergent directions for human resource management: Research in Latin America," in M. M. Elvira, and A. Davila (eds.), *Managing Human Resources in Latin America: An Agenda for International Leaders*, Oxford, UK: Routledge, pp. 235–252.

Frenkel, M. and Shenhav, Y. (2006) "From binarism back to hybridity: A postcolonial reading of management and organization studies," *Organization Studies*, 27(6): 855–876.

Garcia Canclini, N. (1990) *Culturas Híbridas. Estrategias para Entrar y Salir de la Modernidad* [Hybrid cultures. strategies for entering and exiting modernity], new edn., Mexico: Grijalbo.

Great Place to Work Institute (2007) *Best Companies Lists*. Retrieved 11/15/07 from: http://www.greatplacetowork.com/best/index.php.

Hofstede, G. H. (1982) *Culture's Consequences. International Differences in Work-Related Values*, abridged edn., Newbury Park, CA: Sage.

Ibarra-Colado, E. (2006) "Organization studies and empistemic coloniality in Latin America: Thinking otherness from the margins," *Organization*, 13(3): 463–488.

Joo, B.-K. and McLean, G. N. (2006) "Best employer studies: A conceptual model from a literature review and a case study," *Human Resource Development Review*, 5(2): 228–257.

Micheli, J. (ed.) (1994) *Japan Inc. en Mexico. Las empresas y modelos laborales japoneses*, Mexico: Miguel Angel Porrua, Universidad de Colima and UAM-A.

Mills, A. J. and Hatfield, J. (1998) "From imperialism to globalization: Internationalization and the management text," in S. R. Clegg, E. Ibarra-Colado, and L. B. Rodriguez (eds.), *Global Management: Universal Theories and Local Realities*, London: Sage, pp. 37–67.

Mitchell, R. K., Agle, B. R., and Wood, D. J. (1997) "Toward a theory of stakeholder identification and salience: Defining the principle of who and what really counts," *Academy of Management Review*, 22(4): 853–886.

Santiso, J. (2006) *Latin America's Political Economy of the Possible. Beyond Good Revolutionaries and Free-Marketeers*, Cambridge, MA: The MIT Press.

Schuler, R. S. and Jackson, S. E. (2005) "A quarter-century review of human resource management in the US: The growth in importance of the international perspective," *Management Revue*, 16(1): 11–34.

Shimoni, B. and Bergmann, H. (2006) "Managing in a changing world: From multiculturalism to hybridization – the production of hybrid management cultures in Israel, Thailand, and Mexico," *Academy of Management Perspectives*, 20(3): 76–89.

Zabludovsky, G. (1989) "The reception and utility of Max Weber's concept of patrimonialism in Latin America," *International Sociology*, 4(1): 55–66.

# Index

Note: *italic* page numbers denote references to Figures/Tables.